ACLS History E-Book Project

Reprint Series

The ACLS History E-Book Project (www.historyebook.org) collaborates with constituent societies of the American Council of Learned Societies, publishers, librarians and historians to create an electronic collection of works of high quality in the field of history. This volume is produced from digital images created for the Project by the Scholarly Publishing Office and the Digital Library Production Service at the University of Michigan, Ann Arbor. The digital reformatting process results in an electronic version of the text that can be both accessed online and used to create new print copies. This book and hundreds of others are available online in the History E-Book Project through subscription.

Many of the works in the History E-Book Project are available in print and can be ordered either directly from their publishers or as part of this series. For information refer to the online Title Record page for each book. Inquiries regarding this series can be directed to info@hebook.org.

ACLS
HISTORY E-BOOK

http://www.historyebook.org

BURT FRANKLIN RESEARCH & SOURCE WORKS SERIES #97

The Political Activities of the Baptists and Fifth Monarchy Men In England During the Interregnum

PRIZE ESSAYS

OF THE

AMERICAN HISTORICAL ASSOCIATION

The Political Activities
of the
Baptists and Fifth Monarchy Men
In England

During the Interregnum

BY
LOUISE FARGO BROWN, PH.D.

BURT FRANKLIN RESEARCH & SOURCE WORKS SERIES #97

BURT FRANKLIN
NEW YORK

PUBLISHED BY
BURT FRANKLIN
235 EAST 44TH ST.
NEW YORK, N. Y. 10017

FIRST PUBLISHED:
LONDON

1911

PRINTED IN U.S.A.

TO MY MOTHER

PREFACE.

THE purpose of this study is to set forth the attitude toward the English government, in one of the most troubled periods of its history, of two religious bodies which by a large number of their contemporaries were considered enemies of all government, and sworn foes of peace and order. Twice in a period of six years the men belonging to these two parties were actually in a position to affect the policy of the government; for part of the period one of them practically controlled Ireland, and throughout the Protectorate they were a serious problem to Cromwell. I have endeavored to ascertain as far as possible to what extent the political programs of the two parties furnished justification of the popular opinion concerning them, and, in consequence, what was their real importance in the history of their time.

I have used throughout the term Baptist, which in the period under consideration had begun to be employed by the Baptists themselves, in place of the less convenient terms "baptized believer" and "baptized brother". The name Anabaptist, never accepted by the Baptists themselves, was practically the only one applied to them by outsiders. There was, however, great confusion as to its use: Independents and other sectaries usually applied it to the Baptists alone; Royalists, foreigners, and sometimes Presbyterians, made it include the Fifth Monarchy men and all other extreme sectaries, and sometimes it was used yet more loosely as a mere term of reproach.

Of the materials used, the most important have been such collections of contemporary correspondence as the Thurloe Papers, both printed and manuscript, the letters of Henry Cromwell and those of the French ambassador Bordeaux; and contemporary pamphlets, especially the great Thomason Collection in the British Museum. A good deal of information has been pieced together from scattered references in the *Calendars of State Papers,* the *Reports* of the Historical MSS. Commission, the Clarke Papers, and in the Tanner, Carte, and Clarendon MSS. Records of individual churches are unfortunately scarce. Some few are available in manuscript, and several of these have been made accessible in print by the Hanserd Knollys Society and, more recently, by the Baptist and Congregational historical societies of London. The two societies last named are making commendable efforts to publish all existing material for the early history of the Separatist churches. Doubtless the forthcoming volumes of Mr. Champlin Burrage will also contain valuable material.

I wish to acknowledge my indebtedness to Professor C. H. Firth, to Dr. William A. Shaw, to Mrs. S. C. Lomas, and to Dr. Frances G. Davenport, for advice and assistance most kindly given me when I was gathering my material. Grateful acknowledgments are also due to Mr. Frank H. Robinson of the Baptist College of Bristol, and to Dr. W. T. Whitley of Preston, for their courteous answers to letters of inquiry; to Mr. Hubert Hall of the Public Record Office, and to the librarians of the British Museum, the Bodleian Library, the Dr. Williams Library, the Friends' Reference

Library at Devonshire House, the Congregational Library in London, and the Guildhall Library; to the custodians of records at Somerset House, and to the provost of Worcester College. Oxford. I am under a special debt of gratitude to Professor R. C. H. Catterall, who has been my untiring guide and helpful critic from the inception of this work until its completion. I wish also to express my appreciation of the kindness of those who have helped the book through its final stages, especially that of Miss Grace L. Filer, who has aided me in innumerable ways, for which all words of thanks must be inadequate.

L. F. B.

WELLESLEY, MASSACHUSETTS,
September, 1911.

CONTENTS.

CHAPTER I.

Baptists and Fifth Monarchy Men.

It is evident to students of the Protectorate period that the religious views of the men who were directing public affairs, and the attitude of the various sects toward the government, were very important elements in the fortunes of England during those difficult years. The problems of Cromwell, in adjusting to political exigencies his own ideas on the subject of religion and of church organization; his real perplexity and sorrow in dealing with conscientious men whose scruples he understood, and with whose pleas for liberty of conscience he sympathized: these were factors of considerable weight in shaping the destinies of the Protectorate. The curious attempt at government by a body of men chosen for their godliness, and the alternation of governments which gave the country over to confusion in the period which followed Richard Cromwell's abdication: these, as well as the days of the Protectorate, can be better understood after a study of the activities of two bodies of men, frequently confused even by contemporaries—the politico-religious party known as Fifth Monarchy men, and the members of the Baptist denomination. It will be necessary, before beginning such a study, to have a clear idea of the policy and characteristics of each of these bodies.

Of all the forms of Protestantism to which the Reformation gave birth there was one which, more nearly

2

than any other, carried to its logical conclusion the great principle that it is the right of every man to seek God's truth in the Scriptures, and mould his life in accordance with that truth as he sees it. When the great heroes of the Reformation found it expedient to put limitations on that principle, the men called Anabaptists clung to it still, and, harried from land to land, beset with reproachful names, forced to shoulder all the crimes of misguided fanatics attached to the skirts of their movement, carried their faith into all the corners of Europe. The salient feature of that faith was the principle that a church, according to Scripture, is a voluntary association of believers, with whose organization and support the state has nothing to do, and over whose belief and worship no civil power has jurisdiction. The name Anabaptist, applied as a term of reproach, arose out of their contention that, in Scripture, baptism was the sign of admission into the community of believers, and that consequently infant baptism was without validity. All the great leaders of the Anabaptists were apostles of religious tolerance, and many held that no Christian should be a magistrate, engage in warfare, take an oath, or go to law. A small number developed pronounced millenarian views, refused to acknowledge the existing magistracy, and advocated the establishment of Christ's kingdom by force. It was the attempt of this faction to carry out its views in the city of Münster that brought more discredit on the Anabaptists than any other event in their history, and the excesses there indulged in were thenceforth very generally ascribed to all opponents of infant baptism. The term Anabaptism, in the sixteenth and seventeenth centuries, represented to the average man not the doctrines taught by Hans Denck, Balthasar Hübmaier, Caspar Schwenckfeld, or Menno Simons, but those upheld by Knipperdoling and John of Leyden in their short-lived Westphalian kingdom. Yet the credit of these latter had collapsed with their dream of power, while the disciples of the former carried their faith down the centuries.[1]

The Anabaptists of Holland were the spiritual forefathers of the English Baptists. Although scattered persons in England, from Reformation days on, held the distinctive tenets of the Continental Anabaptists, there is no record of any permanent congregation before the early years of the seventeenth century.[2] The first group of English Baptists were dissenters from the English Separatist church in Amsterdam. They had fallen under the influence of the Mennonites there, and from their adoption of the belief in universal redemption came to be known as General Baptists. Members of this group, settling in London, formed the first permanent Baptist church in England in 1611. Their ideas spread, and by 1626 there were at least three General Baptist churches in London, and others in Lincoln, Sarum, Coventry, and Tiverton.[3]

The second group of Baptists, who held Calvinistic views and were consequently known as Particular Bap-

[1] The subject is fully treated in Keller, *Geschichte der Wiedertäufer.* See also Lindsay, *Reformation,* II, 430 ff., and the last edition of Herzog's *Realencyclopädie.*

[2] For the sufferings of these early Baptists, see Crosby, *English Baptists,* I, 33 ff.; *Tracts on Liberty of Conscience* (Hanserd Knollys Soc.), Introduction; Heath, "The Anabaptists and their English Descendants," in *Contemporary Review,* LIX (1891), 392 ff.

[3] Crosby, *English Baptists,* I, 68 ff.; Barclay, *Inner Life of the Religious Societies of the Commonwealth,* 95 ff.; Whitley, ed., *Minutes of the General Assembly of the General Baptist Churches,* 1654-1728, I, xii-xvi.

tists, had their origin in a secession from the Independent church founded in Southwark by Henry Jacob, formerly pastor of an English congregation in Zeeland. The seceders opposed the recognition of the English parish churches as true churches, because they were not formed in accordance with the voluntary principle, and some of them had come to disbelieve in the baptism of infants. The new church was organized under the leadership of John Spilsbury in 1633. Five years later William Kiffin and other seceders from Jacob's church joined their congregation, which afterward split into two equal parts, one under the leadership of Praise-God Barbone, the other under that of Henry Jessey. Hanserd Knollys, a Cambridge man who had spent some time in New England, was for a time a member of Jessey's church, but in 1644 he organized a congregation of his own. In this way the movement spread, until eleven years later there were seven of these Particular Baptist churches in London, and forty-seven in other parts of England.[4]

On account of their doctrinal differences, there was practically no communication between the Particular and the General Baptists. Their organization and customs were, however, very similar, although the General Baptists seem to have retained more of the distinctive customs of the Continental Anabaptists. The congregations of each group were individually independent in government, but gave one another advice and encouragement by means of messengers, and held general meetings at stated intervals to discuss

[4] The existing records of the early London churches are to be found in vol. II, *Transactions* of the Congregational Society, London.

matters of common interest.[5] The organization of the churches was thoroughly democratic. All male members, and in the case of a large number of churches, female members also, were allowed " liberty of prophesying ", that is, of saying during the services whatever they believed themselves inspired of God to say. Officers were elected by the votes of the entire congregation. Any member might be chosen as deacon, but only those who were thought to possess special gifts were elected to eldership, as it was the elders who exercised pastoral duties. The belief that no special education was necessary as a preparation for the work of the ministry led to actual denunciation of higher education by some preachers, and gave rise to the opinion that the Baptists were opposed to learning and to the universities.[6] Moreover, the fact that the men who preached on Sundays frequently worked the rest of the week as saddlers, glovers, felt-makers, and the like, brought upon them the scorn of the Church of England clergy and the Presbyterians.[7] Their unpopularity on

[5] The Free Will Baptists and the Seventh Day Baptists later developed separate organizations, but their numbers were inconsiderable. An apostle of church unity wrote in 1653: " The baptized Churches are subdivided into three parts, one Church is for free will, a second for universal Redemption, a third count themselves more Orthodox in Doctrine, as the Church of England. Neither of these three baptized Churches doe communicate one with another." Erbery, *The Sword Doubled* (Thomason).

[6] For Baptist views on education, see below, pp. 36-37. For the position of women in the churches, see Register Book of the Lothbury Church (Rawlinson MSS., D 828), fol. 28; Barclay, *op. cit.*, 156; Edwards, *Gangraena*, 1646, 29. The preaching of women gave rise to much talk and no little ridicule. See Masson, *Milton*, III, 149, 189.

[7] Edwards, *Gangraena*, 33 ff. An attack on the Baptists published in 1645 has the following: " Q. 'Who are your preachers and what are they?' A. 'There are divers: viz., Mr. Patience, an honest Glover, Mr. Griffin, a reverend Taylor, Mr. Knowles, a learned Scholler, Mr. Spilsby, a renowned cobler, Mr. Barber, a Button maker, and divers others'." *The Anabaptists Catechisme* (Thomason).

this score, as well as on account of their separatism, was shared by the Independents, but their insistence on adult baptism, and the survival of extravagant tales about the Continental Anabaptists, laid them open to especial bitterness of attack, and there is no better index of the spread of Baptist doctrines than the number and violence of the publications which not only opposed Baptist tenets, but, reviving the stories of Münster, represented Baptists as enemies of society and of the state.[8]

The churches responded to the reproaches cast upon them by the publication of confessions of their faith. The earliest of these had been put forth by the General Baptists in the year that they left Amsterdam. It declared the church of Christ to be the company of the faithful, set apart by baptism, and organized in small independent congregations. It stated that magistracy was an ordinance of God, "that it is a fearful thing to speak evil of them that are in dignity, and to despise government", that church members might be magistrates, and that oaths in a just cause might be lawfully taken.[9] In 1644 the seven Particular Baptist churches in London issued a confession. In its doctrinal portion it showed Calvinistic views as opposed to the Arminianism of the General Baptist confession, but like the latter it asserted that the company of baptized believers was Christ's kingdom on earth, that magistracy was an

[8] "I am afraid that Anabaptisme is very rife in England, though not perhaps in one entire body, but scattered . . . here one tenet . . . and there another: yet not so scattered but they meet in one head, which is the hatred of all rule." *A Short History of the Anabaptists of High and Low Germany*, 1642 (Thomason). *Cf. A Warning for England . . . in the famous History of the frantick Anabaptists*, 1642; *Harleian Miscellany*, VII, 382; Featley, *The Dippers Dipt*, 1645; Edwards, *Gangraena*; Baillie, *Anabaptism*, 1646.

[9] *Confessions of Faith* (Hanserd Knollys Soc.), 3 ff.

ordinance of God, and that it was lawful for church members to hold civil office and to take an oath. In addition it maintained that it was the duty of the magistrate to allow liberty of conscience, that obedience to the magistrate was not to extend to anything contrary to conscience, but that punishment for disobedience in such a case must patiently be endured, and that ministers ought not to preach for hire, but should be supported by the free offerings of their congregations.[10]

Here we find the ideas which were to bring the Baptists into the realm of politics. The questions of adult baptism and lay preaching kept them engaged in constant disputes with theologians outside their ranks; differences of opinion as to close communion, laying-on of hands, and the plan of salvation, kept up dissensions within; but it was their attitude toward the relations of church and state which led them to join with the Independents to oppose tithes and a state-controlled ministry, and to go beyond them in championship of liberty of conscience.

In the confession of faith of the church of John Smith, the founder of the first English congregation, occur the words: "The magistrate is not to meddle with religion, or matters of conscience, to force and compel men to this or that form of religion, for Christ only is the king and law giver of the church and conscience."[11] This enunciation of the principle of toleration does not appear in the confession of 1611, published after Smith's death. His flock, however, maintained the principle at length in 1615, in a protest to James I against the prosecution of those who were unwilling to conform to the worship of the Church of

[10] *Ibid.*, 11 ff.

[11] Barclay, *op. cit.*, ch. vi, appendix, xiii.

England, and again in a petition to the same purport in 1620.[12] These, with similar pleas by individuals belonging to their communion, make valid the Baptist claim to stand among the earliest champions of toleration in England.[13]

It is true that the toleration advocated by a large number of Baptists was distinctly a limited one. In a declaration published in 1659, signed for the most part by Particular Baptists, non-Christian faiths and popery were expressly excluded.[14] Still, protests against this limitation were promptly published by two small bodies of Baptists.[15] The General Baptists, too, in a declar-

[12] *Persecution for religion judged and condemned,* in *Tracts on Liberty of Conscience* (Hanserd Knollys Soc.), 83; *A Most humble supplication, ibid.,* 183.

[13] Leonard Busher, *Religion's peace,* 1614, *ibid.,* 1; Roger Williams, *The Bloudy Tenent of persecution,* 1644; Samuel Richardson, *The Necessity of Toleration,* 1647. For an interesting discussion of the importance of the championing of tolerance by English Baptists see Ernst Troeltsch, "Die Bedeutung des Protestantismus für die Entstehung der modernen Welt", in *Historische Zeitschrift,* 1906, 40, 57.

[14] *A Declaration of several of the People called Anabaptists, in and about the City of London* (Guildhall Library).

[15] "We doe declare, That we would have a full and equall Liberty to be granted (and that as the Scope of the Gospel) to all Persons whatsoever, without Exception of one or other, in the matters of there Conscience in the worshiping of God. For why should we not give unto another, that we would (in this case) injoy our selves, or who is he that will Judge another mans conscience; to his own Master, let him stand or fall: if any corrupt, or unsound Doctrine, come into the Church, there is the law of Christ to deale with them by. But what have the members thereof to do to judge them that are without? surely when peace will be upon the Earth, every man shall serve his God, and the Saints shall walk in the name of the Lord their God, therefore our desire is, that God may have that glorious prerogative of Judging mens hearts, according to the Gospel of his Son." *A Declaration of Several Baptized Believers, walking in all the Foundation Principles of the Doctrine of Christ, mentioned in Heb. 6, 1, 2,* December 29, 1659. A copy is in the library of the Congregational Union, London. There are fourteen signatures. The other protest came from a congregation of Free Will Baptists, who were led by one Henry Adis, *Declaration of a small Society of Baptized Believers, undergoing the name of Free-Willers.* January 12, 1660 (British Museum).

ation issued in 1660, and in their confession of faith of the same year, maintain that liberty of conscience ought to be allowed to all men.[16] Again, Baptist toleration, it must be admitted, was too often theoretical rather than practical. There is no indication that when Baptists were in positions of power they were inclined to grant to others that liberty of conscience which they so earnestly advocated. To be sure, it is chiefly from conditions in Ireland that we have to draw our conclusions upon this point, but when all allowances are made, it is hard to believe that, in practice, the majority of Baptists were in advance of their generation in tolerance.[17]

But however they might differ as to its limitations, or be found wanting in its practice, the Baptists of England were all advocates of liberty of conscience. Consequently, at the outbreak of the Civil Wars they were on the side of Parliament, regarding its war as a holy one. And although there were among them some who adhered to the belief of their brethren on the Continent that Christians should not meddle with the sword, they joined the army in great numbers. There, preaching and praying as well as fighting, they carried on a propaganda which daily swelled the Baptist ranks.[18] The spread of their faith, in England as on the Continent, had been largely among humbler folk, and in the

[16] Barclay, ch. x, appendix; *Minutes of the General Assembly*, 19.

[17] See below, 137 ff.

[18] It was among the General Baptists that doubts arose most frequently as to the lawfulness of warfare for Christians. At a quarterly meeting in 1657 it was decided: " 1. In answer to the quiries about fighting we say that in some cases it may be Lawfull, but as the affaires of the nation now standeth and is like to continue till the appearing of the Lord Jesus we account it exceeding dangerous. . . . 2. And for officers of Churches to list themselves either as private souldiers or comission officers that is altogether unlawfull." Register book of Speldhurst church (Add. MSS., 36,709), fol. 131.

early days of the wars most of them served as private soldiers.[19] But promotion was rapid, the tradesman who had enlisted as a trooper at the beginning of the struggle was sometimes a colonel, or even a general officer, at its close, and the churches of humble artisans and small mechanics found themselves with representatives in the high places of the nation.[20] During the same period, Baptist ideas began to take root among people of higher station, until in the latter days of the Long Parliament there were to be found Baptists among the most influential men as well as the most substantial citizens of the state. An attempt to give an exhaustive list would occupy too much space, but the mention of a few names will make it clear that the Baptist element was one by no means to be despised.

The most eminent Baptist in the eyes of men of that generation was Henry Lawrence, later president of the Council of State of the Protectorate. The legal profession was represented by William Steele, Recorder of London, and later Chancellor of Ireland. Among scholars were to be reckoned John Tombes, an Oxford man, eminent as a theologian, William Dell, master of Caius College, Cambridge, Hanserd Knollys, Benjamin Cox, and Francis Cornwall. William Kiffin and Samuel Moyer had unusual reputations as financiers, and

[19] Richard Deane, in 1649, said he knew of but two Baptists in commands before 1648. Letter to Barlow, Crosby, *English Baptists,* II, 2 ff. A Baptist minister, writing in 1659, said he understood that at the time of the king's execution there were none above the rank of captain, and only six captains. Allen to Baxter, May 30, 1659, Baxter Correspondence, IV, 187 ff.

[20] Firth, *Cromwell's Army,* 40 ff., 49 ff. For the way that the churches themselves sometimes formed troops, see the cases of Walter Cradock and Vavasor Powell, *ibid.,* 328, note. For defense of the army preachers by a Baptist officer, see Edmund Chillenden, *Preaching without Ordination . . . proving the lawfulness of all Persons to preach,* 1647 (Thomason).

Samuel Richardson and Praise-God Barbone were substantial merchants. Henry Hills and Francis Smith were successful printers and publishers. The Baptists in the fleet were exceedingly numerous, the best-known among them being Vice-admiral Lawson.[21] In the army the most prominent Baptists were Colonels Robert Bennet, Richard Overton, Charles Howard, Robert Lilburne, John Hutchinson, Richard Deane, Henry Danvers, and John Wigan. A number of those who were Agitators, or took part in the conferences on the Agreement of the People in 1647 and 1648, were Baptists. They were Edmund Chillenden, William Allen, Daniel Axtell, John Barkstead, Alexander Brayfield, Robert Gladman, John Okey, William Packer, Thomas Saunders, and Hierome Sankey.[22] Accustomed in their churches to an atmosphere of democracy and of free discussion, they lent themselves with ease to the ideas, so freely expressed in those conferences, which were to produce the party known as the Levellers. On the other hand, the terminology employed by their sect, with its faith in Christ as head and lawgiver, and their belief that the kingdom of Christ was at hand, crept into the language of the soldiers' agreements, such as that of Manchester, August 1, 1650, which pro-

[21] A General Baptist assembly held in London in 1654 discussed the advisability of sending Baptist chaplains to the fleet. Letter of John Abell, Sept. 3, 1654. Thurloe, *State Papers*, II, 582.

[22] For examples of the different ways in which these men can be identified as Baptists, see Dr. Whitley's list of General Baptist leaders, *Minutes of the General Assembly*, I, xxxv ff. It is scarcely safe, however, to use the signatures to the Propositions to King Charles for such identification. See below, ch. V, note 41. It used to be the fashion to claim Milton as a Baptist, but see Masson, *Milton*, VI, 838 ff. John Bunyan would of course be counted the most eminent to-day.

claimed unwillingness to accept any king but Jesus.[23] Among these fighting Baptists and their Independent brethren, whose favorite relaxation in camp was attendance at a prayer-meeting, there was a fertile field for the development of new religious ideas. And here developed the other party we have set out to consider—the Fifth Monarchy men.

In these army circles, the idea characterizing all the Evangelical churches, that of turning to the Scriptures for justification of every act, was naturally very much at the fore, and it is not strange that the most fruitful sources for the preachers who sought the explanation of current events should be those most obscure and mystical books, the prophecy of Daniel and the Revelation of John. There were certain portions of the book of Daniel which in the seventeenth century gave rise to little controversy, because they were supposed to be so well understood. These were Nebuchadnezzar's vision of the image, and Daniel's vision of the four beasts which succeeded one another. The interpretation of these visions as representing four kingdoms, which were to follow one another on earth, before the coming of the Ancient of Days and the establishment of an everlasting kingdom ruled by the saints, had, in accordance with the accepted ideas of the time, been justified in the successive establishment of the Assyrian, Persian, Greek, and Roman empires.[24] The events of

[23] "We have not only proclaimed Jesus Christ, the King of Saints, to be our King by profession, but desire to submit to him upon his own terms, and admit him to the exercise of his Royal Authority in our hearts." Manchester Declaration, cited by Feake, *Beam of Light*, 1659. The agreements of Triploe Heath and Windsor were also cited by Fifth Monarchy men.

[24] Hearne, in his *Ductor Historicus*, published in 1705, says that objections to this system of chronology have been made, but that he considers them insufficient. 2d ed., I, 131, 292.

the Thirty Years' War gave currency to the idea that the last days of the Roman monarchy were at hand, and that the time was drawing near when the Fifth Monarchy, with Christ at its head, would after much war and tumult be established upon earth. And while England was being rent with civil wars, it is not strange that men began to feel that perhaps these were the wars of the latter days, or that the soldier was inspired to better service by the great thought that the promise might be fulfilled in his lifetime, and that he was one of the saints who were to bring in the new order.

It is difficult in these days to follow with patience, or even with complete seriousness, all the ramifications of Fifth Monarchy speculation, but reduced to its fundamentals, surely nothing could be finer than the simple faith and hope upon which it was founded. Professor Firth, in his life of Thomas Harrison, applies to him the well-known lines of Blake:

> Bring me my Bow of burning gold:
> Bring me my Arrows of desire:
> Bring me my Spear: O clouds unfold;
> Bring me my Chariot of fire!
>
> I will not cease from mental Fight,
> Nor shall my Sword sleep in my hand;
> Till I have built Jerusalem,
> In England's green and pleasant land.

Here speaks the true spirit of the Fifth Monarchy man, and the realization of this lends a dignity to even the wildest projects of these enthusiasts.

In this spirit, indeed, the Parliamentary armies had fought the Civil Wars. The Fifth Monarchy men kept it alive when for others it had lost its potency. Any one who follows the course of events in England between 1642 and 1650 cannot fail to be struck by the prevalence, among the leaders of the forces as well as among the rank and file, of the idea that they were fighting the battles of Christ, and preparing for his kingdom. Soldiers and preachers alike considered the Parliamentary victories as victories of Armageddon.[25]

From the discussions on the Agreement of the People an excellent idea can be gained of the mingling of millenary ideas with notions of government, and of the part of the saints in the warfare of Christ. In referring to the claim of the king to authority in religious matters Lieutenant-colonel Goffe said: "Certainly, this is a mistery of iniquity. Now Jesus Christ his worke in the last dayes is to destroy this mistery of iniquity; and because itt is so interwoven and intwisted in the interest of States, certainly in that overthrow . . . there must bee great alterations of states. Now the worde doth hold out in the Revelation, that in this worke of Jesus Christ hee shall have a companie of Saints to follow him, such as are chosen, and called, and faithfull. Now itt is a scruple amonge the saints, how farre they should use the sworde, yett God hath made use of them in that worke. Many of them have bin employed these five or six yeares."[26] A year later, when the Agreement of the People was again under discussion, Colonel Thomas Harrison said: "The Worde of God doth take notice, that the powers of this world shall bee given

[25] Barclay, *op. cit.*, 186; *Christ's coming Opened in a Sermon before the Honourable House of Commons . . . May 17, 1648, by William Bridge* (Prince collection, Boston Public Library); *The Vengeance of the Temple Discovered in a sermon preached before . . . the Lord Mayor . . . May 17, 1648 . . . by William Strong.*

[26] *Clarke Papers* (Camden Soc.), I, 282-283.

into the hands of the Lord and his Saints; that this is the day, God's owne day, wherein hee is coming forth in glory in the world, and hee doth putt forth himself very much by his people, and hee sayes in that day wherein hee will thresh the Mountaines hee will make use of Jacob as that threshing instrument . . . and he will worke on us soe farre that we are [to be] made able in wisedome and power to carry through thinges in a way extraordinarie, that the workes of men shall bee answerable to his workes." [27]

The convictions of the men of the sword were strengthened by the speculations of divines. In 1642 Henry Archer had published a pamphlet under the title of *The Personal Reign of Christ upon Earth,* in which he analyzed in detail the coming kingdom. It was to be preceded by a general darkness, and troubles among Gentiles and Jews; the Jews would finally be converted, and would then suffer for forty-five years from the Mahometans, heathen, and Papists. Then Christ would come, uplift the saints, and chastise the wicked. He would thereupon withdraw, and the saints would reign until his final coming, a thousand years later. A careful computation, and comparison of Daniel with Revelation, made Archer fix the date for the conversion of the Jews at either 1650 or 1656, and for the coming of Christ at about 1700.[28] John Owen, preaching before the House of Commons in 1649, showed that the preparation for the kingdom of Christ was to be by the destruction of monarchy, and pointed out that a general

[27] *Id.*, II, 185. Goffe was never identified with the Fifth Monarchy party, but Harrison was to be its most distinguished member.

[28] Thomason. In 1650 appeared an elaborate confutation: *The Revelation Unrevealed.* A copy is in the Prince collection, Boston Public Library.

attack on monarchical power was going on.[29] Preaching before the same body again, three years later, on the seventh chapter of Daniel, he declared once more that the wars of the day were those which were to prepare for the kingdom. He had come to believe, however, that it was still far off, since before it came the Turk and the Pope must be overthrown and the Jews brought back to their own.[30] Thomas Goodwin also drew a picture of the Fifth Monarchy, representing it as an earthly kingdom, in which the saints were to have a part, and indicating that it was close at hand.[31]

From across the Atlantic came testimony of the same sort. John Eliot, the apostle to the Indians of New England, wrote of his faith that the work of Christ in the destruction of the Beast was well under way: " The faithful Brethren in Scotland gave the first blow at the dirty toes, and feet of this Image; with whom the faithful brethren in England, presently concurred. But the Iron of the Civil State, stuck so fast to the miry clay, that according to the Word of Christ, they are (beyond all the thoughts of men) both fallen together . . . and all his faithful Word shall be accomplished . . . Christ is the only right Heir of the Crown of England

[29] " Are not all the Controversies, or the most of them, that at this day are disputed in Letters of Blood among the Nations, somewhat of a distinct Constitution from those formerly under debate? . . . Is not the hand of the Lord in all this? Are not the shakings of the Heavens of the Nations from him? . . . Is it not . . . that he may revenge their opposition to the Kingdom of his dear Son? . . . That so the Kingdoms of the Earth, may become the Kingdoms of our Lord Jesus." Sermon preached April 19, 1649; copy in the New York Public Library.

[30] *Sermon . . . concerning the Kingdom of Christ, and the Power of the Civil Magistrate*, preached Oct. 13, 1652; copy in New York Public Library.

[31] This, and two other sermons, were published later in the interests of the Fifth Monarchy party: *A Sermon on the Fifth Monarchy*, 1654; *The World to Come, or the Kingdome of Christ Asserted*, 1655. Both in Thomason.

. . . and he is now come to take possession of his Kingdom, making England first in that blessed work of setting up the Kingdom of the Lord Jesus." Stating that it was the duty of men to seek out the form of government prescribed by the Scriptures, Eliot exhorted those who had been fighting the Lord's battles "That you would now set the Crown of England upon the head of Christ, whose only true inheritance it is, by the gift of his Father. Let him be your Judge, let him be your Law-Giver, let him be your King." As the form of government to be set up, Eliot suggested one he had formulated for his Indians.[32]

This was not the first crystallization of the Fifth Monarchy idea into a serious political proposition. In February, 1649, "many Christian people dispersed abroad throughout the county of Norfolk, and City of Norwich", presented a petition to the Council of Officers, proposing the establishment of the Fifth Monarchy. Starting with the queries, "Whether there is not a Kingdom and Dominion of the Church or of Christ and the Saints, to be expected upon Earth?" and "Whether this Kingdom . . . be not external and visible in the world, yea, extend not to all persons and things universally?" the authors of the pamphlet conclude in the affirmative. This kingdom, they assert, is to be administered "by such Laws and Officers as Jesus Christ our Mediator hath appointed in his Kingdom", will "put down all worldly Rule and Authority

[32] Mass. Hist. Soc., *Collections*, 3d ser., IX, 127-164. This treatise was ordered suppressed by the Massachusetts General Court in 1661. Eliot "recanted", saying he had sent it over to England "about nine or ten years since". It would be interesting to know if there was any connection between the ideas of Eliot and those of William Aspinwall, who after living in New England returned to England, and wrote copiously in behalf of the Fifth Monarchy.

(so far as relates to the worldly constitution thereof) though in the hands of Christians", and is to be expected "about this time we live in". It is not to be established by "humane Power and Authority", but by the gathering, through the spirit of Christ, of a people organized in churches, who, when they shall have attained to sufficient numbers, "shall rule the world by General Assemblies or Church-Parliaments, of such Officers of Christ and Representatives of the Churches as they shall chuse and delegate, which they shall do till Christ come in Person". The duty of the saints is therefore to organize in churches, and "for the present to lay aside all differences and divisions amongst themselves, and combine together against the Antichristian powers of the world . . . whom they may expect to combine against them universally (Rev. xvii, 13, 14)". The petitioners propose that the government encourage the formation of such churches, and persuade Independents and Presbyterians that their interests in the movement are identical. To this end it is urged that only godly preachers be sent out, and that the churches be allowed to elect representatives to the proposed church parliaments, which will "determine all things by the Word, as that Law that God will exalt alone, and make honorable".[33]

This petition, to which it is to be feared the Council of Officers did not give very serious consideration, is the first evidence of any group of people making an organized effort to establish the Fifth Monarchy as the government of England; with it the Fifth Monarchy party emerges into the light. It is to be observed that the petition came from Norwich and its vicinity. There

[33] *Certain Queries Humbly presented by way of Petition . . . to the Lord General and Council of War*, 1649 (Thomason).

are no signatures, and there is no way of determining how wide a movement it represented. Norfolk was, throughout the history of the movement, the chief stronghold of the party outside of London, but only scattered records of its activities there have come down to us.

The first trace of an organization in London dates from the period directly after the battle of Worcester. At that time, a gathering of " divers officers and Members of several Congregations, that had not succumbed to the temptations of the day ", decided to endeavor to stir up Cromwell and his officers to hasten on the Lord's cause, and " to quicken the Parliament to some good work ". These men were Baptists and Independents. Although Cromwell at first listened with interest to their representations, they soon observed that he was taking no steps to put into practice the suggestions they made. They accordingly decided that applications to the government should cease, and dependence be had upon the Lord alone. Therefore, in the latter part of December, 1651, a new series of meetings was inaugurated, at the church of Allhallows the Great, in Thames Street. Here " divers Officers and Members of Churches, among whom some were Souldiers ", agreed to pray for the speedy exalting of Christ's kingdom, the removal of unfit magistrates and ministers, the ending of divisions among the Lord's people, the stirring up of Parliament, army, and people to fulfill their promises, and the prevention, in the coming negotiations with the Dutch, of any step " prejudicial to Christ's cause, and that of his kingdom ".[34] The new movement was at

[34] Feake, *Beam of Light.* Although this account was not published until 1659, there seems no reason to doubt the general accuracy of its statements concerning these early meetings. The negotiations with the

once regarded with suspicion in government, army, and church circles. Some of the leading Independent ministers undertook to persuade the agitators of the error of their ways, and certain of the leaders were persuaded to give up the cause.[35]

The defections were numerous enough seriously to affect the movement for the moment, but in the following spring there was a revival of interest. To this there were several contributory causes. The immediate occasion was the outbreak of the Dutch war, which was regarded as the spread to the Continent of the wars which were to establish Christ's kingdom.[36] In addition, conditions at home were such as would engender discontent in the minds of millenarian enthusiasts. There was danger, in the eyes of advocates of the principle "No king but Jesus", in the wave of monarchical enthusiasm which had followed the publication of Hobbes's *Leviathan,* and under the influence of which even Cromwell was considering the desirability of a return to kingship.[37] The Long Parliament was increasing its unpopularity by disregard of suggestions for the reform of the law, and by its dilatory policy in the matter of the religious settlement, which, it was whispered, might take the form of an intolerant, tithe-supported state church.[38] Well might a new politico-religious party seize this moment to enter upon a fresh stage of activity.

Dutch were those concerning the navigation act, and interference with Dutch trade, which were begun upon the arrival, December 15, of the Dutch ambassadors Cats, Schaef, and Van de Perre; see Gardiner, *Commonwealth and Protectorate,* II, 169.

[35] Feake, *op. cit.,* and circular letter of John Owen, Thomas Goodwin, Philip Nye, and Sidrach Simpson (Carte MSS., 81, fol. 16.) The letter, written in 1654, refers to this earlier effort.

[36] See below, p. 24.

[37] Gardiner, *op. cit.,* II, 75 ff.

[38] *Ibid.,* 82 ff., 98 ff.

Six congregations were invited to send messengers to the new series of meetings, which were held at London House and at some place in Blackfriars. The meetings were " partly to hear those Scriptures opened, which concerned the blessed Interest of Jesus Christ; and partly to wrestle with the Lord again (after our former neglect) for the fulfilling of his Word, in the Destruction of Babylon, and advancement of the Kingdom of his dear Son ". It was left to the messengers " publicly to own and plead the cause of Christ's kingdom ", and they set themselves earnestly to the task, but with varying success, according to the historian of the early stages of the movement, who complained that at this time " the gospel of the kingdom was published with a great mixture of human frailty ".[89]

It is impossible to give with certainty more than a few names of those who were associated with the movement at this time. Apparently the leading spirit was Christopher Feake, a clergyman who in 1646 had begun to have scruples as to infant baptism, and who was in 1649 vicar of Christ Church, Newgate, and lecturer at St. Anne's, Blackfriars. Our knowledge of these early meetings is drawn from an account by him, published some years later, and it seems to have been to the parish of St. Anne's, Blackfriars, that the meetings, which were at first held at Allhallows the Great, were transferred. In March, 1652, there arrived from Dublin an able and zealous young preacher, a Cambridge man, named John Rogers. He had been sent to Ireland by the Council of State the preceding year, and had been preaching in the Dublin cathedral, but left on account of friction with the Baptist pastor there. On his return

[89] Feake, *Beam of Light*; Erbery, *The Bishop of London*, 1653 (Thomason).

to London he again took up a lectureship which he held at the church of St. Thomas the Apostle. It is not known when he embraced Fifth Monarchy principles, but he soon became one of the leading preachers of the party. Next in importance came John Simpson, who held a lectureship at St. Botolph's, Aldgate.[40] Other men who preached Fifth Monarchy doctrines later, if not at this time, were Vavasor Powell, one of the propagators of the gospel in Wales, and John Canne, chaplain to the regiment of Robert Overton. To these early meetings came George Cockayne, who was afterwards one of Cromwell's spies. All of these men except Rogers were Baptists. Of the soldiers attached to the party at this stage we are sure of only one by name, Major Packer. Of those who later became prominent several had taken leading parts in the discussions on the Agreement of the People. They were Thomas Harrison, Nathaniel Rich, Hugh Courtney, William Allen, Edmund Chillenden, John Spittlehouse, Henry Danvers, Thomas Buttivant, and Wentworth Day.

A sufficient number of the writings of these enthusiasts has come down to us to give a pretty clear idea of the doctrines set forth at their meetings. The book of Revelation, and the prophets Zechariah, Ezekiel, and Malachi, furnished them with a large number of their texts, but the book to which they had recourse most frequently was Daniel, and the favorite chapter of Daniel was the seventh. Although the interpretations given by different preachers to the vision of Daniel

[40] For Feake, Rogers, and Simpson, see *Dict. Nat. Biog.* For Rogers, see also Edward Rogers, *Some Account of the Life and Opinions of a Fifth Monarchy Man,* London, 1867, and for Simpson, see Dodd, "Troubles in a City Parish under the Protectorate", in *English Historical Review,* 1895.

varied in detail, their general features were the same. The four beasts were the four great empires of history; the little horn which appeared upon the head of the fourth beast and made war upon the saints was explained as the papacy, William the Conqueror and the remnants of the Norman yoke, the Stuart line, or simply Charles I. The year 1648 had marked the beginning of the dissolution of the Roman power, and the High Court of Justice in that year was the throne of the Ancient of Days. After the destruction of antichristian forms in England, the war would spread to the Continent, and the Pope be driven from his throne. Meanwhile the Jews would return to their own country and make war on the Turk; the righteous alone would flourish, finishing the destruction of the fourth monarchy, and Christ's kingdom would be established, the saints ruling with him.[41] The exact dates of these happenings varied with the individual interpretations of " a time, and times, and the dividing of time ". The date of 1655 was given by one writer for the return of the Jews to Palestine, and 1660 for the final destruction of the " little horn ". According to another, 1660 was the year when the Fifth Monarchy should extend to Rome, and in 1666 it was to be visible over the whole earth. It was to be inaugurated " gradually and mysteriously, yet suddenly ".[42] The methods of computation employed are perhaps worthy of attention. They were summarized by an unsympathetic contemporary as follows:

---

[41] John Canne, *A Voice from the Temple*, 1653; John Rogers, *Sagrir*, 1653; William Aspinwall, *An Explication and Application of the Seventh Chapter of Daniel*, 1654, and *Thunders from Heaven*, 1655. All in Thomason collection.

[42] Canne, *Voice from the Temple; Rogers, Sagrir.*

Some that have heard that the end of Paganism is placed in the year 395 . . . will easily be induced to believe that the famous number, 1260, ought to be added to it, and then . . . 1655 must be pointed out for an apocalyptical epocha. Others pitch upon the year 1656, because, having summed up the lives of the patriarchs in the fifth chapter of Genesis, they find 1656 years from the creation to the flood, and thence infer, that the coming of Christ will be the next year, because it must be as in the days of Noah. To 325 (the Council of Nice was in) add 1332, that is, twice 666, the sum will be 1657. Others will wait three or four years more, hoping that the 1260 years must be reckoned from the death of Theodosius. . . . Nor need we wonder, if we find some confident that eleven years hence we shall see the fatal change, because of the number 666.[43]

There were also differences of opinion as to the exact part the Jews were to play in setting up the kingdom, but it was to be an important one, and therefore they were to be favored, and admitted to England. The war with the Dutch was advocated, for it was by their conquest that a foothold would be gained for the campaign of regeneration on the Continent.[44]

[43] Pell to Thurloe, March, 1655, Vaughan, *Protectorate*, I, 155.

[44] "It was the last Monday preached publicly before a great congregation . . . that if they now made peace with those rogues and dogs the Dutch . . . that God's vengeance would follow upon such a heathenish peace; for where should they have a landing-place, when they went to do the great work of the Lord, and tear the whore of Babylon out of her chair, if they gave back by making a peace with them, a people and land, which the Lord had as good as given wholly up into their hands?" Intercepted letter from London, Oct. 20, 1653 (n. s.), Thurloe, I, 534. See also, *ibid.*, 501. "Thou gavest a Cup into the hand of England, and we drank of it. Then thou carried'st it to Scotland and Ireland, and they drank of it. Now thou hast carried it to Holland, and they are drinking of it. Lord, carry it also to France, to Spain, and to Rome." "I will never believe that this Navy was made on purpose for the breaking of our Neighbours in pieces, and there an end. We shall at last joyn together, and do such work for God as was never done in the world. We shall carry the Gospel with our Navy up and down to the Gentiles, and afterward we shall gather home the Jews out of the Isles first; for those are them shall first be called, and the Ships of Tharsis shall do it." From sermons of Feake at Blackfriars and Christ Church, Aug. 11 and Sept. 11, 1653. Roger L'Estrange, *The Dissenters' Sayings*, 1681.

The immediate duty of the saints was to prepare for the kingdom, by making the existing government accord as closely as possible with the rule of Christ. To this end, none but godly men should be allowed to sit in the seats of the mighty, tithes should be abolished, and the existing laws replaced by the law of God. "Then shall the Oppressor cease and no more complaining be heard in the streets. Taxes should be no more. And Trade and industry should abound. . . . The poor should have bread, and the Army no more in Arrears. Prison doors should be open and Debtors satisfied without Arrests . . . then peace and safety, plenty and prosperity, should overflow the land."[45]

To bring about this happy state of things, the saints must watch and pray, seek union among themselves, and keep apart from the world, as a peculiar people, ready, when the call came, to do their part in the pouring out of the seven vials.[46] They should also direct the government toward the right path, and testify unceasingly against any failure to follow it, serene in the confidence that the Lord would overturn any government that failed to heed these warnings, and would continue to overturn, until one arose which would do his work.[47]

Such was the Fifth Monarchy party's program—a direct result of the belief in the possibility of creating a scheme of things entire through a literal interpretation of the Scriptures. In so far as its members con-

[45] Peter Chamberlen, *Legislative Power in Problems* (Thomason).

[46] Revelation, xvi.

[47] "Thus saith the Lord God; Remove the diadem, and take off the crown: this shall not be the same: exalt him that is low, and abase him that is high. I will overturn, overturn, overturn it: and it shall be no more, until he come whose right it is; and I will give it him." Ezekiel, xxi, 26, 27.

fined themselves to a discussion of the time and circumstances of the millenium, they were of no more importance than any other of the curious sects which were so numerous in the England of that day. But the fact that they regarded themselves as having a further duty, that of admonishing the government of its failings, and suggesting methods of reform, gave another aspect to their activities. It is true that all sorts and conditions of men at this time felt the same duty incumbent upon them, and that the men at the head of the state were constantly receiving from groups of anxious citizens suggestions as to the settlement of the government.[48] But the suggestions of the Fifth Monarchy men were given as from the saints that were to help set up the kingdom, and there was always the possibility that the saints, finding their suggestions ignored, might feel called upon to take upon themselves the work of establishing the kingdom, by force if need be. This it was that from the outset caused the very men who had preached of the imminence of Christ's kingdom, John Owen and Thomas Goodwin, to regard the new party with suspicion. Color was unquestionably given to such suspicions by the language used by members of the party. Sermons which dealt with the destruction of the Image of the Beast, the warfare of the saints, the pulling down of Babylon, as of matters about which men must soon be busy, had a dangerous sound, however figuratively the language employed might have

[48] Among others, *A Model of a New Representative*, 1651, and *A Cry . . . with some Cautions touching the Elections of the (expected) New Representative*, 1651, both in Thomason. A number of Independents and Baptists published a disclaimer of these two: *A Declaration of divers Elders and Brethren of Congregationall Societies*, 1651 (Thomason). The ideas of the authors on government were incidentally given.

been used.[49] Whether it was used figuratively or not was yet to be proved: at any rate it was clear, in the year 1652, that the Fifth Monarchy men felt called upon to meddle with matters of state.

What were the relations of the Fifth Monarchy party with the Baptists? We have seen that its members were drawn from both Baptist and Independent churches. It is quite impossible to estimate the relative proportion of the two denominations represented; it was stated in 1660 that there were quite as many Independents as Baptists among the Fifth Monarchy men.[50] But when it is borne in mind that the common term for Baptist was Anabaptist, and that the term at once suggested the attempt of Knipperdoling and John of Leyden to establish the millennium at Münster, it does not seem strange that those who had no sympathy either with millenary dreams or with antipedobaptism, were content to characterize the new movement as Anabaptist. The fact that the greater number of the preachers were Baptists gave additional verisimilitude to the characterization. It is only by considering the events of each year that we can come to know what actually were the relations of the Baptists in general to the Fifth Monarchy men, and what was the attitude of either party, at different times, to the civil power. It is this which we are to attempt in the pages that follow.

[49] A visitor at Blackfriars in the summer of 1653 wrote, "I heard one prayer and two sermons; but good God! what cruel, and abominable, and most horrid trumpets of fire, murther and flame". Beverning to De Witt, Aug. 26/Sept. 5, 1653, in Thurloe, I, 441.

[50] *Moderation; or Arguments and Motives tending thereunto, by S. T.*, 1660 (Thomason).

CHAPTER II.

GOVERNMENT BY THE SAINTS.

THE Fifth Monarchy men abstained from political agitation during the fall and early winter of 1652. A visitor at one of their meetings described the Baptists and Independents as meeting in different rooms, considering matters of doctrine, and praying for the Holy Spirit, a knowledge of the right way of propagating the gospel, and union among the churches.[1] The army petition of the preceding August, with its request for the abolition of tithes, for law reform, and for the admission of none but godly men to office and to seats in Parliament, must have had their approval; and the favorable attitude toward these reforms which Parliament at first assumed seemed to presage well for the new modeling of the government. But toward the end of the year, when it became evident that no action was intended, the situation changed, and violent attacks upon Parliament began to be heard. At Allhallows the Great, prayers for a new representative were quashed by the government, but at Blackfriars and elsewhere the Fifth Monarchy men continued to preach vehemently against the Long Parliament.[2] An additional cause of offense was furnished by the negotiations with the Dutch. Moreover, the rejection of the bill continu-

[1] Erbery, *Bishop of London.*

[2] Extracts from Clarendon MSS., March 18, April 8, 15, 1653, in *English Historical Review*, 1893, 528-529; Gardiner, *Commonwealth and Protectorate*, II, 232, 248 ff.

ing in authority the commissioners for the propagation of the gospel, an action iniquitous enough in itself, in the eyes of members of the gathered churches, struck home with particular force to the Fifth Monarchy men, for Thomas Harrison was one of the commissioners, and Vavasor Powell one of the ministers who would be displaced through the failure of the act.[3] The refusal of Parliament to consider the bill for a new representative brought matters to a head, and when Cromwell, suspicious of the plan of Vane and his party to prolong indefinitely the power of the members then sitting, violently drove out the Parliament which had continued so long, Harrison was following out the ideas of his party in acting as his lieutenant.[4]

The Fifth Monarchy preachers were loud in their praises of Cromwell's act. The dissolution of Parliament proved conclusively that the Ancient of Days had set up his throne in England. Parliament had finished the work the Lord had set for it, and now Cromwell had been raised up to purge the throne it had begun to dishonor. A new and wonderful rule was to be inaugurated, bringing with it every blessing.[5] As a news writer quoted Powell, preaching at Whitehall, "Law should streame downe like a river freely, as for twenty shillings what formerly cost twenty pounds, impartially as the saints please, and it should runn as rivers doe, close to the doors."[6] It was to be a government by the saints, and the Fifth Monarchy men considered it their duty, as saints, to suggest the means by which it should be instituted.

[3] *Ibid.*, 249.
[4] *Ibid.*, 255.
[5] Canne, *Voice from the Temple.*
[6] *English Historical Review*, 1893, 533.

"We humbly advise that forasmuch as the policy and greatnesse of men hath ever failed, yee would now at length (in the next election) suffer and encourage the saincts of God in his spirit, to recommend unto you such as God shall choose for that worke."[7] So ran a message from North Wales. A London congregation, whose pastor was the Fifth Monarchy Baptist, Edmund Chillenden, proposed that three times the desired number of men be nominated, and the selection made from them, according to scriptural precedent, by lot.[8] Another suggestion was that the choice be made from the army, since it represented the gathered churches.[9] A meeting of the congregation of John Rogers at St. Thomas Apostle's resulted in a set of proposals, the substance of which was that the government be put into the hands of a Sanhedrim of seventy godly men, chosen by Cromwell, and set apart for the work by prayer.[10]

When it finally became known that Cromwell and his advisers had decided to put into practice the principle at the root of these suggestions, that is, to summon an assembly of godly men, the Fifth Monarchists were jubilant, and Cromwell was hailed as the Moses who was to establish the new order, the chief ruler appointed

[7] "A voice out of the hearts of diverse that wait for the Lord Jesus in Denbighshire, in North Wales", in Nickolls, *Letters and Papers of State*, 120.

[8] "The humble representation of the congregation of Jesus Christ meeting at the Chequer without Aldgate", *ibid.*, 121. Approbation was expressed of the qualifications for nomination suggested in the *Declaration* of 1652, mentioned above, ch. I, note 48.

[9] Spittlehouse, *The Army Vindicated*, 1653 (Thomason). A few weeks later he had decided that Cromwell ought to do the nominating. Spittlehouse, *A Warning Piece Discharged* (Thomason).

[10] Rogers, *A Few Proposalls* (Thomason).

by God.[11] There were, however, dissenting voices. The discovery that Cromwell had adopted the plan with some reluctance, and had desired to modify it by giving seats to such men as Fairfax, who had no connection with the gathered churches, gave rise in some hearts to the feeling that perhaps the leading rôle in the new order was to be reserved for some one more enlightened regarding it. Naturally that other would be Harrison, the chief champion of the new plan in the Council of Officers. Harrison was said to have made no secret of his dissatisfaction with Cromwell's attitude, and the drifting apart of the two men seems to have dated from this time.[12] Still, in spite of some signs of disaffection, the general attitude was one of hopefulness, and when at last the Little Parliament assembled, the work of regeneration was breathlessly awaited.[13]

Whatever Cromwell's misgivings as to the wisdom of attempting a government by the saints, his speech on opening the assembly which was to put the experiment to the test, was enthusiastic enough to satisfy the most extreme supporters of the theory; indeed, expressed their very hopes, that the day of the fulfilment of proph-

[11] Spittlehouse, *A Warning Piece Discharged.* Rogers, much encouraged, wrote another letter to Cromwell, suggesting reform of the law, abolition of tithes, and so forth. Extract from introduction to *Beth-shemesh Clouded,* in Edward Rogers, *Fifth Monarchy Man,* 53 ff.

[12] Gardiner, *op. cit.,* II, 274, 276.

[13] Letters of John Portman, July 8, 20, *Calendar of State Papers, Domestic, 1652-1653,* 15, 39. The *Faithful Scout,* July 8, 1653, greeted the Parliament with a reference to "these Overturning, Overturning, Overturning dayes", and expressed the hope that it would "endeavor the directing of the Kingdom of Jesus Christ to the uttermost parts of the Earth". Border, the author of the *Scout,* was a Baptist, and strongly sympathized with the Fifth Monarchy party. See the issue for Oct. 27, 1652.

ecy was perhaps at hand.[14] While it was a question of deciding upon the best settlement of the nation, Cromwell's strong common sense had allowed no millenary enthusiasm to blind him to the practical drawbacks of placing the government in the hands of a body of men chosen for their godliness alone, and quite without political experience. But, now that he was committed to the experiment, he gave free rein to the other side of his nature, and to the hope that, since the best government ought surely to be a government carried on by good men, these good men were to be made instruments for the welfare of the nation.

The assembly in which such high hopes were centered, called in later days after a worthy Baptist among its members who was conspicuous for his name as well as for his activities, was stigmatized by contemporaries as a company of Anabaptists.[15] It was certainly a body unique among English Parliaments, but it would be a mistake to think of it as composed chiefly of fanatics and enthusiasts. The changes made by the Council, together with the moderate men among the nominees of the churches, reduced the number that advocated an

[14] "I say, you are called with a high call; and why should we be afraid to say or think, that this way may be the door to usher in things that God hath promised and prophesied of, and [so] set the hearts of his people to wait for and expect? We know who they are that shall war with the Lamb against his enemies; they shall be a people, called, chosen, and faithful. . . . Indeed I do think something is at the door. We are at the threshold, and therefore it becomes us to lift up our heads and to encourage ourselves in the Lord. And we have some of us thought it our duty to endeavour this way, not vainly looking on that prophecy in Daniel, *And the Kingdom shall not be delivered to another people.*" July 4, 1653. Stainer, *Speeches of Cromwell*, 113, 114.

[15] Intercepted letter, August 1/11, 1653, Thurloe, I, 393. "Il seroit difficile de descrire les quallités et conditions de ces nouveaux ministres: il y en a de tous arts et professions, et leur plus grand talent est de prescher." Bordeaux to Brienne, July 4/14, P. R. O. Transcripts.

extreme program to not more than sixty out of the one hundred and forty members.[16] Still, in organization and regularity of attendance, the radical party went far toward making up its deficiency in numbers, and, by the expedient of dispensing with a regular clergyman, and having the prayers offered by different members in turn, it proceeded to impart to its sittings the atmosphere of a gathered church.[17] When a debate arose as to the name by which the assembly should be known, some of the radicals advocated the term Parliament, "because of the lowness and innocency of the title, having little of earthly glory or boasting in it".[18] In the declaration which they issued on July 12, the members stated that Gods' people were looking for strange changes, as they were before Christ's birth; that the records of no nation so showed the actings of God as did England's; that they hoped to be the instruments to complete his work, by promoting the gospel, breaking yokes, and removing burdens.[19] It was resolved that none but religious men should be employed, and the nation was invited to join in a service of prayer.

[16] Gardiner, *op. cit.*, II, 281, 307 ff. Among the radical members those who can be identified as Baptists or Fifth Monarchy men are the following: Praise-God Barbone (B.), Robert Bennet (B.), John Browne (F. M.), John Carew (F. M.), Hugh Courtney (F. M.), John Crofts (B.), Henry Danvers (F. M., B.), Thomas Harrison (F. M.), Samuel Highland (B.), Dennis Hollister (B.), John James (B., F. M.), Francis Langdon (F. M.), Samuel Moyer (B.), Richard Price (F. M.), William Reeve (B.), William Spence (B.), Arthur Squib (F. M.), John Williams (B., F. M.).

[17] *Exact Relation*, reprinted in *Somers Tracts*, VI, 266 ff. Firth believes this account to have been written by Samuel Highland, Gardiner, *op. cit.*, II, 288, note 4. It was by contemporaries attributed to Praise-God Barbone. See *A Faithfull Searching Home Word*, 1659 (Thomason).

[18] *Exact Relation.*

[19] *Cal. St. P., Dom., 1653-1654*, 21.

4

These preliminaries once out of the way, Parliament proceeded to attack the great subject of tithes. On July 15 it was proposed that no minister receive his maintenance from tithe after November 3. The question of putting to vote this sweeping measure was defeated by sixty-eight votes against forty-three. After some discussion and substantial modification, the question was, by a vote of fifty-six to forty-nine, referred to a committee. In both divisions, Harrison acted as teller for the minority.[20] This was the first check for the reformers. The tithe system as it existed was quite generally regarded as objectionable, but the moderate party insisted that it should not be abolished until some other mode of supporting the clergy should have been devised. The radicals, as one of them expressed it, proposed to " have it removed as a grievance in the first place, and then to make provision as God should direct ".[21] The same policy guided them with regard to the Court of Chancery, and here they had the support of the moderates. On August 5, without a division, a vote was passed for the abolition of that court.[22] In the Marriage Act, too, the radicals were able to establish the principle that marriage is a purely civil institution, and to make obligatory that registration of births, marriages, and deaths which had for years been customary in the Baptist, and in some of the Independent congregations.[23]

The attitude of the Parliament with regard to law reform sheds light upon the real strength of the Fifth

[20] *Commons Journals*, VII, 285, 286.

[21] *Exact Relation*. John Rogers, at the request of some of the members of Parliament, argued before the committee on tithes in September, *Fifth Monarchy Man*, 78 ff.

[22] *Commons Journals*, VII, 296. The act never went into effect.

[23] Barclay, *Religious Societies of the Commonwealth*, 397, note, 406.

Monarchy party in the House. One of the moderates complained that all members were "unsainted and condemn'd into the Fourth Monarchy, and looked upon as obstructors of Reformation, and no longer fit for the work, if not thorough-paced to all the Principles of Reformation held forth by Mr. Feake and others at Black fryers and other places".[24] Now among the things demanded from Fifth Monarchy pulpits and in Fifth Monarchy pamphlets was the abolition of the existing laws of England as a remnant of the Norman yoke, and the substitution for them of the laws of God as laid down in the Scriptures.[25] Most people were agreed that the laws of England were in need of simplification and reform. Cromwell was later to urge action in that direction on his Parliaments repeatedly. Members of the gathered churches had clear ideas in what direction reform should proceed. John Coke wanted them cleared of everything "either properly and directly, or collaterally and obliquely, repugnant to the law of God".[26] All the radicals, and even some of the moderates would wish to further some sort of legal reform, and there was no difficulty about the appointment of a committee to take charge of the matter. For the use of this committee the results of the labors of a similar committee of the Long Parliament were ordered printed.[27] But on August 9 a committee was appointed "to consider of a new Body of the law." Its existence

[24] *An Answer to a Paper entituled, a True Narrative of the Dissolution of the late Parliament*, 1654 (Thomason).

[25] Rogers, *Sagrir*, 1653 (Thomason); Aspinwall, *The Legislative Power is Christ's peculiar Prerogative*, 1656, and *Explication*, 1654 (Thomason).

[26] Cited by Robinson, in *Select Essays in Anglo-American Legal History* (Boston, 1907), I, 481.

[27] Somers, *Tracts*, VI, 177-245.

however, gave currency to the story that a movement was on foot to abolish the laws of England, and substitute the Mosaic code. The apologist of the radicals claimed that this report was due to the substitution by the clerk of the expression "new body of the law" for "new model of the law", and indignantly denied that the intention was "to destroy the law, and take away the Laws we had been fighting for all this while as our birthright and inheritance". He claimed that the objection to the laws was their volume and intricacy, and "incongruity in many things with the word of God", and that what was desired was their reform and simplification, "not a destroying of the law, or putting it down".[28] The reasonable conclusion is, that the Fifth Monarchy men in the House, while they could depend upon the support of the Baptists and a large number of the Independents for measures of law reform, and even for the unqualified abolition of tithes, found themselves in a hopeless minority when it came to the more extreme part of their program, and therefore did not urge a plan in which they undoubtedly believed.[29]

While it was Fifth Monarchy doctrine that laid the assembly open to the reproach that it meant to abolish the laws, it was probably the Baptist attitude which seemed to justify a rumor that it contemplated abolishing the universities. William Dell, a well-known Baptist who was master of Caius College, Cambridge, had in the preceding April published an argument intended to prove that the universities were in no way essential for the training of ministers. He argued, however, that

[28] *Exact Relation.*

[29] See Gardiner, *op. cit.*, II, 314, note, 322, note 2.

"if the Universities will stand upon a Human and Civil account, as Schools of good Learning for the instructing and educating youth in the knowledge of Tongues and of the liberal Arts and Sciences, thereby to make them useful and serviceable to the Commonwealth . . . and will be content to shake hands with their Ecclesiastical and Antichristian Interest, then let them stand . . . but if they will still exalt themselves above themselves and place themselves on Christ's very Throne . . . then let them . . . descend into the darkness out of which they first sprang".[30] The principle of the Baptists that all men who felt a call to preach were thereby qualified for the task had brought them to this feeling that universities were not absolutely indispensable institutions, and it is not at all unlikely that the Baptists as well as many of the Independents in the Parliament were inclined to favor reform along the lines advocated by Dell. There may even have been some enthusiast imbued with the ideas of Samuel How, the Baptist preacher of earlier days, who in the House proposed their unconditional abolition, and thus gave rise to the single report that has come down to us that such a thing was contemplated.[31] If so, his following was very limited, as otherwise the matter would have attracted more notice.

It was early evident that the reform party in Parliament was not inclined to favor the ideas of the Levellers. Certainly those who were Fifth Monarchists had no sympathy with them, for though the two parties agreed in their objection to tithes and existing legal

[30] *The Stumbling Stone*, 1653 (Thomason).

[31] Pauluzzi to Morosini, Dec. 15/25, 1653, P. R. O. Transcripts. For Samuel How, see Barclay, *op. cit.*, 502, 503.

institutions, their principles were fundamentally at variance. While the ideal of the Levellers was government by the people, that of the Fifth Monarchists was government by the elect, and while the Levellers longed for a full and free Parliament, the Fifth Monarchy men yearned for a dispensation from Heaven. There seems to have been no representative of the Levellers' cause in the Little Parliament, and whatever individual sympathy there was at the outset for the case of John Lilburne soon wore itself out. Refusing at first to intervene in order to secure a suspension of his trial, Parliament later imprisoned some petitioners in his favor, and finally, on his acquittal, ordered him kept in prison. His supporters issued an attack on Cromwell and his "so-called Parliament", and invited the people of England to convene on October 16 to elect a true Parliament.[32] On that day it happened that Edmund Chillenden's congregation, which had had its hand in suggesting the composition of the "so-called Parliament", was listening to a sermon by its pastor in one of the chapels of St. Paul's, which it had been occupying since the preceding June.[33] The mob that gathered in answer to the bidding of the Levellers showed its opinion of the sentiments of these godly folk by throwing stones through the windows. Chillenden was a man of war as well as a preacher, and a riot ensued, which was dispelled only by the intervention of the

[32] See Gardiner, *op. cit.*, II, 296 ff.

[33] See above, p. 30, *Cal. St. P., Dom., 1652-1653*, 423. Several years earlier this congregation had presented to the committee for propagating the gospel a petition against tithes and a national church. Grey, *Examination of Neale's Puritans*, 149.

mayor and sheriffs, who by good fortune were worshipping close at hand.[34]

Although like the rest of the sectaries the Fifth Monarchy men had until this time approved and supported the Parliament, yet as the weeks went by and none of the great reforms begun so boldly were carried through, they began to get uneasy, and when the elections to the Council of State on November 1 gave the moderate party a majority in that body, which it was surmised might take steps to end the war with the Dutch, uneasiness gave way to hostility. This hostility extended to the " Parliament, army, Council of State, and all men in power ", but Cromwell came in for the largest share of abuse.[35] The chief center of disturbance was Blackfriars, and Feake was the most violent, though Harrison also called attention to himself by open criticism from the pulpit of Cromwell and the Dutch peace.[36]

The position of Cromwell was a difficult one. Early in August he had begun to show dissatisfaction with his Parliament. The radical party in that body was supported in the Council of State by Harrison and his adherents. Yet Cromwell was held responsible by

[34] Bordeaux to Brienne, Oct. 17/27, 1653, P. R. O. Transcripts; *The Madman's Plea, or a sober Defence of Captain Chillington's Church*, by W. E[rbury] (Thomason); *Cal. St. P., Dom., 1653-1654*, 200, 205; newspapers for the week of Oct. 16, 1653. Gardiner, *op. cit.*, II, 304, note 2, comments on the fact that about this time Chillenden, who was a captain in the army, was cashiered for some unknown cause. A letter from a member of his congregation shows that he was the following month excommunicated for immorality, and, in accordance with the strict discipline of the army at the time, this may be the reason why his commission was taken from him. The letter contains some interesting details as to the chapel. Samuel Oates to Robert Jeffes, Nov. 15, 1653, Rawlinson MSS., A 8, fol. 127.

[35] Bordeaux to Mazarin, Nov. 7/17, 1653, P. R. O. Transcripts; *Moderate Publisher*, Nov. 19-Dec. 2; Thurloe, I, 396, 442, 501, 519, 534.

[36] *Ibid.*, 610, 612, 621.

the public for the actions of both bodies. While the November election gave the numerical majority in the Council to the moderates, in the House their majority was, as we have said, counterbalanced by the fact that they were irregular in attendance. The radicals took their responsibilities more seriously. Several reforming acts of real importance and moderation were passed, but in the renewed attack on Chancery the most impracticable measures were proposed, and the opposition to the assessment bill was very disquieting to those who had to meet the expenses of the government. Moreover, when the great question of church settlement was attacked in any of its phases, it became quite evident that the barriers to an agreement were insurmountable. With the denunciations of Levellers and Fifth Monarchy men ringing in his ears, it is not strange that Cromwell began to consider with favor plans to limit the power of Parliament and strengthen the executive.[87] Nor can there be any doubt that he approved the bill for a High Court of Justice, introduced on the ground of danger from the Royalists, but providing a means of dealing with such utterances as were being hurled at him from the pulpits. By a stroke of irony this bill was hurried through the House while those who would have opposed it were absent, listening to one of the orators at Blackfriars.[88] Harrison left

[87] A letter to Cromwell, dated Nov. 16, deals with the Blackfriars attacks on Parliament, army, and Council, warns him that such talk will injure the reputation of the government abroad, and advises him to settle the government on a firm foundation. Rymer, *Foedera,* XX, 719.

[88] *Exact Relation.* This, with the *Answer to a Paper entituled: A True Narrative . . . ,* gives the account of affairs from the radical and the moderate point of view respectively. Although Glass has devoted much research to his study of this Parliament, Gardiner's account, *op cit.,* II, chs. xxvii, xxviii, is still the most impartial and reliable one we have.

town the following day, the general opinion being that it was on account of the weakening of his party and the displeasure of Cromwell with his actions.[39] Lambert, who had in the days following the dissolution of the Long Parliament advocated a strong central government in opposition to Harrison's scheme, appeared in London, and presided over a meeting of officers that discussed the state of affairs.

These events aroused the Fifth Monarchy preachers to a new outburst of opposition, and it is quite possible that their activities, as an index of what might be expected if he should countenance another *coup d'état,* influenced Cromwell in his refusal to assume supreme power at this time. At least it was while his negotiations with Lambert's faction were proceeding that he interviewed Feake and some of the other preachers, and remonstrated with them for strengthening the enemies of the Commonwealth abroad by sowing dissension at home. They thereupon accused him of "assuming exorbitant power", and maintained that it was their duty to give voice to the inspirations of the Holy Spirit. Unable to make any impression upon them, Cromwell sent them away. The next day Harrison was back in town, and Lambert had returned to the country.[40]

In the mean time the struggles in Parliament over church reform continued. In the middle of November the radical party had succeeded in carrying, by a close

[39] Bordeaux to Brienne, Nov. 26/Dec. 6, 1653, P. R. O. Transcripts.

[40] Gardiner, *op. cit.,* II, 321. Later Cromwell sent Sterry, one of his chaplains, and other ministers, to argue with them. Bordeaux to Brienne, Dec. 1/11, P. R. O. Transcripts; intercepted letter, Thurloe, I, 621. In October Sterry and Caryll had approved a pamphlet intended to confute Fifth Monarchy errors. Homes, *The Resurrection Revealed,* 1654 (reprinted, London, 1833).

vote, a motion to abolish patronage. On December 1 it was ordered that a bill to that effect be brought in on December 6. On the following day the committee on tithes made a report embodying a scheme for commissioners to eject unfit ministers, and for the continuance of tithes, with a provision that any who scrupled tithe should be allowed some other form of payment. After protracted discussions, the first clause was rejected on December 10 by a majority of two. The moderates had endeavored to present in this report a compromise acceptable to all, but this vote convinced them that no compromise was possible. They therefore concocted and carried out the scheme whereby the Parliament resigned its powers back into the hands of Cromwell.

Thus ended the Little Parliament. There could be no better illustration of the tenacious spirit of the radicals than was furnished by the little band of twenty-eight or thirty, headed by Harrison, who sat doggedly on, declaring that they had been " called of God to that place, and that they apprehended that the said call was chiefly for the promoting the interest of Jesus Christ ".[41] It was therefore necessary for a file of soldiers to put an end to the solitary attempt to govern England by an assemblage of the saints.

The attempt to rule England by means of a body of men chosen for their godliness was a failure because those men were unwilling to temporize, to accept half measures when the complete attainment of their ideals was plainly impossible, to agree upon what was expedient instead of insisting upon what they believed to

[41] *Commons Journals*, Nov. 17, Dec. 1, 2, 10, 12; *Great Britain's Post*, Dec. 14-21, 1653; *cf. Politique Post*, Jan. 4-11, 1653/4.

be right. They were not all willing to go the same lengths: the Fifth Monarchy men among them advocated a program far more radical than did the Baptists and Independents; but they all agreed that the laws of England needed reformation, and that the system of tithe should be abolished. Their numbers were sufficient to obstruct legislation on controversial subjects, and since the uncompromising minority had failed to devise what has remained undevised from that day to this—a means of carrying on any government short of absolute despotism without compromise, without temporizing, without the acceptance of a little good when a greater good seems unattainable—government by the saints was forced to give way to another form of government.

CHAPTER III.

THE PROTECTOR AND THE SAINTS.

THE establishment of the Protectorate was a great blow to the Fifth Monarchy men. They objected to it, not as did the Levellers and Parliamentarians, because it was a government set up by the army, but because it was a government by a single person. The only government with a single person at its head which they felt that they could conscientiously support was the Fifth Monarchy, or kingdom of Christ. The manner in which the new order was established was also a source of offense. "Yesterday the General was proclaimed protector", wrote Hugh Courtney, "I will not insert the solemnities, which were too much after the old fashion, and so grievous to many. It is hard now to tell you where the greatest joy is; but I am sure some rejoice with trembling, their sorrow being oppressed by reason of the present shame and reproach they judge to be upon the gospel and the profession thereof."[1] "My heart is full, and often akes to consider what is come to pass, and what is at the door."[2] "The people of God are highly dissatisfied."[3] "Mr. Powell is very hearty, high, and heavenly."[4]

These were not the adjectives applied to Powell by an adherent of the new order who heard him say in a

[1] Hugh Courtney to John Jones, Dec. 20, 1653, Thurloe, I, 640.
[2] Same to Hugh Mason, same date, *ibid.*, 639.
[3] Same to Morgan Lloyd, same date, *ibid.*, 639.
[4] Same to Daniel Lloyd, same date, *ibid.*, 640.

sermon on December 19, that it was a great pity that any of the saints should be supporting the government of Cromwell, which was bound to be but temporary: indeed, "a small matter should fetch him down with little noise". He intimated that Cromwell was the "vile person" referred to in Daniel, xi, 21, "to whom they shall not give the honor of the kingdom, but he shall come in peaceably, and obtain the kingdom by flatteries". "Lord", he cried, "have our army men all apostatised from their principles! What is become of all their declarations, protestations, and professions? Are they choked with lands, parks, and manors? Let us go home and pray, and say, 'Lord, wilt Thou have Oliver Cromwell or Jesus Christ to reign over us?'"[5] Feake, preaching at the same meeting, declared that Cromwell was the little horn of Daniel's prophecy, who was to make war upon the saints, and whom the saints would finally destroy. On the preceding day these two had held similar discourse at Blackfriars, where one of them called Cromwell "the dissemblingest perjured villain in the world", and on the day following, while preaching in the chapel at Whitehall, they were arrested and brought before the Council of State. As their behavior there was far from conciliatory, they were sent to prison.[6]

They were released after a few days, and as the Blackfriars meetings had been prohibited, Powell

[5] Information of Marchamont Needham, Dec. 20, 1653. *Cal. St. P., Dom., 1653-1654*, 304 ff.

[6] Intercepted letter, Dec. 22, 1653, Thurloe, I, 641; *Cal. St. P., Dom., 1653-1654*, 308, 309; Bordeaux to Mazarin, Dec. 22, and to Brienne, same date, P. R. O. Transcripts; *Severall Proceedings*, Dec. 29, 1653. Hugh Peters, in a sermon preached December 18, advised the people who were looking for Christ's coming to do so at home, peaceably. *Moderate Publisher*, Dec. 21-23, 1653.

preached at Christ Church. One of his hearers noted with approval the peaceable tone in which he concluded his discourse, " perswading his brethren to meddle no more with Civil matters, but to speak of spiritual glories, which he held forth in the Reigne of Christ, and the Saints with him on earth ".[7] However, this sermon was reported less favorably to the government, and on the following day a warrant was issued for his arrest. He escaped into Wales, but before leaving he preached at Christ Church and Blackfriars, declaring that some ruled as kings, without the advice of the saints, whom the Lord would pull down, for the present government was not of God, and would soon be destroyed.[8]

Feake and Simpson, less fortunate than Powell, were arrested under the new ordinance which declared any deliberate attack upon the existing government to be treason, and were imprisoned at Windsor Castle, whence they wrote copiously to their respective congregations, bidding them wait on the Lord, and declaring their imprisonment a season of great spiritual comfort.[9]

[7] Erbery, *An Olive Leaf: or, Some peaceable considerations to the Christians meeting at Christs-Church in London* (Thomason).

[8] *Faithful Scout,* Jan. 27-Feb. 3, 1653/4; *Cal. St. P., Dom., 1653-1654,* 353. Efforts were made at this time by some of the leading Independent divines of London, both to clear themselves of the suspicion that they shared the ideas of the Fifth Monarchy men, and to prevent the movement from spreading. A circular letter, signed by John Owen, Thomas Goodwin, Philip Nye, and Sidrach Simpson, was addressed to the " Churches of Christ ", concerning " those high and open attempts of some of our Brethren in London: who in pursuit of an opinion concerning the Kingdom of the Saints, or Fifth Monarchy, to be administered by the Saints, by immediate Commission from Jesus Christ, have decryed all other Government that is the Ordinance of men, as peices of the fourth monarchy, to which Christ in this juncture of time they must suppose hath put a period ". January 9, 1653/4, Carte MSS., 81, fol. 16.

[9] *Cal. St. P., Dom., 1653-1654,* 449; *Faithful Scout,* Jan. 27-Feb. 3, 1653/4; *Severall Proceedings,* Feb. 2-9; *Moderate Intelligencer,* Feb. 16-23; *Loyal Messenger,* April 3-10; *Weekly Intelligencer,* April 4-11.

Not all the Fifth Monarchy preachers took part at the outset in the denunciation of the Protectorate. John Rogers, mindful, perhaps, of how nearly in accordance with his proposals had been the composition of the Little Parliament, addressed to Cromwell, under his new title, a set of propositions for the new government. In them Cromwell is urged to defend the cause of Christ as opposed to earthly interests, giving no protection to the state clergy, and rising superior to outworn state policies, carnal counsellors, and heathenish laws. He has been an " Instrument ", and the saints are praying that he may continue one. Rogers promises that if he will " freely oblige for Christ and his Interest, the Faith and Prayers of the Saints, (which were never higher than now) shall protect you sufficiently in all emergencies; but if you will ingage for Antichrist and his Interest, the loud crying Faith, and incessant high-spirited Prayers of the Saints, will all ingage against you, and never give Jehovah Nissi, the Lord our Protector rest, till the excellency of Jacob have prevailed. Take heed what you do." It is possible that Rogers was not ingenuous in these proposals, but it seems probable that he actually hoped that something would come of them. He was an eager, sanguine enthusiast, and was at this time under the spell of an extreme admiration for the personality of Cromwell.[10]

That spell was no longer potent for Cromwell's old comrade-at-arms, Thomas Harrison. He forfeited his commission rather than consent to act under the Protectorate, and his example was followed by Nathaniel

[10] *The humble cautionary proposals of John Rogers,* 1653 (Thomason).

Rich, John Carew, and other officers of lesser note.[11] The newspapers commented on his sermons and prayers in Fifth Monarchy meetings, and he was soon asked to retire to his father's house in Staffordshire.[12] It was a matter of common report abroad that Harrison was the leader of a strong party against the government, and however unlikely it might be that he would attempt an insurrection, open criticism, coming from a man of his prominence, was dangerous. His being sent into the country saved him, doubtless, from arrest under the treason ordinance.[13]

With the withdrawal or imprisonment of the leading agitators came an interval of comparative quiet. Samuel Highland of the Little Parliament, Captain John Spencer, and Henry Jessey the Baptist minister, carried on the meetings at Allhallows, and though there was talk of persecution, and of the imprisonment of the saints, it was comparatively innocuous.[14] Yet the actions of the new government were such as to make a new outburst probable. The court ceremonial, the knighting of the mayor, the issue of an ordinance regulating the appointment of ministers and establishing the triers, the failure to deal with the question of tithes, the negotiations for peace with the Dutch—all

[11] *Perfect Occurrences*, Jan. 27-Feb. 6, 1653/4; *Weekly Intelligencer*, Jan. 29-Feb. 8; Thurloe, I, 641. Harrison, referring to this period when on trial as a regicide, said: "When I found those that were as the apple of mine eye to turn aside, I did loathe them. Rather than to turn as many did that put their hands to this plough, I chose rather to be separated from wife and family . . . though it was said, 'sit at my right hand', and such kind of expressions." *Dict. Nat. Biog.*

[12] *Cal. St. P., Dom., 1653-1654*, 387; *Certain Passages*, Feb. 10-17, 1653/4; *Moderate Intelligencer*, Feb. 16-23; *Weekly Intelligencer*, March 7-14.

[13] Intelligence from Paris, Jan. 7, 1654 (N. S.), Thurloe, I, 650.

[14] Marchamont Needham to Cromwell, Feb. 7, 1653/4, *Cal. St. P., Dom., 1653-1654*, 393.

these were as sparks to the tinder of Fifth Monarchy indignation.

A particularly effective witness for the stirring up of men's minds at this time was a certain Hannah Trapnel, a member of John Simpson's church. In a cataleptic state, which lasted sometimes for days, she saw visions and dreamed dreams, which she proclaimed in verse.[15] She insisted that it was her duty to declare for the Fifth Monarchy, and although she prayed for Cromwell, and counselled the people of God not to revile, but to exhort him, she enumerated his shortcomings in great detail, intimating that he was the Little Horn, and she meddled with matters of policy such as the Dutch peace. After creating a nine-days wonder in London, she went about the country accompanied by two members of the radical party in the Little Parliament, spreading the doctrine of discontent. She was finally arrested in Cornwall and sent up to London. She was imprisoned in Bridewell, whither great crowds flocked to see and hear her.[16] The effect of her utterances was particularly great on account of the belief of a large number of her hearers that they were directly inspired of God. Were not such manifestations of a piece with the miraculous ebb and flow of the Thames, the fall of one of the walls of St. Paul's, the comet, and the reputed appearance of Charles I's ghost at Whitehall—all of them signs of divine displeasure with the new government?[17]

[15] *The Cry of a Stone*, Feb. 20, 1653/4; *Strange and Wonderful News from Whitehall*, March 11; *A Legacy for Saints*, July 24 (all in Thomason).

[16] *Cal. St. P., Dom., 1653*, 393, *1654*, 86, 89, 197; *Severall Proceedings*, Jan. 12-19, 1653/4; *Mercurius Politicus*, April 13-20; *Weekly Intelligencer*, May 30-June 6; *Perfect Account*, June 7-14.

[17] B. T. to ——, 21, 10 mo., 1654, *Clarke Papers*, II, xxxiv.

The fresh outburst of opposition was led by John Rogers, whose confidence in Cromwell had been considerably shaken in the interval between December and March. As early as January he had shown signs that he was developing distrust of the Protector's intentions, and in the last week of March he called a meeting at the church of St. Thomas Apostle's to consider the breaking-up of the last Parliament; the present apostasy; the ordinance on treason and other signs of persecution; the deadness of spirit among the little remnant of the saints; the existing ministry; the temptations of the court; and such miscellaneous evils as hypocrisy, pride, oppression, and the prevailing drought.[18] By the end of May he had worked himself up to a state of violence. A visitor at his church informed the authorities that he prayed for the hastening of the time "when al absolute power shal be devolved into the hand of Christ; when we shal have no lord protector but our Lord Jesus . . . Look in mercy upon thy saints att Windsor, that are imprisoned for the truth and the testimony of Jesus . . . Remember thy handmaid, who is brought to town, and threatned by the worldly powers, who crucify Christ Jesus in the spirit every day. Heare the blasphemies of the court, and regard their ridiculous pomp and vanity. And now Christ Jesus is proclaimed kinge, pour forth thy vials upon the worldly powers, the powers of Antichrist". He then preached from a text in the gospel of Matthew, demonstrating that the present government was opposing the kingly office of Christ, and applying the most

[18] *The Grounds of meeting at Tho. Apostle, the 28th day of the first moneth 1654, in solemn humiliation before the Lord, beginning at 7 a clock in the morning,* Thurloe, II, 196.

opprobrious epithets to Cromwell and his court.[19] In conclusion he read a letter from Feake at Windsor, and then a hymn was sung, composed for the occasion, and beginning: "Come, glorious king of Zion, come to defend thy cause against all earthly powers, and to work deliverance for thy captives." [20] In spite of these

[19] Information, May 28, 1654, Thurloe, III, 483. Other passages are cited in Gardiner, *Commonwealth and Protectorate,* III, 114.

[20] Several examples of Fifth Monarchy hymnology have come down to us. One of them, by Powell, "Mr. Powell's hymn at Christ Church, Dec. 18," *Scout,* Jan. 27-Feb. 3, 1653/4, is as follows:

To Christ our King, let us praise sing,
Who is our Savior dear,
Who is our Protector and our Rock,
Who will come and soon appear.

His Saints shall reign with him on earth,
And great ones they shall bow;
The Battle and the Battle ax
And men of war shall know

That he will arise, and he will rule,
And their power will fall,
And Christ our great Commander, He
Shall be our General.

Hast Lord, come quickly down,
Thy Saints do wait and pray,
And men would fain, if they knew how
Thy prophets kill and slay.

But they shall live, and eke stand up,
And give their testimony
Against the Monarchs of the Earth
That sit and reign on high.

John Rogers produced verses of a somewhat better quality, to judge from a fragment (Thurloe, III, 137):

For God begins to honour us,
The saintes are marching on;
The sword is sharpe, the arrows swift,
To destroy Babylon.

Cf. Mr. Feake's Hymne at Christ Church, Aug. 11, 1653 (Thomason).

utterances Rogers was allowed his liberty until July, when he was finally sent as a prisoner to Lambeth Palace.[21]

The imprisonment of these leaders by no means put an end to their influence. The very fact that they were in prison without trial witnessed against the government, and during their captivity they saw their friends, preached sermons, composed pamphlets about the Fifth Monarchy and their own sufferings, and wrote letters of encouragement and counsel to their congregations. "Rouze up, my dearest hearts", wrote Feake to the Coleman Street church, "in the might of your God, and go on in the name of your Captain-General, and by your secret, inward, invisible weapons, wound this base, upstart, private interest under the fifth rib". [22]

Observe that it is the weapons not of the flesh but of the spirit that Feake bids his followers employ. Although the kingdom is to come from above, wrote one very able advocate of the cause, and it is impossible for any one to hasten its coming, "Is it therefore for us to sit still, and to keep no watch, nor make preparation for that day? Whether is it not the duty and safety of all men, Rulers, Teachers, and people, of the whole Camp of Israel, to cast up and remove the stumbling block out of the way of the Lord?" This was to be done by reminding the rulers of their duty, and persuading them to set up the laws of God. He asked "Whether between an immoderate and unruly Spirit

[21] *Cal. St. P., Dom., 1654*, 263, 438; *Perfect Account*, Aug. 2-9, 1654; *Severall Proceedings*, Aug. 3-10.

[22] *The New Nonconformist*, May 24, 1654 (Thomason). This is a collection of letters to the different congregations. A few days after its publication, the Council of State ordered that Feake and Simpson be kept close prisoners, and debarred from preaching. *Cal. St. P., Dom., 1654*, 188.

on the one hand, despising and trampling upon Authority, which is a beam of God, and a spirit of baseness and flattery on the other hand, dawbing over unrighteousness, and having the persons of men in authority in admiration, because of advantage, is there not between both a middle way, wherein the Spirit of God upon a man may lead him forth to bear his witness against the unrighteousness or backslidings of the Rulers, and yet in the same Act hold an holy reverence to the Authority it self, and a meek acquiescence in the administration of providence disposing the Authority into such a hand, either in an active or permissive way?" [23] About the same time were published some sermons preached by Thomas Moor the preceding November at Blackfriars, the meeting most given to seditious utterances. In these he warned believers against trying to hasten the fulfilment of the prophecies, and bade them be subject to the powers in being. He declared that the saints were not called upon to take arms for the realization of Christ's coming; they might help it forward, but not with material weapons. "Nor indeed will there be any long setling of the Kingdom or Glory upon any sort of men (which may be a comfort to you) nothing but overturn, overturn, overturn, till he whose right it is do come . . . nor till then is it your time, as Saints, to wish for or execute vengeance on them that as such, and for his name sake, do trouble you." [24]

[23] *Sighs for Righteousness,* June 2, 1654 (Thomason). There is also a copy in the Boston Public Library.

[24] *Mercies for Men,* June 15, 1654 (Thomason). John Rogers, in an open letter to Cromwell, which came into Thomason's hands June 10, said: "As Luther wrote to the Duke of Saxony, so do we humbly to you, my Lord. 'I would not', saith he, 'but all have free liberty, yet if any transgress Gospel bounds, and would raise up seditions or wars against you, then you may repress them.' . . . So, my Lord, if we stir up people

With such admonitions before their eyes, the millenarian enthusiasts kept reasonably peaceable during the summer of 1654.[25] Whatever may have been the differences of opinion in their ranks as to the propriety of submitting quietly to Cromwell's rule, all probably agreed that it was advisable to wait and see what attitude would be adopted by the coming Parliament. However, in order that there might be no doubt in the minds of members of Parliament and of people in general as to the position of their party, they issued a manifesto the week of Parliament's assembling.

This manifesto is entitled, *A Declaration of several of the Churches of Christ, and Godly People in and about the Citie of London, concerning the Kingly Interest of Christ, and the present sufferings of his cause and Saints in England.*[26] It is a violent attack on the government, and an arraignment of the army for deserting its old principles. "Did we ever think to see so many hopeful Instruments in the Army, Churches, and elsewhere, to be so fully gorged with the flesh of Kings, Captains, and Nobles etc. (i. e. with their Lands, Mannors, Estates, Parks, and Palaces) so as to sit with ease and comply with Antichrist, the World, Worldly Church and Clergie?" Godly people, it goes on to say, have been deceived as to the principles of the

---

to risings, tumults, or carnal warfare, as men falsely charge us, then punish us as you please, for it is contrary to our principles so to do." *Mene, Tekel, Perez,* quoted in Rogers, *Fifth Monarchy Man,* 121.

[25] John Rogers, preaching on June 18, took the treason ordinance into the pulpit with him, and commented on it. He professed abhorrence, however, of plots directed against the lives of those in power. In spite of these asseverations, he was considered seditious, and his arrest occurred during the following month. *Perfect Account,* June 14-21, Aug. 2-9, 1654; *Mercurius Politicus,* July 27-Aug. 3.

[26] Sept. 2, 1654 (Thomason).

Fifth Monarchy party, which declares for the kingly interest of Christ, and disowns any participation in "carnal plots", for its warfare is spiritual. Announcement is made that there will be a weekly debate, to which all the enlightened are invited, on the time, laws, offices, and other features of the Fifth Monarchy.

The paper has one hundred and fifty signatures, and the statement is made that the meeting at which it was drawn up had ruled that only these, out of all the signatures that were obtained, should be published. The names are arranged by congregations, and at first sight it would appear that the document was issued by the churches of Feake, Chamberlen, Rogers, Raworth, Knollys, Simpson, Jessey, Barbone, Lieutenant-colonel Fenton, and Samuel Highland. A closer examination, however, reveals that while signatures were made specifically in the name of the whole churches of Chamberlen and Rogers, in the other cases the names are given simply as belonging to members of the congregations, and the names of Knollys, Jessey, Barbone, Fenton, and Highland, are conspicuously absent.[27] That these churches did not officially support the manifesto, and that some protested against this apparent misrepresentation, appears from a query in a pamphlet by the Baptist pastor, Samuel Richardson: "Whether the wayes some take in opposing the present Government, doth not declare their opposition is not from God, witness their publishing of a Libel, called, a Declaration in the names of severall Churches, with severall hands to it, as if it

[27] The names are printed in columns, in blocks, and opposite the several blocks the words "Of the church that walks with Mr. Feake", "In the name of the whole Church that walks with Dr. Chamberlain", etc.

were signed by those said churches, and upon examination it is proved false and counterfeit." [28]

Knollys, Jessey, Barbone, Fenton, and Highland were well-known Baptists, and this apparent ranging of their congregations, whether wholly or in part, on the side of the Fifth Monarchy party, brings up the question of how far the Baptist churches were affected by the movement, and what was the attitude of Baptists in general toward the Protectorate. As we have seen, a large number of the members of the Fifth Monarchy party from its inception were Baptists, and the fact that Feake, Simpson, and Powell belonged to that communion makes it easy to understand that the Fifth Monarchy agitations in the early days of the Protectorate should frequently be referred to as "Anabaptist".[29]

There were indeed, as we shall see clearly in the case of the Baptists in Ireland, aspects of the Protectorate to which the Baptists strongly objected. Some of them felt that the very term Protector was an impiety if applied to any but the Deity.[30] The ceremonial of the new court, too, offended the Baptist ideas of simplicity, and they looked with suspicion upon the steps taken to regulate the ministry. Yet a proposal to protest against the government, introduced into Baptist circles by Henry Danvers, a Baptist who was also a Fifth Monarchy man, met with no success.[31] The General Bap-

[28] *Apology for the Present Government* (Thomason). John Spittlehouse, in his *Answer to one part of the Lord Protector's Speech* (Thomason), rejoins that there are the signatures for all to see.

[29] This was especially the case in the despatches of Bordeaux and other foreigners.

[30] "Oliver Cromwell called Lord Protector when as God alone was the protector of his people, but we sinned." *Broadmead Records* (Hanserd Knollys Soc.), 43.

[31] Edmund Chillenden to Cromwell, Thurloe, IV, 365. Chillenden took to himself the credit of having caused the failure of the movement, his purpose in this letter being to prove his loyalty.

tists, at a meeting of representatives from all parts of England, issued a formal declaration of their submission to the government. In it they stated that the question of the " dueness or undueness " of the call of persons to rule did not, to their way of thinking, relieve them of the responsibility of peaceable submission to the powers in being. They knew of no grounds for believing that the saints were to rule, as saints, before the coming of Christ's kingdom on earth, and expected rather to suffer patiently, as the saints hitherto had done, until that time. As honest and faithful men they ought to serve the government when called upon to do so, and they hoped that any dissatisfaction expressed by individual Baptists would not be attributed to the Baptist churches, or to the generality of their members.[82] Three of the leading Particular Baptist ministers in London wrote to their brethren in Dublin soon after the establishment of the Protectorate, disowning the ideas held forth at Blackfriars, and declaring that the new government had saved the country from anarchy and gave promise of unprecedented protection and freedom of worship for the saints. They begged that the Baptists in Ireland would do nothing to justify the prevailing misconception regarding Baptist principles, " Which is, that we deny authority, and would pull down all Magistracy. And if any troble should arise, either with you or us, in the nations, which might proceed to the shedding of blood, would it not all be imputed and charged upon the baptized churches? . . . This we can say, that we have not had any occasion of sorrow in this matter from any of the churches in this

[82] *Confessions of Faith* (Hanserd Knollys Soc.), 328, 329.

nation, with whom we have communion; they with one heart desiring to bless God for their liberty, and with all willingness to be subject to the present authority ".[33]

It appears, then, that the leading Baptists in England, while disbelieving on principle in a government which maintained a church establishment by means of tithes, and exercised a supervision over its ministry, yet considered such a government preferable to anarchy, and found it not inconsistent with their consciences to recognize it. Some of them went further, accepted office under it, collected tithes, and even sat on the board of triers.[34] They were, for the most part, shrewd, practical men, prosperous merchants and the like, who realized the practical difficulties in the way of sweeping away established institutions, especially financial institutions, with a wave of the hand, and considered themselves justified in accepting, and even profiting by, the existing order, until Cromwell should see his way to bettering it.[35] Personal loyalty to Cromwell would stand for something with some of them, as in the case of Henry Lawrence, the president of the Council of State, and Samuel Richardson, who was one of the most eloquent defenders of the Protectorate.

Such men would be able to influence the congregations to which they belonged against taking up with extreme views, but many less practical members, while not forsaking their communion, would be irresistibly

[33] The letter was signed by William Kiffin, John Spilsbury, and Joseph Fansom, London, "the 20 of the 11 mo." [1654], Nickolls, 159-160.

[34] Jessey, Tombes, and Dyke were triers. A large number of Baptists held livings throughout the period. A Quaker complains: "The Baptist sues us for the very tithe eggs." Cited by Barclay, 204.

[35] William Kiffin and Hanserd Knollys were conspicuously successful men of business. Samuel Moyer is said to have had the greatest financial reputation of his time. Glass, *Barbone Parliament*, 77.

attracted by such assemblies as the Monday meetings at Blackfriars. One of the boasts of the Fifth Monarchy party was that association with it did not preclude membership in any other body of Christians, and we have seen that a large number of its adherents, from the beginning, belonged to the Baptist communion.[36]

The single Baptist church which signed the Fifth Monarchy manifesto as a unit was that of Dr. Peter Chamberlen, a visionary deeply imbued with Fifth Monarchy ideas. The other leading spirits in his church were John More and John Spittlehouse, also Fifth Monarchy men, and the French physician Naudin, who in May was implicated in a plot against Cromwell.[37] As early as February the church had discussed the question "Whether we have a call from God to visit the L. Pr.? If yea, upon what account, or to what end?" The decision was in the affirmative: "If we ought to tell our Neighbour of his faults, much more a Ruler, because the goode or evil of a K. is more conse-

[36] An example of the charm exercised by the Fifth Monarchy preachers is furnished by a letter from an apprentice to one of them—probably John Rogers—which was intercepted by one of Thurloe's agents. His master had forbidden him to go to hear Powell, Feake, Simpson, and their associates preach, and he could not resign himself to the deprivation. The master finally consented to submit their dispute to the arbitration of two ministers, Richard Baxter and the man to whom the apprentice was writing. There is nothing in Baxter's correspondence to indicate whether this strangely assorted committee met; it must have been an interesting interview, if it did occur, and one would know the position that Baxter must have taken, even if we did not possess his answer to a similar request from an apprentice as to the advisability of going to hear some moderate Baptist preachers. Rawlinson MSS., A 47, fol. 27 ff.; Baxter Correspondence, IV, fols. 229-231.

[37] Gardiner, *op. cit.*, III, 125 ff. Naudin's scheme for the government had at least the value of simplicity. "After the protector was cut off, all that were in command, from the general to the least officer, should be in command but eight days, and every one take their turns." Examination of Buller, Thurloe, II, 352. There is no evidence to show whether or no any of Naudin's fellow church members were in this plot.

quence." The prophets testified before rulers, and Paul was to bear the name of Christ before kings. Among the points set down for mention were, the poor, lawyers, tithes, persecution, malignants, taxes, excise. It is easy to see that here was a body in excellent mood to be approached by the advocates of the Fifth Monarchy manifesto.[38]

Two days after the appearance of the manifesto, Cromwell stood in the Painted Chamber to address the first Parliament of his Protectorate. As he looked over the assemblage which was to put to the test the Instrument of Government, his mind must have flashed back to that very different company which had come together at his bidding fifteen months earlier. Only four of the radicals who had sat there then were before him now. The attempt to rule by a body of men chosen for their godliness had proved a failure, and the other great principle of the Puritan revolution—government of the people through their elected representatives—was to have its trial. The new Parliament had been chosen while the defects of the Little Parliament were still fresh in men's minds, and the spirit of reaction had brought about the election of a body with a distinct Presbyterian bias.[39] According to report, one or more Anabaptists had stood for election in most of the con-

[38] The records of this church, which from 1652 to 1654 met in Lothbury, are in the Bodleian Library, Rawlinson MSS., D 828. The account of this debate is on fol. 33 a. John More, as the result of a quarrel with Chamberlen, had withdrawn from the church in April, and joined Knollys's church. It may have been his influence that won from that body the signatures credited to it in the manifesto.

[39] The Dutch ambassador wrote on August 11/21, 1654, that two-thirds of those elected were Presbyterians, " or at least such as do hold for a firm ministry, with goods and orders in the churches ". Thurloe, II, 538. See also Bordeaux to Brienne, July 17/27, Sept. 7/17, P. R. O. Transcripts.

stituencies, and made violent efforts to win votes, but people were glad to exhibit their aversion to men of that sort " whom for their covetous, vexatious, violent and cruell practices (that will have all judgment, no mercy) they cannot love ". Some few had been successful, but not enough to create a faction, had they desired to do so.[40]

Cromwell, too, was of a different spirit. No one had suffered more than he on account of the deadlock caused by the impracticable projects which the enthusiasts in their honest zeal had championed. And since the establishment of his Protectorate he had learned certain things. He had been taught from the pulpits of Christ Church and Blackfriars the force of absolute sincerity and unbounded religious ardor linked to fantastic notions. From the same source he had been shown what a danger to a newly-established government could be a few opponents strong in the belief that scripture and right were behind their arguments. He could foresee nothing but ruin for the state if such fanatics, with the Levellers and ever-plotting Royalists at their elbows, should remain unbridled. And it is little wonder that he had come to regard as undesirable " that heady way . . . of every man making himself a Minister and a preacher ",[41] and that these disorders were developing in him the belief that an unorganized church, like an unorganized state, meant anarchy, and that a state church, even along Presbyterian lines, would be the only arrangement that could bring order out of chaos, and peace out of discord. In addition, he knew

[40] George Green to ——, Sept. 4, Clarendon MSS., XLIX, fol. 57; Ludlow, *Memoirs,* I, 545; Thurloe, II, 546, 565; *Severall Proceedings,* Aug. 31, Sept. 14.

[41] Stainer, *Speeches,* 140.

that if he wished to gain the support of Parliament in carrying on the government as he believed it should be carried on, he must conciliate the strong Presbyterian element. For this purpose a castigation of the errors of an extreme Independent faction would have its value.

The castigation was thorough. He spoke bluntly of "the mistaken notion of the Fifth Monarchy. A thing pretending more spirituality than anything else. A notion I hope we all honour, wait, and hope for, that Jesus Christ will have a time to set up his reign in our hearts, by subduing those corruptions and lusts, and evils that are there, which reign now more in the world than I hope in due time they shall do. . . . But for men to entitle themselves on this principle, that they are the only men to rule kingdoms, govern nations, and give laws to people . . . truly, they had need give clear manifestations of God's presence with them, before wise men will receive or submit to their conclusions. . . . Notions will hurt none but them that have them. But when they come to such practices,—as to tell us, that liberty and property are not the badges of the kingdom of Christ, and tell us that instead of regulating laws, laws are to be abrogated, indeed subverted, and perhaps would bring in the Judaical law instead of our known laws settled amongst us,—this is worthy every magistrate's consideration ".[42]

[42] *Id.*, 134 ff. A Baptist-Fifth Monarchy critic of Cromwell, referring to this speech, quoted the well-known verses (Proverbs, xxx, 18, 19) beginning: "There be three things which are too wonderful for me, yea, four that I know not"; and remarked "And if it were honest and lawful to add to Scripture, one might put in a fifth way, viz., The way of a Protector in his Speeches, and between them and his actions, for no man that follows him there, is able to find him out ". *The Protector, So called, in Part Unvailed*, 1655 (Thomason).

Small as was the number of radicals in the Parliament thus harangued, the imposition of the Recognition made it much smaller, excluding as it did all the extreme Republicans, and with them all who would conceivably have favored any applications made by the sectaries. Such an application had apparently been contemplated. A rumor was in circulation of a petition which declared the present government far more arbitrary than that of the late king, and begged that an end be put to its tyranny. Many thousands were declared ready to aid such a work at the hazard of lives and estates.[43] The movement apparently originated in Wales, where Vavasor Powell had been at work since the beginning of the year. It will be remembered that he had escaped thither to avoid arrest. Almost immediately had come news that he was busily stirring up sedition. He was seconded by Captain John Williams, one of the radical party in the Little Parliament, who was already engaged in a campaign against the government, and a certain Morris Griffith. These three went from place to place preaching, and it was bruited about that they and their hearers were scouring up pistols and making other martial demonstrations. Powell was indeed so vehement as to alienate some of his adherents, and many of the members of his church refused to sign the remonstrance he was preparing. The fact that the justices of the peace in the neighborhood were his fellow church-members, made it difficult to have any action brought against him, and although he was finally indicted, nothing came of it, and by autumn he was able to promise twenty thousand saints who would hazard

[43] Greene to ——, Sept. 23, 25, 1654, Clarendon MSS., XLIX, 38, 39; Bordeaux to Brienne, Sept. 14/24, P. R. O. Transcripts.

their blood for the cause.[44] However exaggerated his estimate, it was certain that he had a following of some sort, and the government began to investigate the matter, beginning by the arrest of Harrison, who, it was said, had promised to present the petition. But as the alteration in the character of Parliament had made it impossible that the petition, if presented, would lead to anything, Cromwell invited Harrison to dine at Whitehall, admonished him in a friendly way to give up "those deceitful and slippery ways whose end is destruction", and with "good counsel and more civility" restored him his liberty, and sent him back to the country.[45]

Meanwhile the Fifth Monarchy men were carrying on their campaign in print. Early in September John Spittlehouse felt that he was inspired of the Lord "(In the absence of Mr. Feake, Mr. Rogers, etc., now prisoners of the Lord Jesus) to mind our present Rulers and Army of their Persecutions and Apostacies, and what is likely to follow them for so doing, if they repent not".[46] His diatribe arraigned the government for imprisoning the saints; attacked the Instrument of Government; and called upon the army to give up its apostacies, to be ruled by the Scriptures, and to set up the rule of King Jesus. The *Observator*, in which Marchamont Needham was at this time defending the Protector's policy, published a response to this pamphlet in its first number, and from the pen of Samuel

[44] H. Williams to A. Griffiths, Jan. 20, 1653/4, Thurloe, II, 44; intercepted letter, Feb. 2, *ibid.*, 64; J. Phillips to J. Gunter, n. d., *ibid.*, 93; G. Lloyd to D. Griffith, ult. Feb., and intercepted letter, April 11, *ibid.*, 226; information of Rogers's jailer, Feb. 3, 1654/5, *ibid.*, III, 137.

[45] Greene to ——, Sept. 25, 1654, Clarendon MSS., XLIX, fol. 5 a.

[46] *Certain Queries Propounded to the most serious Consideration of those Persons Now in Power*, Sept. 11 (Thomason).

Richardson, the Baptist pastor, came an elaborate defense of the government.[47] The author maintained that Feake and Rogers were in prison, not for religion, but for meddling with politics. If the army had seen error in its declarations, it was well that it had not kept to them. As for tithes, he had heard that the Protector meant to abolish them. The triers were a useful institution. "I doe from my heart believe", he concluded, "that it is best for this whole Nation, to bee content with this Government, and quietly to sit down under it, and to thanke God that things are not worse than they are: indeed I look upon this Government in which we enjoy liberty in matters of religion, to be a blessed Government; if the offense of Tith were removed, I believe wee should injoy as much freedome and liberty under it, as any doe under any Government in all the whole world!"[48]

In November William Aspinwall published a picture of the Fifth Monarchy men as persons humble, meek, and patient, "without any secret plots and designes; of a quiet temper, taking meekly loss of estates and imprisonment", who mind not abuse, but "wait for and pray for, and preach for, and suffer for the Kingdome of Christ, which they know will assuredly come, and is now at hand, even at the doores".[49] From prison Feake sent forth a statement of his personal position. His congregation had written to him that they could not take steps to gain him his freedom without in so doing recognizing the government, which would be

[47] *Observator,* Oct. 17-24, 1654; *An Apology for the Present Government, and Governour,* Sept. 30, 1654 (Thomason).

[48] *Ibid.*

[49] *A Premonition of sundry sad calamities yet to come,* Nov. 30 (Thomason).

"a bowing the knee to the image of the Beast". He had responded that he himself, in accordance with God's commands, "owns the powers in being, and renders tribute where tribute is due". This statement had been interpreted as apostacy to his former principles, and he proceeded to justify himself, and at the same time refute the accusation that he was against magistracy, ministry and government. He explained that he must own, either the powers that be, or anarchy, and that anarchy was even worse than monarchy. Passive obedience should be rendered, in all things contrary to Christ's law, and punishment for disobedience in cases contrary to conscience should be patiently borne, as he was bearing it. Taxes should be paid, but no active part should be taken in the government: for example, saints should not vote in Parliamentary elections. As to honoring the government, he did so; he took off his hat to Cromwell, and stood when in his presence; none the less was it his duty to witness against him. In answer to the argument that ministers should not meddle with affairs of state, he cited the example of the eminent divines, John Owen and Thomas Goodwin. He considered it one of the arguments against the support of ministers by the state, that it took away their freedom to attack the vices of the state.[50]

Apparently Cromwell saw in this last utterance of Feake an indication that he had taken up a position less extreme than his former one, for several days after its publication he gave him a hearing at Whitehall, in the presence of some members of his congregation. Feake must have fulfilled his principle that beyond passive

[50] *The Oppressed Close Prisoner in Windsor Castle, his Defiance to the Father of Lyes*, Dec. 19, 1654 (Thomason).

obedience it was a minister's duty to bear testimony against wickedness in high places, for he was not set at liberty.[51]

Cromwell sent also for John Simpson "to come and conferre with him as a brother and a christian, and to bring three or four of the Church along with him".[52] Simpson had been released from prison in July, with orders not to preach within ten miles of London.[53] Having heard that Cromwell had attributed his obeying the order to fear, and that it had appeared in the public prints that he had changed his principles, he came up to London the latter part of December, and preached at Allhallows and elsewhere, inveighing bitterly against the triers, and proclaiming that Christ's kingdom was at hand. Answering Cromwell's summons he and his friends spent a whole day at Whitehall, sturdily refusing to touch the Protector's food, and indulging in unlimited plain speech. Their principal accusations were, that he had taken away liberty from the saints by instituting the triers, had broken his promise to take away tithes, and had failed to keep his engagement to maintain the just laws of the land, and to support no government by a single person. Cromwell answered their arguments patiently, but gave them no encouragement to hope for a change in his policy, and dismissed them with an admonition to sober behavior.[54]

[51] Newsletter, Dec. 23, 1654, *Clarke Papers*, III, 15.

[52] Letter from a member of Simpson's church, *id.*, II, xxxiv.

[53] Gardiner says Simpson broke prison in December, but the order for his release is in the State Papers. *Cal. St. P., Dom., 1654*, 253, 438; *Certain Passages from Every Daies Intelligence*, July 27. *Severall Proceedings*, under date of August 10, spoke of Simpson as one "who now owns and prayes for the present Powers".

[54] Intercepted letter, Dec. 21, 1654, *Clarke Papers*, II, xxxv ff. Gardiner has given an account of this interview, *op. cit.*, II, 264 ff.

These efforts made by Cromwell to win over some of the party leaders were undoubtedly prompted by news which came to him of renewed activity in Fifth Monarchy circles, not only in London, but in the country also. In Norfolk some fifteen churches met to consider the best means of witnessing against the government, and the London churches talked of sending messengers to different parts of England and Wales to ascertain the spirit of the people. It appears that there was a feeling in these London churches that the time was past for such half-hearted measures as had been advocated by the radicals in the Little Parliament. "Now the indignation of the Saints against Babylon is so heightened that when they come to the Lorde's worke againe no less will serve then the utter eradication of all what is planted, or built by the Manne of Sinne . . . many being strongly perswaded that the Lord looketh for more from his servants, then faith and prayer. . . . My perswasions are great that a terrible destruction will suddainely be brought upon Babylon's workes and workmen in England." A curious feature of the attitude taken by some of these extremists was that they feared Cromwell might make some concessions, such as taking away tithes and reforming the laws, "and so deceive the minds of the simple, and enrage all the more against the non-complyers".[55]

It is not likely that any large number of Fifth Monarchy men shared, at this period, the impression that Cromwell might yield on some of the points which made his government so unpopular with them. Any faith they may have had in him had received its death-

[55] Intercepted letter, Dec. 19, *Clarke Papers,* II, xxxii.

blow from his speech at the opening of Parliament. And if they had retained any lingering hopes of Parliament's attitude, the position it took with regard to church matters in the early days of December had effectually dispelled them. The only hope left to them now was in the army, and it is a noteworthy fact that from this time forward a prominent place in all their pleas was given to the argument that the soldiers, in supporting the Protectorate, were guilty of the most frightful apostasy, since in the civil wars they had repeatedly declared themselves upholders of the cause of Christ and opponents of government by a single person.

Similar arguments had already been brought into play by a purely political party, the Levellers. The principles of the Levellers and of the Fifth Monarchy men were, as we have already pointed out, diametrically opposed. Yet there were certain points where they could meet on common ground. Both parties believed in absolute liberty of conscience. Both found much to criticize in the existing legal system. The arguments of the Levellers against the imprisonment of John Lilburne applied with equal force to that of the Fifth Monarchy preachers. Finally, both parties were unanimous, although on differing grounds, in their opposition to Cromwell's assumption of power. It is, therefore, not at all strange that we find Fifth Monarchy pamphleteers borrowing arguments from the Levellers, and Levellers utilizing Fifth Monarchy men for carrying on their agitations.

The connection between Levellers and Baptists was of a different sort. The only Levelling principles for which any organization of Baptists would have stood sponsor, as Baptists, were those of liberty of conscience and separation of church and state. Yet the political theories of the Levellers had been developed in the favorable atmosphere of the gathered churches, and a large number of their most prominent members were Baptists. There is, however, no reason for believing that any Baptist organization ever lent itself to the designs of the Levellers. But when a number of Baptists were named in connection with any Levellers' project it was promptly considered Anabaptist, in accordance with the theory that the Baptist ranks were honeycombed with John of Leyden principles.

Such a project was the one which came to a head in the fall of 1654. Three Baptist colonels, Alured, Saunders, and Okey, the first of whom had been recalled from Ireland in the spring for speaking against Cromwell, began in September to attend meetings held by the Levellers Wildman and Sexby. Sexby is said to have been a Baptist, and other Baptists present at some of the meetings were Vice-admiral Lawson and Colonel Hierome Sankey. Robert Overton, too, had met with Wildman in the spring, and expressed dissatisfaction with the government. At the same time he had also declared his scruples to Cromwell, but had promised that if the time ever came when he could not conscientiously serve the government, he would inform him.[56] The immediate result of these meetings was the famous declaration of the three colonels, in tone a Levellers' manifesto, but signed by Saunders, Okey, and Alured, and therefore promptly stigmatized as

[56] Examination of Colonel Alured, Rawlinson MSS., A 41, fol. 560; Overton to ——, Jan. 17, 1654/5, Thurloe, III, 110 ff; Thurloe's notes, Gardiner, *op. cit.*, III, 228, note 3.

Anabaptist.[57] The paper was prepared for circulation among the officers, but was seized in Alured's rooms before any other signatures could be obtained. The three colonels lost their commissions, and Alured, against whom there were other charges, was committed to prison. Almost simultaneously with the petition of the three colonels appeared one from the seamen of Penn's fleet. While it asked for the redress of undoubted grievances, it also referred to the army's declarations, and to the liberties of the free born people of England, in language highly reminiscent of the Levellers. The Baptists were exceedingly numerous in the fleet, and Gardiner thinks it probable that the petition was drafted by the most prominent of them, Lawson.[58]

The prompt dealing with these two petitions put an end for the time to the Levellers' plans for England, but their negotiations with the army in Scotland went much farther.[59] How far they made known to their Baptist allies their plans, which were to seize General Monck and force Overton to take command, is not known. Probably they did not reveal the real nature of the design. Two Baptists who were active in gathering volunteers for the plot, Major John Bramston and Samuel Oates, chaplain of Pride's regiment, declared, both publicly and in private letters to friends, that nothing more was intended than a remonstrance to be presented to the government through Monck, and even the most careful examination has failed to reveal that

[57] *The Humble Petition of several Colonels of the Army*, Oct. 18, 1654 (Thomason).

[58] Gardiner, *op. cit.*, III, 214 ff.

[59] Word was brought of a general movement in England, and Colonel Eyre, a Baptist, was arrested on susupicion of connection with it, but the details did not become known. See Gardiner, *op. cit.*, III, 226.

Overton knew more than the fact that such a paper was in circulation among the officers.[60] However, as Gardiner points out, it was dangerous to have a man of his views in the important position which he held as governor of Hull.[61] He was arrested and committed to the Tower, and the occasion was seized to rid tne army "of persons of those principles, viz. Levellers and Annabaptists".[62]

The papers found in the possession of Oates and Bramston on their arrest for participation in the plot, afford some insight into the mental processes of these opponents of the government. Oates's papers were largely miscellaneous jottings very obviously inspired in good measure by a Levelling production that had appeared some months earlier.[63] He recognized, however, some good things in Cromwell's administration. "How hard a thing it wil bee", he reflected, "for the people of God to oppose the Lord Protector in anything, seeing hee hath bin soe great an Instrument in many things for their good. And all the great things which the people of God have had don for them have been don by him." With regard to civil war, he resolved: "First not to have a tongue moveing or a hand wageing in another. Rather myselfe bee in bondage or dye . . . 2ndly, Not to omitt in a Christian passive way to offer something to the present power if they

[60] Oates to Parkinson, Dec. 2, 1654, Nickolls, 132; same to ——, Firth, *Scotland and the Protectorate*, 241; Hedworth *et al.* to Holmes, Dec. 18, Thurloe, III, 29-30; Whalley to Cromwell, March 8, 1654/5, *ibid.*, 205-206; *cf.* Gardiner, III, 228.

[61] Gardiner, III, 228 ff.

[62] Thurloe to Pell, Jan. 26, 1654/5, Lansdowne MSS., 751, fol. 254.

[63] *Some Mementos for the Officers and Souldiers of the Army*, Oct. 19, 1654 (Thomason).

call for me to endeavour my satisfaction or to give an accompt of my dissatisfaction ".[64]

Major Bramston was more sweeping in his condemnation. Among his papers was a set of eight arguments by Paul Hobson, an officer and a prominent Baptist preacher, intended to prove that all church members who signed loyal addresses to the Protector ought, for so doing, to be excommunicated.[65] The idea appealed to Bramston, and as Hobson's arguments were addressed primarily to soldiers, he drew up another set, of eighteen instead of eight, applying to all saints. Both productions bristle with citations from Scripture, and contain the arguments made familiar by the petition of the three colonels, that the people of God had broken their covenants, built again that which had been destroyed, and thus brought discredit on themselves.[66]

It is probable that Bramston intended to enclose his "Reasons" in a letter he had written to the members of one of the Baptist churches in London, with whom, not having heard from them anything "tending to the awakening of Zion", he felt compelled to remonstrate. He upbraided them for being at peace with the government, and for justifying "all that wickednes and treason trut[h] and Covenant breaking which hath of Late been acted by many of us who are your bretheren". Then he demanded: "Have you not—nay, doe you not—condem those just men as bisey bodey and such as sufer as evle doers, who are now in

[64] Rawlinson MSS., A 34, fol. 49 ff. The paper is undated, but there is a copy among the Clarke MSS., among other copies of the papers found on the prisoners.

[65] Copy among the Clarke MSS.

[66] Add. MSS., 4159, fol. 195 ff. See also Bramston's examination, Firth, *Scotland and the Protectorate*, 241-242.

bonds for the testemony of a good conscienc; have you forgot sinc you your selves were called factius, and such as wear the disturbers and troublers of Israll . . . have you so soon forgoten your old resalutions which was that you would have no King but Jesus . . . o is it not a sad thing that you who have soe much abhored the Court prid and vanety shold now becom fawners and flaterers there as som of you are . . . have not I heard and seen you deny to pray for saints that ware in prison becaus they did contend with the corupt pourz of the Earth? . . . the day of the Lord is coming, it is ny att hand, and if judgment begin at the Hous of God wher shall the ungodly and siners apeare?"[67]

According to the principles of Hobson and Bramston, the entire Baptist churches of Leith, Edinburgh, and St. Johnstons ought to have been declared excommunicate, for they promptly issued a loyal address to the Protector disclaiming any part in the plot that had come to light. They declared that they owned and prayed for the government, and regretted having fallen under suspicion of participation in the recent plot, "through the defect of one; we knoweing noe more under suspition of guilt (in this matter) of our Society".[68]

This address appeared in the public prints, and efforts were made to create the impression that it represented the position taken by all moderate Baptists.[69]

[67] *For the Church of Christ Assembled at the Glas House in broad street, London, 25 of the 10 moneth* [1654], Add. MSS., 4459, fol. 145 ff.

[68] *The Humble Address of the Baptized Churches, consisting of officers, soldiers and others, walking in gospell order at Leith, Edinburgh and St. Johnstoun*, Clarke MSS., 27, fol. 133. See Firth, *Scotland and the Protectorate*, 242.

[69] *Mercurius Politicus*, Feb. 8-15, 1654/5.

Such expressions of loyalty were very valuable to Cromwell at a moment when Levellers, Commonwealth's men, and Royalists were all directing attacks upon him, and his Parliament was persistently refusing to come to any agreement which would put into his hands the power he needed in order to deal with them. It was over the question of control of the army that the deadlock finally came, and when he seized the earliest possible moment allowed by the Instrument of Government for the dissolution of Parliament, he performed an act which surely should have won him the approval of the army, towards which its policy had been in the highest degree irritating, and of the sectaries, who had been given no reason to hope that it would ever be willing to assure to them what was their breath of life—liberty of conscience.

CHAPTER IV.

SAINTS IN PRISON AND OUT OF PRISON.

CROMWELL'S championship against Parliament of the cause of liberty of conscience did not lack its reward. " Many, very many of the Churches of Christ ", wrote Thurloe to Monck, " as well those under baptisme as others in Scotland and England, have acknowledged the Government in writeing under theire hands since the disolution of the Parliament." [1]

One of the Baptist addresses has come down to us. It is entitled *The Representation and petition of Christ's servants, and your Highnesse loyal subjects, walking in the profession of faith and baptisme in Northumberland, Yorkshire, and Darbieshire.* Disowning any part in the agitations against the government, these Baptists speak of the present " halcyon daies of peace, plenty and liberty ", salute the Protector and his Council as the " happie powers ordained of God ", and rejoice in " that excellent instrument, the Saints Magna Charta, for the government of this Commonwealth, wherein such blessed provision is made for the tendet Lambs of the Lord Jesus, seconded by the late affectionate fatherly breathings of your Highnesse, at the dissolution of the last Parliament ". [2]

It would be pleasant to see in this nothing more than spontaneous enthusiasm for the rule of Cromwell, and

[1] *Clarke Papers,* II, 245. See also Bordeaux to Brienne and Mazarin, Jan. 23/Feb. 4, Feb. 8/18, 1654/5, P. R. O. Transcripts.

[2] February 11, 1655, Nickolls, 134.

for the excellences of the Instrument of Government. But, though the address is undoubtedly sincere, it is impossible to avoid ascribing some of its fervor to *odium theologicum.* In the middle of the paper occur the words: "Let such as are infatuated with Atheism, and poysoned with the dregges of Arminius, cry up a self-advancing power in Creatures, whiles we adore the Prince of the earth, who giveth the kingdoms of the world to whomsoever he pleaseth." Now Thomas Tillam and the Hexham church, who head the list of signatories, were at this time engaged in a fierce dispute with the Baptists of Newcastle over points in the doctrine of the latter which Tillam and his followers considered strongly Arminian.[3] Paul Hobson was the champion of the Newcastle church, and that church had, less than a fortnight before the appearance of the address from which we quote, been holding a meeting with churches of the neighborhood to take into consideration Hobson's "8 diabolical reasons" why all who subscribed loyal addresses to the Protector should be declared beyond the pale of the church. Most radical views had been expressed, and the dissentients had decided to publish something to clear themselves of blame.[4] Presumably this was the address we have been considering; at any rate its publication at this time could not have been unconnected with the action of Hobson's supporters, and it cannot be considered an indication of unanimous approval of the government among the Baptists of the northern counties.

While Paul Hobson was the center of Baptist discontent in the north of England, Adjutant-general

[3] *Hexham Records* (Hanserd Knollys Soc.).
[4] Topping to Thurloe, Feb. 5, 1654/5, Thurloe, III, 138.

William Allen was suspected of playing a similar part in the south. Recalled from his post in Ireland on account of speeches against the Protectorate, he had received some good advice from Cromwell, and had retired to his father-in-law's house near Exeter, resolved "to bee silent, to wait, and se what God would bring forth".[5] Apparently silence was beyond his powers. Word came to Cromwell that his disaffection was a matter of common report, and that his activities were especially noticeable among the Baptist churches of the neighborhood, whose meetings he was attending "disguised with kind of vizard".[6] The presence in the neighborhood of Hugh Courtney, who also was criticizing the Protectorate, increased the suspicion of the government agents. Cromwell sent friendly messages to the Baptist church at Exeter, which returned a prompt and loyal response, so it was evident that the dissatisfaction there had not proceeded far. Allen was probably quite truthful in his protestation that he dared not lift a hand against the government, or advise such a course. But he had indulged in free criticism, and Cromwell judged it expedient that he be laid under restraint.[7]

Cromwell's position with regard to these enthusiasts was an exceedingly difficult one. There was undoubtedly a good deal in the contention of Fleetwood that to put men like Allen in prison was likely to have worse effects in inflaming public opinion than their agitations would have were they ignored.[8] Yet he could scarcely

[5] Allen to Cromwell, Feb. 7, 1654/5, *ibid.*, 140-141; same to Axtell and Carteret, same date, *ibid.*, 141.

[6] Unton Croke to Cromwell, Feb. 7, *ibid.*, 143.

[7] *Id.*, and report of Coplestone and Croke, *ibid.*, 140; Allen to Cromwell, *ibid.*; Cromwell to Croke, Jan. 2, *Letters and Speeches*, II, 400.

[8] Fleetwood to Thurloe, March 14, 1654/5, Thurloe, III, 246.

avoid doing as he had done, especially at this juncture, when plots and rumors of plots were the order of the day. Levellers and Cavaliers had their uprisings planned, and the government had information of a rumored Fifth Monarchy plot which was about to come to a head.[9]

However, when opportunity offered, Cromwell spared no efforts to make it clear that he was not keeping men in prison without cause. The members of John Rogers's congregation resolved, after several days and nights of prayer, that it was their duty to go to Whitehall " and demand the Lord's prisoners and bear their testimony against those in present powers ". They thereupon chose by lot twelve members of the congregation—because twelve was " the Lord's number against the Beast, and the root and square number of the hundred, forty-four thousand in Rev. xiv ". The twelve, each with a Bible in his hand, presented themselves at Whitehall with a message addressed, without any titles, to Oliver Cromwell. The message stated that " in the name of our Lord Jesus, and of that whole society who have entrusted us on this errand, we are to DEMAND the Lord's prisoners . . . whom ye have so unchristianly rent and torn from us . . . and neither we nor they know for what to this day, but we are persuaded it is for their Faith and Conscience in the Truth and Testimony of Jesus Christ, against the foul apostacies and sins of the times ". Cromwell very naturally objected to the peremptory tone of the application, and said that Feake and Rogers were in prison, not for conscience' sake, but as " evil doers and busie

[9] Examination of Ellen Aske, Feb. 17, *ibid.*, 160.

bodies in other mens matters ". He promised, however, to give Rogers a hearing in their presence.[10]

For our knowledge of this interview with Rogers we are chiefly dependent upon an account written from notes taken at the time by one of the twelve, and published to confute the report that their leader "stood confounded". Spite of the partisan bias of the whole, a great deal of it bears the impress of a verbatim account, and gives an extremely vivid notion of what must have been an extraordinary conversation.[11] Rogers began by taking the position that he would answer no questions except in open court, at a legal trial. This demand for a legal trial was the strong feature of his position, and the only answer which Cromwell had for it was that he was kept from trial through kindness, as, if tried, he would be put to death under the treason ordinance. When confronted with reports of his utterances from the pulpit and in prison, taken down by government spies, he challenged the wording here and there, but admitted that the matter was substantially correct. He proclaimed his readiness to defend his words, and "to side with just principles", whether "*praedicando, precando,* or *praeliando*". At this Sir Gilbert Pickering, alive to the question of Rogers's readiness to take arms, inquired, "Said you not '*praeliando*'?" "Yes", was Rogers's response, "in the Spirit of the Lord, for the case was never so clear as now it is. . . . For the controversy . . . is now be-

[10] *The Faithfull Narrative of the Late Testimony and Demand made to Oliver Cromwel, and his Powers, on the Behalf of the Lords Prisoners,* March 21, 1654/5 (Thomason), reprinted in Rogers, *Fifth Monarchy Man,* 175 ff.

[11] The official account, a brief one, was given in the *Weekly Intelligencer,* Jan. 6-Feb. 13, 1654/5.

tween Christ and you, my Lord, Christ's government and yours; and which of these two are the higher Powers for us to side with and be obedient unto, judge ye." Thereat Cromwell exclaimed: "Ha! who denies the case to be clearer now? But I heard indeed it is some of your principles to be at it. Why, you long to be at it—you want but an opportunity." Rogers's rejoinder was: "The Remnant of the Woman's seed must be at it when they have the call." Continuing, he launched into a discourse upon the Beast's dominion. Cromwell impatiently said that he knew nothing of such matters. On the subject of triers, tithes and the national ministry he endeavored to make Rogers understand his point of view, but failed to cope with the accusation that his government depended upon "the long sword".

Among the members of the court party who were present was William Kiffin, who exhibited some hostility to Rogers. Rogers's supporters said that Cromwell, in making the statement that his duty was to keep the peace, pointed to Kiffin, and said that "there were Anabaptists who would cut the throats of those not of their forms", as would Presbyterians and Fifth Monarchy men. Rogers replied to this that the Fifth Monarchy principle was of such a latitude that it took in all saints, without regard to the form of religion which they professed. It was very evident that there was no possibility of converting this skilful disputant, and he was sent back to prison.

As he was being conducted across the palace yard, he met Harrison, Rich, Carew, Courtney, and others, who were coming as delegates from another congregation to demand the release of the "Lord's prisoners".

Cromwell told this delegation, made up of men as well known as the others had been obscure, that there was no one in England in prison on the Lord's account, that Feake and Rogers had been arrested for speaking against the government and for inciting people to arms. It was by this time late in the day, and Cromwell, who must have had enough of argument by that time, asked them to come to him at a more convenient season. He sent for them on three different occasions, but they failed to appear. Thereupon, having had information that the four named were endeavoring to stir up a revolt, he had them taken into custody. He gave them a hearing in the presence of a number of people, clergymen and others, among whom were two Baptists: Cradock, a Welsh minister, and Recorder Steele. At the request of the prisoners he invited also Simpson, a certain Banks, and the Fifth Monarchy preacher, John Pendarvis of Abingdon. The prisoners explained that their reason for not obeying his summons was that doing so would have implied a recognition of the government, which they considered Antichristian and Babylonish. Carew said that when the Little Parliament was dissolved Cromwell "tooke the Crowne off from the heade of Christ, and put it upon his owne".[12] They objected to parliaments on the

[12] Carew, when about to be executed as a regicide, gave the following testimony of his faith, from the scaffold: "There are many things laid upon many of those that profess the Kingdome and glorious appearance of Jesus Christ, as if they were enemies to Magistracy and Ministery, and as if so be we were for the destruction of the laws and properties of mankind; therefore shall I speak a few words unto that. And if indeed we were such, we were fit to be turned out of the world. . . . There is no such thing; I desire to bear witness to the true Magistracy, that Magistracy that is in the Word of the Lord. And that true Ministery . . . that . . . hath his holy Spirit. That testimony I desire to bear, and that testimony I desire to stand faithfull in, with integrity to the

ground that power belonged to Christ and not to the people, and they refused to promise to live peaceably. All four were thereupon committed to prison. Cromwell took pains to make clear the grounds of their imprisonment: that it was not alone for contempt of the government, but for special offenses in each case. Harrison was charged with countenancing opposition to the government and maintaining the lawfulness of taking arms against it; Carew, with the same offenses, and with having endeavored to seduce some important officials from their trusts; Rich, with having interfered with the raising of the tax; and Courtney with having fomented sedition in Norfolk and different parts of the west country. None of them had any response to make to these charges. Harrison was sent to Portland, whence he was later transferred to the Isle of Wight; Carew to Pendennis Castle in Cornwall; and Courtney to Carisbrooke Castle. Rich was allowed his liberty for a time, because his wife was dying, but he was later sent to Windsor.[13]

In commenting on their imprisonment the *Scout* said: " 'Tis very observable, that at several meetings at their respective churches, sundry times they declared, That although the Constitution of this present government was both ratified and confirmed, contrary to what they formerly expected, yet they would not lift up a hand against the Lord Protector, to pull him out, but by

---

Lord Jesus, as King of Saints, and King of Nations. And therefore it is, I say, to have a Magistracy as the first, and counsellors as at the beginning, men fearing God, and hating covetousness. And that Ministry as doth preach the everlasting gospel." *The Speeches and Prayers of some of the late King's Judges,* 1660.

[13] *Faithfull Narrative;* Thurloe to Monck, n. d., *Clarke Papers,* II, 242 ff.; Newsletter, Feb. 24, 1654/5, *id.,* III, 23; *Ralph Josselin's Diary* (Camden Soc., *Publications,* 3d. ser., XV), 109, 110.

their Spiritual Weapon of Jesus Christ they doubted not but to pray him out." [14] Probably the friendly *Scout* and the unfriendly Thurloe, who reported that they maintained the right to take arms against the government, were both correct. Their position was that while opposition to tyranny was lawful, it was the duty of the saints to endure the existing order until they received a definite call from God; that untimely action would hinder, instead of hasten, the promised kingdom. They could not promise to abstain from opposition, for the call might come at any time, and meanwhile they must bear witness.

If any people in England heartily wished for the release of the "Lord's prisoners", it was those who had them in custody. Rogers early in the year had complained of the treatment he was undergoing at Lambeth, and his jailer responded with an account of how he was encouraging his party, "a handfull of Scum, the very raf of Billingsgate, Redriffe, Ratliffe, Wappen, etc.", as he characterized them; telling them that they would soon possess the government, "that the Antichrist, the Babilon, the greate dragon, or the man of Sin, Oliver Cromwell, at Whitehall, must be puld down". One of them, preaching in Rogers's chamber, had said "that wee did not live in an age to expect miracles; that Babilon cannot be destroyed, nor the sainte at Windsor bee released by only faith and prayer; but you must bee of good courage, and make use of materiall instruments, and proceed by force"." [15]

Some of Rogers's visitors, the jailer's epithets to the contrary, were persons of quality and standing. The

[14] *Scout*, Feb. 23-March 2, 1654/5.
[15] Thurloe, III, 136, 486-487; Rogers, *Fifth Monarchy Man*, 201.

report of their numbers, together with Rogers's unquiet behavior, and the request of those who were responsible for him that he be either released or sent to some other prison, led to his being transferred to Windsor Castle in March.[16] Here Feake was already causing trouble to the governor, praying for the throwing down of "the three grand tyrants of the Nation, the Army, the Law, and the Clergy", calling Cromwell by no terms more polite than "Apostate, Covenant breaker, Jugler, Traitor, Usurper, Tyrant, and Persecuter", and teaching his little son to sing "The Protector is a foole", and "The Protector shall goe downe forty times together". When Rogers arrived, the poor governor was between the two driven quite to his wits' end. For a time the violence of their preaching led to their being closely confined, without the solace of each other's society, or that of the friends who came down from London to see them. Later, through representations made by the latter, an order of the Council directed that they have the freedom of the castle. They had been forbidden to preach in public, but on the following Sunday they strayed into the chapel at service time, when part of the congregation had assembled. Feake, entering the pulpit, began to pray. Rogers took up his position on the pulpit stairs, and when the regular minister entered, refused to make way for him. The governor, coming in with the garrison, bade the two come down and return to their chambers. They refused, saying that if they were to go they would have to be dragged, like Paul and Silas. The governor ordered some soldiers to put them out, and they had the opportunity of emulating those scrip-

[16] *Cal. St. P., Dom., 1655,* March 30.

tural personages to their hearts' content. Feake clung to the pulpit until it cracked with the strain. Rogers, having been ejected from the chapel, took up his stand on a stairway and began to pray in a loud voice. When efforts were made to dislodge him he grasped one of the stones in the wall, and maintained his hold until it was pulled from the mortar. When the two had finally been locked in their rooms and sentinels placed at the doors, Feake took up his position at his window, and when the congregation appeared on its way home from the service, began to harangue the people on a curiously irrelevant text from Revelation.[17] The drums were beating as the garrison came forth, but Feake succeeded in making himself heard above the tumult, and, when his voice failed, Rogers took up the discourse from his window until Feake had gathered strength enough to begin again.

Both prisoners subsequently declared that they would preach themselves to death rather than allow their liberty to be interfered with. Their preaching began to undermine the discipline of the soldiers, and their churches sent a gift to a sergeant who refused to use force against Rogers. Most irritating of all, they posed as martyrs when, as the governor of the castle complained, that was the rôle unwillingly enacted by the officers of the garrison: "For what martyrdome can there be greater then to persons who desire to employ their courage and fidelitie according to their Conscience to be crowed over by persons whom both their imprisonment and crimes should have taught an-

[17] "And when he had opened the seventh seal there was silence in heaven about the space of half an hour." Probably Feake laid his emphasis on the succeeding verse: "And I saw the seven angels which stood before God; and to them were given seven trumpets."

other civility." As their congregations maintained that they were being treated with undue severity, Cromwell appointed a commission to investigate the situation.[18] The findings of this commission are not on record, but apparently it was decided that all restraint on their "liberty of prophesying" should be removed, for by October their invectives were attracting so much attention that it was deemed expedient to remove them to the Isle of Wight.[19]

They were at first imprisoned at Sandown, and there is a mixture of the absurd and the pathetic in Feake's account of the hardships there, the unwholesomeness of the air, and the horrors of the bed provided for them, which was not only damp, but was stuffed with hops. To be sure, they were offered facilities for drying the bed, and a keeper assured them that hops were wholesome, but they preferred not to run any unnecessary risks, and slept in their clothes upon the floor, comforting themselves with the reflection that Nehemiah and his followers were once in a situation where they did not remove their clothes except for washing.[20]

The importunities of Feake's wife led to his being in time transported to the mainland, and given his liberty

[18] "A Paper from Coll. Whichcock [*sic*] Governor of Windsor Castle concerning Mr. Feake and Mr. Rogers", May 18, 1655, Rawlinson MSS., A 26, fol. 239 ff.; "A True relation of the Unchristian dealings exercised by the Governor of Windsor Castille, and the Soldiers under his commaund and in his presence towards Mr. Christopher Feake and John Rodgers (the lords prisoners there) of which we underwritten were ey and eare witnesses", *ibid.*, fol. 252 ff.; Account of a meeting at Allhallows, Thurloe, V, 756; *Weekly Intelligencer,* May 1-8, 1655.

[19] In June, Feake was visited by John Tillinghast, a Baptist clergyman from Norfolk who held Fifth Monarchy views. Going up to London, Tillinghast obtained an interview with Cromwell, to whom he used language so violent that the bystanders cried shame. Tillinghast died a short time after, from over-excitement, his biographer thinks. See his life, *Dict. Nat. Biog.*

[20] Thurloe, V, 757-758.

in a small town, with an order from the Protector bidding him remain there. He consulted the Scriptures to ascertain whether he was bound thus to be his own jailer. "At length came into my mind the case of Peter and John in the 4th of the Acts, who being called before the high priest Ananias and Caiaphas, were by them commanded not to preach in the name of Jesus. Now suppose, that either of their highnesses had sent Peter and John an order, enjoyning them to confine themselves to such a village, as Saron, or Joppa, or the like, and forbear coming to preach at Jerusalem: suppose, I say, an order had come to them upon that account, signed by either of their highnesses Ananias H. or Caiaphas H. like this with Oliver P. do you think they would have obeyed it, and been confined to a village? We find the contrary, for they preached the more boldly in the city of Jerusalem. Then having my warrant here from the scripture, I resolved for London, notwithstanding the order of Oliver P." When he was heard of in London, preaching as usual, he was sent back to his village, with a soldier to keep an eye upon him, and remained there until an order came for his release in December, 1656.[21]

Rogers, in spite of the efforts of his friends, was destined to remain long in what he considered exile from his native land. For a time he was quartered in a private house at the western end of the island, but as he continued to declaim against the government, and it was difficult to restrain people from flocking to hear him, he was removed to Carisbrooke Castle, with his family. Here he had the solace of companionship with

[21] *Ibid.*; Feake's preface to *The Prophets Malachy and Isaiah*; *Clarke Papers*, III, 61; *Cal. St. P., Dom., 1656-1657*, 194.

Courtney and Harrison, and with the latter he established a firm friendship. As he still insisted on preaching to all who would listen, he gained the ill-will of his jailers here, as at Lambeth and Windsor, and was subjected to many hardships. Later, Sir Henry Vane became his fellow prisoner, and the two became very intimate, solacing the hours of captivity by conversations on all manner of topics, including the coming kingdom. To them, as to Feake, the order for release came in December of 1656.[22]

Although their leaders were in prison, and their meetings attracting less attention, the zeal of the Fifth Monarchists had not waned. Several important pamphlets came out in the spring of 1655, and in the summer of that year the members entered upon a new phase of activity.[23]

Certain events which had followed Cromwell's dissolution of Parliament—his proclamation on religious liberty, and his championship of the Savoy Protestants—were such as could not fail to win the approbation of the Baptists. Moreover, the Royalist plots which threatened to bring back the days of episcopacy naturally suggested the advisability of support of the existing government in fear that worse might come. It is true that Charles Stuart had hopes of Baptist support, but although throughout the period individual Baptists were to be found supporting his cause, there is no evidence of any concerted movement made by them in his

[22] *Jegar Sahadutha,* in Rogers, *Fifth Monarchy Man,* 250 ff.; *Cal. St. P., Dom., 1656-1657,* 194.

[23] Aspinwall, *Thunders from Heaven,* and *The Work of the Age;* Postlethwaite, *A Voice from Heaven* (Thomason); Llanvaedonon, *A Brief Exposition upon the second Psalme* (Thomason).

favor.[24] On the contrary, some of the Welsh Baptists took arms to help put down the March insurrection, incurring thereby the suspicion that their movement was for the release of Harrison; and Vavasor Powell, at the head of his supporters, himself captured some of the plotters.[25] The Fifth Monarchy men were far from approving such signs of loyalty to the Protectorate, and they began what seems to have been an organized campaign for the purpose of winning Baptist support away from the government.[26]

One day toward the end of August all London was talking about some mysterious *Queries,* which had been scattered about the streets in the night, and which to many seemed to presage an Anabaptist plot. The main purport of these queries, which were entitled *A Short Discovery of his Highness's Intentions concerning the Anabaptists in the Army,* was that the Baptists were being systematically weeded out of the army in the course of the reorganization of the forces, although there had been a time when Cromwell was very glad of their services.[27] The authorship of this paper was pretty conclusively fastened upon John Sturgeon, a

[24] Intelligence from Manning, April, 1655, Thurloe, III, 355; *Calendar Clarendon Papers,* III, 51.

[25] Gunter to Goffe, March 21, 1654/5, Thurloe, III, 291; Nicholas to Cromwell, March 16, *ibid.,* 252.

[26] For an attempt to quicken Baptist zeal on the subject of liberty of conscience, see the circumstances of the arrest of Kiffin under the old ordinance on heresy, immediately following the mention of that ordinance in connection with Biddle's arrest. *A True state of the Case of Liberty of Conscience,* July 14; *The Spirit of Persecution again broken loose,* July 21; *The Petition of Divers Gathered Churches,* Oct. 23, 1655 (all in Thomason).

[27] Reprinted in Thurloe, III, 150. It is there called *Queries for his Highness to answer to his own conscience.* See also *Perfect Proceedings,* Aug. 23-30, 1655; *Weekly Intelligencer,* Aug. 28-Sept. 4.

member of Cromwell's lifeguard, and a Fifth Monarchy Baptist.[28] The idea that Cromwell had adopted as a definite policy the removal of Baptists from the army was not a new one. In April of the preceding year the French ambassador had written home that such a policy had been inaugurated, and then and later enough Baptists of Fifth Monarchy or Levelling principles had been dismissed to give color to the charge.[29] If we add to these the officers who voluntarily gave up their commissions rather than own the government, we shall not find it difficult to understand the large reduction in the number of Baptist officers since the establishment of the Protectorate. That Cromwell should plan to remove Baptists on account of their religious affiliations was quite out of keeping with his character; moreover, as we have seen, the Baptists had not, as Baptists, given any evidence of being a menace to the government. However, the plausibility of the suggestion won it a certain credence.[30]

The second attack on the government that contained a special appeal to the Baptists came out in October. Its title is a summary of its contents: *The Protector, so called, in Part Unvailed: by whom the Mystery of Iniquity is now Working, or a Word to the good*

[28] Thurloe, III, 738 ff.; Rawlinson MSS., A 29, fol. 268; *Clarke Papers,* III, 51. For Sturgeon see *Dict. Nat. Biog.* Close upon this affair came the Order of Council against unlicensed printing, and the disappearance of all newspapers except the government organs.

[29] Bordeaux to Brienne, April 17/27, 1654, P. R. O. Transcripts. The dismissals were particularly numerous in consequence of the army plot in Scotland, and Thurloe's words in that connection would seem almost a confirmation of Sturgeon's charge. See above, p. 72.

[30] In the *Queries,* the intentions of Cromwell were said to have been expressed in a conversation with Lord Tweeddale. The latter promptly issued a denial that any such conversation had taken place. *Public Intelligencer,* Oct. 8-15, 1655. The letter is dated from Edinburgh, Sept. 22.

People of the Three Nations . . . Informing them of the Abominable Apostacy, Backsliding, and Underhand dealing of the Man above mentioned, who having Usurped Power over the Nation, hath most wofully betrayed, forsaken, and cast out the good old Cause of God, and the Interest of Christ, and hath Cheated and Robbed his People of their Rights and Priviledges. By a late Member of the Army, who was an Eye, and an Ear witnesse to many of these things.[81] Borrowing many of the arguments, and frequently the language, of the petition of the three colonels, the author depicts the government as one that no man with the spirit of a true Englishman ought to be willing to serve in any capacity, civil or military. But it is the Baptists who have especially disappointed him, " for I thought if any people in the world would be valiant for God they would ". He refers pityingly to those Baptists who have been deceived by Cromwell's policy of using the support of the saints to keep down the Fifth Monarchy men. A Baptist acknowledgment of the government from Kent, indeed, he thinks was not drawn up there, but in London, by Baptist adherents of the court, and sent down into Kent for signatures, " which acknowledgment was cast out by several of the Saints both in and out of the churches, as an abominable thing. . . .[82] And truly the baptized people are more to be condemned, then the rest, because in siding with the Court they do own and countenance those very things, as to the pomp, pride and glory of the world, which they abhor and cast out among themselves; yet because one or two that are eminent among them do follow the

[81] Thomason's date is October 24.

[82] This may possibly be the address given in Nickolls, 152.

Court, and wander after the Beast, and a baptised Person is President of the Councel", many Baptists are blind to the fact that the chief end of the government is to put down the spirit and principle for which the Baptists stand.

A third appeal to the Baptists came in *A Ground Voice,* published a few weeks later. It was addressed to the army, "with Certain Queries to the Anabaptists in particular that Bear any Office, either in Court or Army, under the present self-created Politick Power". The first part is a turgid Fifth Monarchy address to the soldiery, bidding them come out of Babylon, and separate from the crew of Antichrist; and an arraignment of Cromwell, not merely as a traitor, but as a murderer, guilty of all the blood spilt at Hispaniola. In the second part, the Baptists who are serving the state are asked if it is not dishonorable, and a denial of their professions, to hold any employment from the present court. Besides, it is urged, they are only being used as baits, to prevent the alienation of their churches, and will be cast out when the Protector is more firmly seated. They had best withdraw at once, of their own accord, and put a distance between the righteous and the wicked.[83]

The reference to the disaster at Hispaniola is one that appeared from this time forward in all these attacks on the government. The belief that the failure of Cromwell's West Indian expedition was a direct judgment from God for his wickedness in seizing the supreme power, was one that made a strong appeal to pious

[83] Thomason's date is November 16. The pamphlet concluded with the request to meditate on such verses as Revelation, xviii, 4; II Corinthians, vi, 17; Jeremiah, li, 6, 45, and l, 8; Isaiah, lii, 2, etc.

souls. Fervently held by the Fifth Monarchists, it was in their hands a potent weapon in the battle to win away supporters from a government set apart by this plain sign for destruction. It was perhaps the most effective argument which they used in their efforts to influence the Baptists, and those efforts were already showing signs of success. Members of groups that had long been silent were seen heading deputations at Whitehall. Cromwell's ill-health at this time, if not caused by disappointment at the failure of his plans, and sorrow on account of the expressions of dissatisfaction that were daily brought to him, was certainly not improved by them.[34] Fleetwood, who was an extreme Independent, and who always displayed great sympathy with the Baptists, many of whom were his close friends, was of service to the administration at this juncture. He had gained quite a reputation for skill in dealing with discontented sectaries in Ireland, and he was able to enlist the services of Hierome Sankey, a Baptist recently returned thence, who was at this time supporting the Protectorate. Together they had a series of meetings with Simpson, Jessey, and others, and did what they could to alter their views, though without conspicuous success.[35]

The establishment of the major-generals provided Cromwell with a means of watching the movements of the sectaries in all parts of the country. Goffe, in Lewes, reported that a petition was being circulated for the reformation of the law, the abolition of chancery, tithes, and oaths, and the bringing to trial of pris-

[34] Sankey to Henry Cromwell, Oct. 2, 1655, Lansdowne MSS., 823, fol. 120.

[35] *Ibid.*, and same to same, Oct. 9, *id.*, 821, fol. 24; Bordeaux to Brienne, Oct. 22/Nov. 1, P. R. O. Transcripts.

oners. The Baptists were very generally signing it, and the members of the largest congregation in the town—that of Postlethwaite, a Fifth Monarchy preacher—were refusing to sign, not because of its tenor, but because it recognized the Protectorate, addressing Cromwell as " his highness ". Goffe went to hear Postlethwaite preach, and found him quite moderate, his chief grievance being the imprisonment of Harrison and Feake.[36]

In Wales, the behavior of Vavasor Powell and John Williams was once more suspicious. Major-general Berry sent for Powell, and told him that he had heard that he and his friends were " about some designe, that tended to put things into distraction ". Powell replied that they would die rather than do such a thing; that the project in hand was merely the securing of signatures to a petition which was to be presented to Cromwell; that they hoped for redress of their grievances, and were in any case in duty bound to make public their " dissatisfactions and desires ", but that, this done, they intended nothing further. Berry, who understood Welshmen, and did not believe in taking their notions too seriously, talked with him at length, saying that he thought such a petition, if privately presented, was justifiable and harmless, but that it would be unadvisable to publish it. He thought he had made an impression, and told Powell he might preach, provided he avoided vexed questions. Pleased with the moderation of his sermons, Berry invited him to dinner, and had another friendly conversation with him. When he left, assuring Berry that he was always glad to be convinced when in error, and that, though he had been

[36] Goffe to Thurloe, Nov. 5, 7, 1655, Thurloe, IV, 151, 161.

given a bad name, " it neither was his purpose or practice to preach anything tending to faction ", the major-general felt that fears of danger from that quarter were quite superfluous.[37]

That his confidence was based on insufficient grounds became apparent during the ensuing fortnight. The petition was duly presented, and Berry, warned that the matter had better be investigated, was still inclined to make light of it, having heard that some of the signatures had been affixed without the knowledge of their owners, and believing that the whole affair was merely the result of misunderstanding and misplaced "Brittish" zeal.[38] But within a few days the petition appeared in print, and it was at once evident that the government had now to deal with one of the most bitter attacks that had as yet been directed against it.[39] It was addressed to Cromwell, not as Protector, but as captain-general of the forces, and warned him that on the day of judgment he must answer for his " slighting and blaspheming of the spirit of God . . . the hard measure you give his people, by reproaches, imprisonment, and other oppressions, and where pride, luxury, lasciviousness, changing of principles, and forsaking of good ways, justice and holiness will not have the smallest rag of pretence to hide them from the eyes of the judge, which things (whatsoever you say for yourself) are (even at present) to be read in your forehead, and have produced most sad effects everywhere ". To the usual

[37] Berry to Thurloe, Nov. 17, 21, Thurloe, IV, 211, 228; *Mercurius Politicus*, Nov. 21.

[38] Same to same, Dec. 1, Thurloe, IV, 272.

[39] " A word for God, or a testimony on truth's behalf, from several churches, and diverse hundreds of Christians in Wales (and some few adjacent) against wickednesse in high places, with a letter to the lord general Cromwell." Reprinted in Thurloe, IV, 380 ff.

grievances, including the expedition to the West Indies, is added a complaint of the preferment accorded to Cromwell's relatives and friends. Finally, the petitioners announce that they " withdraw, and desire all the Lord's people to withdraw from these men, as those that are guilty of the sins of the later days, and that have left following the Lord, and that God's people should avoid their sin, lest they partake with them in their plagues ".[40]

This proclamation was greeted with acclamations by the Fifth Monarchy men in London. Cornet Day read it at Allhallows on the day of its publication to five hundred hearers, to whom he and Simpson denounced " the theeves and robbers at Whitehall, and the great theife Oliver Cromwell, the tyrant and usurper ". Day was arrested, and Simpson went into hiding.[41] Powell was arrested before the publication of the petition, but toward the end of December he was again at liberty, and expressed to Berry regret that Day had made that use of the paper.[42]

Berry continued to regard the trouble as unimportant, but the advice of men like Broghill, Whalley, and Haynes was for repression rather than neglect. Whalley expressed surprise that Cromwell had so long tolerated Simpson; Haynes felt that " if a special regard

[40] Thurloe, commenting on this petition in a letter to Henry Cromwell, said, " I will make noe observations, though many others doe, that it is evident they will call up againe the old parliament, which they themselves were the great occasion of destroyinge; appeale to the generality of the people for justice and righteousnes, comend parlaments chosen by the people (the thinge they most of all hate) or doe any other thinge, rather than misse of their end of bringinge thinges to trouble and confusion ". Jan. 1, 1655/6, Thurloe, IV, 373-374.

[41] Thurloe to Henry Cromwell, Dec. 17, 25, 1655, *ibid.*, 321, 343.

[42] Newsletter, Dec. 22, *Clarke Papers*, III, 62; Berry to Thurloe, Dec. 28, Thurloe, IV, 359; *Word for God*, *ibid.*

be not had of condign punishment of them, your friends that serve you have but little encouragement soe to doe ".[43] " Since the All-hallowes men wil be still mad ", wrote Broghill, " 'tis a mercy they appeer soe evidently that we must confess tacitly they speake the truth, unless we punish them openly for speakinge of such horrid lyes. I know it has greived many an honest hart, that they have bin suffered so longe; and 'twould satisfy them, if they were tollerated noe longer. I feare indulgency will rather heighten their evell, then win them from it." [44]

Cromwell could not bring himself to consent to harsh measures against men whose opposition to him was conscientious, however misguided. He preferred to be guided by the excellent principle upon which Berry acted, that there is nothing like persecution for making a cause flourish.[45] Yet the voices from Allhallows were far-reaching. Henry Cromwell put his finger on the real danger. " You write me worde in your laste of Daye's and Sympson's carriage ", he wrote to Thurloe. " Dare they be soe bolde, if they had not good backe? Howe longe have the Anabapt. and they bin at odds? From whence comes John Sympson? " [46] The Fifth Monarchy party in itself was perhaps a negligible quantity, but if the Baptists should be won over to their side the situation would be serious. And the campaign for that purpose was in full swing. What looked like an organized distribution of the *Word for God,* the

[43] Whalley to Thurloe, Dec. 12, *ibid.*, 308; Haynes to same, Dec. 20, *ibid.*, 329.

[44] Broghill to Thurloe, Dec. 25, *ibid.*, 342.

[45] Berry to Thurloe, Dec. 28, 1655, Jan. 5, 1655/6, *ibid.*, 359, 394.

[46] Dec. 26, 1655, *ibid.*, 348.

Protector Unvailed, and the *Queries,* was going on in different parts of the country.[47]

The government was soon supplied with materials for carrying on a counter campaign. Samuel Richardson again appeared as the defender of the Protectorate, declaring that " Nature, Reason, and the word of God " required all men to support a government which was established of God, gave a freedom hitherto undreamed of in matters civil and religious, and had under consideration all grievances which were still unredressed.[48] From South Wales came a paper with some nine hundred signatures, decrying the *Word for God,* and declaring that the majority of the Welsh people were loyal to the government.[49] These two papers the authorities took steps to circulate throughout the country, and among the Baptists in the navy.[50]

The agitation which seems to have been most widespread at this time was in Norfolk. In December the government was apprised that efforts were being made

[47] *Mercurius Politicus,* Dec. 14, 1655; Whalley to Thurloe, Jan. 11, 1656, Thurloe, IV, 412.

[48] *Plain Dealing,* Jan. 23, 1655/6 (Thomason). This effort of Richardson's did not go unrewarded. See Richardson to Thurloe, May 17, Rawlinson MSS., A 38, fol. 487. A much abler response to the *Word for God* was the *Animadversions upon a Letter and Paper,* attributed by Gardiner to William Sedgwick of Ely. But as a defense of the government Richardson's pamphlet was much more acceptable to the court party, and, as the work of a Baptist, it was especially useful for circulation among Baptists. See Goffe to Thurloe, Jan. 23, Thurloe, IV, 445, and Thurloe to Henry Cromwell, Feb. 5, 12, *ibid.,* 505, 531.

[49] *The Humble Representation and Address to his Highness, of several Churches and Christians in South Wales and Monmouthshire. Presented Thursday, January 31* (Thomason). Its asseverations did not hold good for North Wales. Thomas Cooper, one of Cromwell's Baptist supporters, was there at this time, and was much cast down by the spirit displayed. Cooper to Thurloe, Feb. 21, 1655/6, Thurloe, IV, 551.

[50] Butler to Thurloe, Feb. 16, *ibid.,* 540; Goffe to same, Feb. 11, *ibid.,* 525; Vice-admiral Goodson to Thurloe, June 24, Rawlinson MSS., A 39, fol. 433.

by Day's faction to win over churches in Norfolk and Suffolk.[51] Late in January came word that some of the most godly men in the neighborhood of North Walsham were carrying on an agitation, which had spread to Norfolk churches hitherto considered free from the Fifth Monarchy taint. A general meeting was appointed to take place in Norwich in March, to discuss " the visible kingdom of Christ, and the present duty of the Saints in reference to the present Government of the world ". The more violent party, among the leaders of which were the Baptist Colonel Danvers, and Thomas Buttivant, a former member of Cromwell's lifeguard, was prepared to advocate an appeal to arms. They were even said to have arms and horses in readiness. It was arranged by the authorities that some moderate Baptists should attend this meeting, that they might furnish counsel of moderation.[52] The messengers of twelve churches, Baptist and Independent, were present, and the advice of the sober-minded so far prevailed that the government newspaper was able to announce that they " generally declared to each other, That they believed Christ should have a visible and glorious kingdom, and also that they accounted it their duties to be subject to the present Powers, and to pray for them: and if any should be otherwise minded, it would bee to them great sorrow and grief of heart, as also an offence ".[53] A few weeks later there was held a meeting of those who dissented from this decision, with the purpose, it was averred, of presenting a letter to Cromwell, in the spirit of the *Word for God*. Major-

[51] Haynes to Thurloe, Dec. 20, Thurloe, IV, 329-330.

[52] Brewster to Thurloe, Jan. 28, March 5, 1655/6, Thurloe, IV, 472-473, 581; Thurloe to Henry Cromwell, March 18, *ibid.*, 629.

[53] *Mercurius Politicus*, March 13-20, 1655/6.

general Haynes talked with the leading pastors and messengers, and made all possible efforts to check the growth of the spirit of discontent. In the end, not more than about thirty took part in the meeting.[54] Doctrinal matters were pushing political questions into the background, and many of the Fifth Monarchy men, here and in other parts of the country, were undergoing the rite of baptism. Some of them, too, were becoming Seekers and Quakers.[55]

On the whole, the indications during the spring and summer of 1656 were that the Fifth Monarchy party was declining in numbers. To this fact the spread of the Quaker propaganda unquestionably contributed. It is not necessary to go back to the seventeenth century for examples of eagerness to embrace the latest thing in religion, and by 1656 the Fifth Monarchy movement had for many become *vieux jeu*. On the part of the leaders, however, with very few exceptions, zeal for the cause was unabated. And since some of them, like Powell, were also enthusiastic evangelists, it was difficult for outsiders to be sure whether or no politics were entering into their activities. For example, Powell in early June presided over a meeting of more than four hundred people, come together out of seven or eight counties, and a much larger meeting was projected for the same month.[56] Hannah Trapnel had been since the preceding December in Wales, with companions who did not own the government. In May it was reported that she was getting little encouragement, and was thinking of crossing the sea. At the same time there

[54] Haynes to Cromwell, April 9, 23, Thurloe, IV, 687, 727.

[55] Haynes to Thurloe, April 23, June 27, July 5, *ibid.*, 727; *id.*, V, 166, 188; *Mercurius Politicus*, April 17-24.

[56] —— to Whitelocke, June 12, Thurloe, V, 112.

were being held in that part of the country many meetings of "Fifth Monarchmen, Quakers, etc., who though they differ in other things, agree in destroying magistracy and ministery".[57] John Sturgeon, the reputed author of the *Queries,* was addressing large meetings in Reading, though he was avoiding public attacks upon the government.[58] In Hull, too, the activities of John Canne were so suspicious that he was ordered to leave the place.[59] It was impossible to ignore reports of this sort, despite rumors of dwindling numbers and lessening credit. Fifth Monarchy men become Baptists did not necessarily become peaceful ones: in fact, the reverse was sometimes known to be the case.[60] The very fact that there was no evidence of a plot in connection with any of the agitations made it impossible to deal with them effectively, and their existence was one of the elements which contributed, in the minds of many sober-thinking folk, to the conclusion that it would before long become necessary to settle the government upon some firmer foundation.

[57] *Publick Intelligencer,* Dec. 24-31, 1655; *Mercurius Politicus,* May 29-June 5, 1656.

[58] Goffe to Thurloe, May 1, 1656, Thurloe, IV, 752.

[59] *Cal. St. P., Dom., 1656-1657,* 41. See also *Eng. Hist. Rev.,* 1907, 314.

[60] "Our North Walsham fifth monarchy bretheren, who weare lately dipped, are synce grown exceeding high in their expressions, and that tending to bloud." Haynes to Thurloe, July 16, 1656, Thurloe, V, 220. See also *ibid.,* 219.

CHAPTER V.

Kingdom Building.

In the early part of the year 1657 there were two attempts, both unsuccessful, to re-establish monarchy in England. One of these attempts was due to the belief of lawyers and other conservative men that the only hope of securing a permanent settlement, and of maintaining at the same time the good results secured in the civil wars, was by restoring the one form of government recognized by English laws, and placing the crown on the head of Cromwell. The other arose out of the conviction of certain enthusiasts that there was no hope for any settled government in England until they, as God's chosen people, had overthrown the existing order and established divine kingship in the person of Jesus Christ. Thus, at the same moment, but in very different ways, the hottest heads and the coolest heads in England were dreaming of crowns.

The attempt of the idealists came first. To understand it we must retrace our steps, and study the inner development of the Fifth Monarchy party since 1654. From its inception the party had exhibited two very different tendencies. One was toward the support of the principle that the existing government was to be overthrown by the prayers of the saints, who were to separate from the world, and endeavor to live pure lives; testifying against evil, but submitting peaceably to the government, even though they could not conscientiously own it. The other tendency was toward the belief in armed resistance—in establishing by the sword the rule of the saints.

The principles of the moderate wing were well set forth by William Aspinwall in the summer of 1656. While waiting for the Fifth Monarchy, he says, it is right for the saints to obey the fourth, and even hold office under it, however corrupt it may be. The Fifth Monarchy men are "the best and truest friends unto Government, and count it their duty to be faithful unto their trust, be the Rulers what they may, or the form of government what it will. Only they take themselves bound in Conscience to rebuke sin, and bear witness against unrighteousness, in any person, of what quality soever, and in any form of Government whatsoever".[1]

John Simpson, formerly one of the most violent of the warlike section, had already adopted principles similar to these. At a meeting in February, 1656, he preached that the Fifth Monarchy was not to be expected before the personal coming of Christ, and declared that he was utterly against the project of some of the party, both in London and the country, to appeal to arms. An uproar arose straightway, and the assembly broke up in confusion.[2]

Delighted at what seemed an indication that the views of the party's leaders were moderating, Cromwell took steps to ascertain whether it would be advisable to liberate some of those who were in prison.[3] Cradock,

[1] *The Legislative Power is Christ's Peculiar Prerogative*, August 20, 1656 (Thomason).

[2] Thurloe to Henry Cromwell, Feb. 19, 1655/6, Thurloe, IV, 545; Hartlib to Worthington, March 10, *Worthington Diary* (Chetham Soc.), I, 79.

[3] *Cal. St. P., Dom., 1655-1656*, 190, 202.

the Baptist minister, was sent to interview Harrison at Carisbrooke Castle, and to intimate to him that the Protector was willing to restore him his freedom, provided he would give a pledge to remain peaceably at his country home and refrain from action against the government. Fleetwood went on a similar errand to Rich, who was his personal friend. After their first interview Rich wrote him a long letter, in order to make clear his position.[4] He laid weight upon the entire injustice of his imprisonment, and maintained that, were he to consent to any condition whatever in order to secure his liberty, it would be a tacit concession that there had been some warrant for the treatment he had undergone. He declared that his only course was to remain quietly in prison "till conviction of the errour be actually acknowledged by looseing bonds without any other cry or petition but their own injustice . . . I envy not those in power, but pity and pray for them, but it is that their workes may be burnt and their soules saved so as by fire, which if such fooles as I am should attempt to kindle 'twould perhaps scorch me as much or more then them. . . . I leave them to the Lord; he is the best judge of his owne wrong or mine if any be; if they feare us raysing armys surely it could not be in the cloudes; their courage, wisedome and conduct are more honourable guards from new or old enemys, then putting freinds in durance. If it be not such an outward but a more spirituall, invisible and inward appearance that is suspected, alas, what walls or force

[4] The first part of the rough draft of this letter was printed in Thurloe, VI, 251. The latter part was misplaced among the papers of 1657, and has never been printed. It is to be found in the Rawlinson MSS., A, 60, fol. 458 ff. It is written on rough paper, in poor ink, with numerous corrections and interlineations.

can confine the anointing? Can it be thought that violent suspensions practised upon that invincible spirit which breathes not but in innocent purity, justice, and righteousnesse, doe portend more then the will and weaknesse of man, which intends but cannot obtaine its suppression?" Harrison's answer was in the same spirit. Both men professed a preference for captivity, as an occasion of spiritual profit, and an opportunity to benefit by the prayers of the saints. However, notwithstanding their refusal to give pledges, freedom was forced upon them. Although the order for their release was stayed on March 1, when rumors of a rising were rife, Harrison was set free on March 22, and Rich probably about the same time.[5] Harrison retired to his father-in-law's house at Highgate, which now became, according to Thurloe, the center of resort for the disaffected party.[6]

The party in London which believed in an appeal to arms, though small in numbers at this time, was great in zeal. It was probably during the preceding winter that its members had organized five meetings in different parts of the city. According to information which reached Thurloe, each of these meetings consisted of twenty-five members, and only one member of each meeting knew of the existence of the other four. From these organizations representatives were sent out to carry on the propaganda in different parts of the country.[7] The headquarters were in Swan Alley, Cole-

[5] Rogers, *Jegar Sahadutha*, in *Fifth Monarchy Man*, 277. Rich was arrested in August, and imprisoned at Windsor till Oct. 4, when he was ordered confined at his country house. *Cal. St. P., Dom., 1656-1657*, 71, 112, 130, 582.

[6] Thurloe to Henry Cromwell, April 16, 1656, Thurloe, IV, 698. For Harrison's attitude during this summer, see Harrison to Jones, 12th 5th mo., *Correspondence of John Jones*, 257.

[7] Thurloe's account, Thurloe, VI, 184 ff.

man Street, and here were held both the public meetings, and private ones, to which only the faithful were admitted. The auditory was wrought to the pitch of tears and lamentations by means of expositions on such texts as the following: "If I whet my glittering sword, and mine hand take hold on judgment; I will render vengeance to mine enemies, and will reward them that hate me. I will make mine arrows drunk with blood, and my sword shall devour flesh; and that with the blood of the slain and of the captives, from the beginning of revenges upon the enemy."[8] These meetings were much frequented by young apprentices, who quite relished being told that they were God's people chosen out of an apostate nation which had adopted a hypocritical government; that the time of deliverance was at hand, and that they should be as the lion terrible to the rest of the beasts.[9]

Through the conversation of some of these apprentices rumors came to the ears of the authorities in March, 1656, of a boasted force of six thousand men, armed and ready to join any rising against the government. There was talk of plots to put Cromwell and the Lord Mayor to death, to punish the aldermen, and to set Harrison and the other prisoners free.[10] These were the reports which caused the stay in the proceedings for the liberation of Harrison and Rich, which were continued after some investigations had been made. No foundations for the rumors were discovered, and the

[8] Deuteronomy, xxii, 41, 42.

[9] Information, May 26, 1656, Thurloe, V, 60. Another place of meeting was White's Alley, Coleman Street.

[10] Examinations and information, March 15, 17, 26, *id.*, IV, 621, 624, 650.

reports from the country indicated that the propaganda there was having no signal success.[11]

However unsuccessful in winning converts, the little body of enthusiasts in London worked on with zeal undiminished. At a meeting on July 8 it was decided that the time for pulling down Babylon and its adherents had come, and that the saints must do it, and by means of the sword. To avoid discovery, it was decided that one man should be chosen out of each meeting, to whom his fellow-members were to communicate " what readiness they are in, with what force they have, what arms, what money, and when to be ready ". Thus only one in each assembly knew the names of those who were engaging in the conspiracy.[12]

Rumors of these transactions came to the ears of other discontented factions. The Commonwealth men had some Fifth Monarchy men among them, and it was hoped that an understanding between the two parties might be brought about, and some joint action decided upon. A meeting was arranged, and among the twelve present were Colonel Okey, Arthur Squib, John Portman, and Thomas Venner, with Vice-admiral Lawson and four captains of the navy.[13] Squib belonged to the radical party in the Little Parliament, Portman was a Baptist who held a minor position in the admiralty office, and Venner was a wine cooper who had held a post in the Tower, but had lost it the preceding summer for suspected implication in a plot there.[14]

[11] Thurloe to Henry Cromwell, April 15, 1656, Thurloe, IV, 698; same to Montague, April 28, Carte, *Original Letters*, II, 104.

[12] " The effect of the meeting of the Fifth Monarchy men." Thurloe, V, 197.

[13] Thurloe's account, *id.*, VI, 185.

[14] Barkstead to Cromwell, June 6, 1655, Thurloe, III, 520. Venner had lived for a long time in New England. See Banks, " Thomas Venner," in *New Eng. Hist. and Gen. Reg.*, 1893.

The basis of the proposed agreement between the two parties was the *Healing Question* of Sir Henry Vane. The point upon which a settlement promised to be difficult was the manner of procedure. The Commonwealth party advocated the assembling of a select few of the members as their authority, while the Fifth Monarchy men desired immediate action, with no preconcerted plan, the issue to be left to Providence. Appeal was made to Harrison and Rich to help settle the differences of opinion, but they refused to be drawn into the affair. The meetings dragged along, the government keeping its eye upon the men known to be concerned, until on July 29 Lawson, Okey, Portman, and Venner were ordered brought before the Council. Venner eluded the vigilance of the authorities, and the others were dismissed with admonitions.[15]

The agitations of the Commonwealth party had been begun as a result of the news, made public on June 26, that a new Parliament was to be elected. Cromwell had endeavored to avoid calling a Parliament at this time, but the absolute necessity of raising money had forced him to it. Straightway efforts were made to bring to the polls in opposition to the Cromwellian policy a large number of Commonwealth men, Levellers, Baptists, Fifth Monarchy men, and Royalists.

It will be remembered that one contention of some of the leaders of the Fifth Monarchy party was that the saints ought not to take part in parliamentary elections. To men with such scruples was addressed that

[15] Thurloe's relation, Thurloe, VI, 185-186; Barkstead to Thurloe, July 25, 1656, *id.*, V, 248; Thurloe to Henry Cromwell, Sept., 1656, *ibid.*, 317; Thurloe to Montague, Aug. 28, Carte, *Original Letters*, II, 111.

very able piece of campaign literature, *England's Remembrancers.* Its plea was that the present call for a Parliament was the voice of God, "saying, Gather the people, call a solemn assembly, go and reason together". It opened the way to escape from the existing tyranny. Those who refused to do any thing that implied a recognition of the government were told that the exercise of the suffrage was not such a recognition, since it was an inherent right, unconnected with writs of election. Those who believed "that God requireth at this time higher ways of advancing Christ's kingdom than by parliaments" were assured that there could be no higher way, and no better means of advancing Christ's kingdom, than the election of a body of able and godly men.[16]

Copies of this pamphlet were distributed during a prayer made by Venner in a private meeting in Coleman Street, Swan Alley, on August third.[17] Other copies were distributed throughout the country. Those sent to Norwich were traced to Buttivant, one of the Fifth Monarchy leaders there.[18] Its suggestions bore some fruit, in so far as can be judged from the reports that Fifth Monarchy men took part in the tumultuous elections that followed.[19] Rich and Alured were ar-

[16] Printed in Thurloe, V, 268 ff. Thomason's date is August 1, and he adds "Scattred about the streets".

[17] Informations, Thurloe, V, 272.

[18] Haynes to Thurloe, Aug. 10, 1656, *ibid.*, 297; examinations, *ibid.*, 342.

[19] An interesting example of the confusion in men's minds regarding parties and principles is furnished by the election of William Kiffin for Middlesex. The opposition to him was organized by the Fifth Monarchy Baptist Chillenden, who of course opposed him because he was one of Cromwell's supporters. Kiffin, however, was mobbed at the polls by the country people, whose slogan was, "Noe Anabaptist". Thurloe to H. Cromwell, Aug. 26, 1656, Thurloe, V, 349; Titon to Kiffin, Aug. 8, *ibid.*, 286.

rested in connection with these tumults, probably on suspicion that they had had something to do with the appearance of the pamphlet in question.[20]

Despite all agitation, the results of the elections were not such as to promise much encouragement to unyielding opponents of the Cromwellian régime, and the plans of the warlike party of the Fifth Monarchists were again pushed to the fore. In September a declaration of their position was in print. It announced that the saints constituted a state by themselves, and as such were justified in exercising their royal authority and using " all honest and just means to defend themselves, and offend their enemies, and to contend against those that doe or shall oppose them in their worke and busines, which is accordinge to the patterne shewed unto them in the mount and law of Christ, ordained and declared throughout the Scriptures ". The work of destruction must precede the setting up of Christ's kingdom, and to prepare for this work the saints must separate from the state church, and from the gathered churches which do not believe in the war against Christ's enemies, and must not serve or own the civil power.[21]

The organizers of the rising were all obscure men. The only name among them which is at all familiar is that of Venner, who achieved notoriety through another plot in post-Restoration days. The plans were drawn up at night meetings by a few leading spirits, and then submitted to the larger assembly. It was de-

[20] Gardiner, *Commonwealth and Protectorate*, IV, 262.

[21] *The Banner of Truth Displayed: or, a testimony for Christ, and against Anti-Christ. Being the substance of severall Consultations, holden and kept by a Certain Number of Christians, who are waiting for the Visible appearance of Christ's Kingdome, in and over the world: and residing in and about the city of London*, Sept. 24, 1656 (Thomason).

cided "that principally we endeavour and engage against the army, and principles of the army, . . . and that according to reason and wisdom, we do not separate colours, and engage against many strong enemyes at once, as the priests and lawyers ". The organization of the conspirators was as nearly as possible along biblical lines. The forces were to be divided into three bands, according to the precedent established by Abraham, Jacob, Gideon, and David; the officers were chosen by lot. "Such gayne and spoyle as is due to the Lord, and to the treasury and work of the Lord, according to the rule and practice of the Scripture, both of gold, brasse, and precious things", was to be brought into a common treasury, "and that which is for the brothers, for their particular encouragement" was to be equally distributed among those who went into action and those whose duty it was to "stay with the stuffe". A seal was chosen, bearing a lion couchant, and the motto "Who shall rouze him up?" The plan was to begin by falling upon a troop of horse, executing the officers and all the soldiers who refused to submit, and seizing the horses, "because the Lord hath need". Spies were sent out to view the country for a suitable spot for such an enterprise, and a rendezvous was selected in Epping Forest.[22] Messengers were to publish in all the large market towns a proclamation asserting that testimony had been given against the apostasy of the government, that God had set his seal upon that testimony by blasting the Hispaniola design, and that the saints were now

[22] The greater part of the deciphered copy of the conspirators' minutes, in the Add. MSS., 4459, fols. 111-122, has been published by Mr. Champlin Burrage in the *Eng. Hist. Rev.*, 1910, 725-737. They were deciphered by Jessop and several of the members of Richard Cromwell's Parliament. Burton, *Diary*, III, 494.

justified in rising against evil doers, since Parliament and army in the past had shown that it was " no resisting of Magistracy to side with just principles ". This proclamation, which was later printed and circulated, outlined the government of the coming state. Christ was to be the supreme legislative power; the Scriptures, the body of the law; a Sanhedrim of godly men was to be the chief magistracy, having control of the militia. There was to be no taxation without the consent of the people, no tithes, and no interference of the civil power in religious matters.

" We do now ", the proclamation concluded, " in the name and Authority of the Lord King-Jesus, call upon the Lord's people, our Brethren, Sisters, and Friends, with every one that professeth the name of God, that are yet in Babilon . . . to come out of her . . . for the houre of his Judgment is come."[23] When sufficient forces should be assembled at the rendezvous, the conspirators expected to march into Norfolk and Suffolk, " because there is most Churches and Christians of the faith, and the Countrey generally enclosed and soe

[23] *A Standard Set Up. Whereunto the true Seed and Saints of the most High may be gathered together into one, out of their severall Forms: For the Lambe against the Beast, and False Prophet in this good and honourable Cause. Or, the Principles and Declaration of the Remnant, who have waited for the blessed Appearance and Hope. Shewing, how Saints as Saints, men as men, and the Creation shall have their blessings herein, as in the Deliverance of the True Church out of Babylon, and all Confusion; as in the most Righteous and Free Common-Wealth-State; as in the Restitution of all things. Subscribed W. Medley, Scribe. . . . Who shall Rouse Him Up? Lift up a Standard for the People, whereunto the true Seed and Saints of the Most High may be gathered together*, May 17, (Thomason). Cromwell was informed that this proclamation was the work of a leading spirit in the Little Parliament, *Letters and Speeches*, III, 79. It may possibly have been by John Browne, one of the Welsh radicals, who was a Fifth Monarchy man. See letter of Browne to John Wright, Rawlinson MSS., A 47, fol. 30.

most fitt for our purpose". A certain number of horses, and some arms and ammunition were in readiness. The "sisters", who met by themselves, had charge of the proclamations, which were to be distributed among the churches and elsewhere after the expedition had set out. Such, in its naïve simplicity, was the plan, the details of which the brethren were allowed to reveal only so far as was needed for bringing in recruits.

The propaganda had little success. For one reason and another the recognized leaders of the party refused to join the plotters. Feake, who had finally been given complete liberty, was no more reconciled to the government than he had ever been. Coming up to London he had harangued a gathering in Newgate market until it was broken up by the marshal and his men. The following day he spoke for some three hours at a meeting of churches at Allhallows, where Simpson and Kiffin were present. He gave a detailed account of his sufferings in prison, and with his accustomed vigor attacked the Babylonish government, with its relics of popery, its lawyers, and its triers. He declared that so far from bewailing divisions among the churches, he believed they ought to be increased; that the churches were becoming corrupt, and allying themselves with Babylon, and that those who were still faithful ought to be stirred up to come out of them.[34] Kiffin and Simpson undertook to defend the government against his strictures, winning for themselves from the audience the epithets of "courtier" and "apostate". It would seem from this incident that Feake was in a mood to

[34] Account of a meeting at Allhallows, Thurloe, V, 755 ff.; newsletter, January 6, 1656/7, *Clarke Papers*, III, 86.

join the extremists, and he was, indeed, invited to preach at one of their meetings, but for some reason he was excluded at the last moment. Nothing daunted, he made his way to an upper room and preached there, to the disturbance and indignation of those below.[25] The breach thus made was not healed, and the plotters had to do without the aid of this able leader. Similar ill fortune awaited them in other directions. Rogers had been warned against them by the churches of Ipswich and Abingdon, and would have nothing to do with them.[26] Harrison, Carew, and "the rest of the prisoners", sought an interview with the leaders, and expressed regret at the differences of opinion which existed within the party. They said that the conspirators were not of a gospel spirit, and refused to join them. Similar refusals were met with from people of less note. One speaker in a Coleman Street meeting compared Venner and his associates to Korah, Dathan, and Abiram. They had great hopes of winning over the Baptist church to which Portman belonged, and judged from the replies the Baptists made to their overtures that they too were waiting for the call, and were organized, with officers and a set of reasons for their position. It turned out, however, that there was

[25] Conspirators' minutes. A Mr. Chapman was also excluded. This may have been Livewell Chapman, the publisher of most of the Fifth Monarchy pamphlets.

[26] Thurloe had heard that the first plan of the plotters had been to begin the rising at Abingdon, at the funeral of John Pendarvis, the Fifth Monarchy Baptist. The funeral services were prolonged for several days, and were finally interrupted by a detachment of soldiers. If the government had been misinformed, and there was no connection between the Abingdon group and the Venner group, as appears from a passage in a pamphlet entitled *A Witnes to the Saints in England and Wales,* 1657 (Thomason), the hostility of the Abingdon church would easily be understood.

a grave difficulty in the way. According to the statement in Revelation, xi, the Gentiles were to tread the court of the holy city for forty-two months. At the end of that time the rule of the Beast would be over, and the reign of Christ would begin. This exact limitation set upon the Protectorate—for the Protectorate was without question the rule of the Beast—had already helped Fifth Monarchy men to endure patiently.[27] Now although the forty-two months would not be at an end until the sixteenth of June, 1657, Venner had arranged for his rising to take place early in the second week of April. Probably his faction believed that two months' time was not too long to allow for undermining the foundations of the Beast, but the Baptists in question refused to stir before that time. They were strengthened in their refusal by the knowledge that Harrison and the other ex-prisoners disapproved of the enterprise. In the end a few of these Baptists allowed themselves to be persuaded to join the conspirators, but the majority of them held aloof.

There were dissensions, too, in the plotters' ranks—jealousies as to the choice of officers, and so on; and at one time even doubt whether their call was sure. They put doubts behind them, however, and although their pledged force finally numbered no more than eighty, they thought of the thousands who would flock to their

[27] "And were it not to fulfil the word of God (Rev. xi) that this present death is upon us for three years and a half, I should be so astonished at it as not to know what to make of it. . . . Yea, the shrill heaven, heart, and earth tearing call of saints, past, present, and to come . . . to maintain their cause, to revenge their blood and the Lamb's, and to be UP AND DOING for the Lord Jesus, the King of Saints, it is NOW within a year or two, as we shall show you." Rogers wrote these words in 1655, *Fifth Monarchy Man*, 138-139.

standard when once it was set up, and took courage. The date finally set for the rising was midnight of April 9, 1657. The forces were to gather in three different parts of London, whence they were to march to the common rendezvous at Mile End Green. At seven o'clock in the evening of that day, word was brought to Whitehall that there were Fifth Monarchy men assembling in Bishopsgate Street. A troop of horse was sent out, which found Venner and twenty-three others, in a house in Shoreditch, booted and spurred, and praying for the success of the enterprise. Some arms, a standard bearing the lion device, and packages of the proclamations were found at the rendezvous, and supplies of arms and ammunition were discovered in a house in Swan Alley. Harrison, Lawson, Rich, and Danvers were sent for by the Council and questioned, but nothing further was done. The authorities had possession of the papers which showed the relations of Harrison and his friends to the plotters, and they did not implicate these men. Cromwell took a friendly tone toward Venner and his followers, when they were brought before the Council, but they responded with bitterness and insolence. They were sent to the Tower, and the attempt to establish the Fifth Monarchy by overthrowing the Protectorate was at an end, or practically at an end. A single report has come down to us of a body of Fifth Monarchy men gathered near Epping at the end of April or in the early part of May, but easily dispersed by a party of horse. As some sixty were said to have been captured in this attempt, it would seem to have been a more considerable one than

Venner's, but whether it was connected with his, or an independent movement, it is impossible to say.[28]

Thurloe gave an account of the conspiracy of Venner's party to Parliament, and there was some debate upon it. Highland, among others, felt strongly that the conspirators should be severely dealt with. However, the affair came during the debate on the kingship, and was set aside for the matter of larger moment.[29]

Absurd as were the details of the conspiracy, and inconsiderable as were the numbers and standing of the persons engaged, it represented a very real danger, as Professor Firth has pointed out, because of the insecure status of the government, and the fact that there were other bodies of malcontents who would have been glad to take advantage of the outbreak, had it not been stamped out at the beginning.[30] Its occurrence at this particular juncture was very useful in pointing a moral in connection with the kingship project. As Henry Cromwell put it, writing to his father, " These wylde notions concerning the right of saints to reign, and the imaganary immediate government of Christ upon earth, must needs call aloud for some settlement both in church and state, such as the parliament hath lately advised your highnes unto ".[31] Though there were differences of opinon with regard to the desirability of the form of settlement advised by Parliament,

[28] Cited by Firth, *Last Years of the Protectorate,* I, 218, note. Most of the sources for Venner's plot are quoted by Burrage, *Eng. Hist. Rev.,* 1910, 725-737.

[29] Burton, *Diary,* II, 2 ff.

[30] Firth, *op. cit.,* I, 218. The discovery of the plot was of course a signal for an attack on all that the party stood for, including its opposition to a church establishment. See *The Downfall of the Fifth Monarchy, or, The personal Reign of Christ on Earth, confuted,* April 20, 1657 (Thomason).

[31] April 22, 1657, Thurloe, VI, 222.

English people generally were in agreement with young Henry as to the desirability of some change in the government.[32]

Though Thurloe tried to obscure it, the fact remains that the offer of kingship to Cromwell, while it did not inspire, certainly furnished a spur to Venner's outbreak. It says something for the unwillingness of a large body of the Fifth Monarchy party to appeal to arms, and also indicates a falling away in the numbers of the party as a whole, that the plot, during the weeks when Cromwell's acceptance of the crown was considered very probable, received no more encouragement. In any case, the lack of generalship shown in the plans of Venner and his men, their quarrelsome spirit, and the difficulty of getting any considerable number of persons to agree on the interpretation of the chronology of the book of Revelation, was bound to preclude his gaining many converts. But the lack of any noteworthy expressions of opposition to the kingship project on the part of Fifth Monarchy men in general, indicates a certain indifference on the subject. Probably it seemed to them that the Protectorate was practically as bad as a monarchy, and that the proposal for a change in title was in itself a forerunner of the change that was to end the Beast's dominion; each change in the condition of affairs bringing so much nearer the great change which was to establish Christ on his throne.

The most conspicuous opposition to the project for making Cromwell king came not from Fifth Monarchy, but from Baptist, ranks. The great mass of the Baptists

[32] Cromwell himself used the conspiracy as an argument when he was urging the adoption of the Petition and Advice without the title of king. *Letters and Speeches*, III, 68.

untouched by Fifth Monarchy views had accepted the Protectorate, after the first, with something like resignation. Many of them, and this would be particularly true of the Baptists in the army, were governed by personal esteem for Cromwell. As a worthy Norfolk individual looked at it, "There is a principall of tyrany in the government, and were not his person better then the government, we should soone see and finde what manner of government wee are under".[83] Others probably had the same experience as Samuel Richardson, who at the outset believed that the title of Protector was unlawful, but was later persuaded by arguments based on Scripture that it was not.[84] Like Richardson, the mass of Baptists awaited the time when Cromwell should find it possible to remove the abuses which grieved their hearts. But by the end of the year 1656 they had begun to grow impatient.

Much currency had been given to a report that Cromwell, at the beginning of his Protectorate, had told Jessey, the Baptist minister, that he might call him juggler if tithes were not taken away by September 3, 1654. When reproached in December of that year with having broken his promise, he said that he could not remember whether he had said such a thing or not, but that in any case his Council was against the taking away of tithes, and he could not carry it against such opposition.[85] When he opened Parliament in the fall of 1656, his anxiety to remove tithes was not con-

[83] R. B. to ——, July 30, 1655, Thurloe, III, 686.

[84] *Plain Dealing*, 1656 (Thomason). He was induced to change his opinion by a sermon by John More on Nehemiah, ix, 27.

[85] B. T. to ——, *Clarke Papers*, II, xxxiv; *The Protector, So called, In Part Unvailed; A looking Glass for, or, An Awakening Word To, the Superior and Inferior Officers*, Oct. 22, 1656 (Thomason).

spicuous. Declaring the importance of a state maintenance of the ministry, he averred, " I should think I were very treacherous if I should take away tithes, till I see the Legislative power to settle maintenance to them another way ". Nor did he make it a strong point with Parliament that its duty was to discover that other way.[36] Consequently the Baptists, who were unable to follow Cromwell in his gradual change of attitude on the church question, began to complain.[37]

However, no discontent was immediately apparent. At an assembly of General Baptists held in London this same month it was decided that " The church ought to behave herself to the present power in all humility to do as they command or suffer as they inflict, in matters pertaining to men willing to obey. And in things concerning Worshipe, if it be by them commanded Contrary to God's Law, to suffer meekly ".[38] Certain Welsh Baptist churches, too, in November announced that it was the saints' duty to be subject even to unrighteous government, and all the more to the present one, which was righteous. They should pray for it and work for it, privately admonishing, but not publicly rebuking, any evil tendencies it might exhibit.[39]

But when the proposal to adopt monarchical forms, often meditated, was actually adopted by Parliament and urged upon the Protector, all the earlier opposition

[36] Stainer, *Speeches*, 240.

[37] " The Anabaptists sayes [*sic*] you are a perfidious person, and that because you promised them att a certaine day to take away tythes, but did not perform with them." Bradford to Cromwell, March 4, 1656/7, Nickolls, 141.

[38] Whitley, ed., *Minutes of the General Assembly of General Baptist Churches*, I, 6.

[39] *An Antidote Against the Infection of the Times*, Nov. 15, 1656 (Thomason).

to those forms was revived. All the appurtenances of monarchy were distasteful to these folk, who were constantly preaching simplicity of life, the eschewing of costly apparel, and the avoidance of pride and pomp.[40] Its association in the past with a policy of intolerance in religious affairs was not easily forgotten, and, finally, the reconstruction of that which had been destroyed in the wars meant to them, as Cromwell himself expressed it, the rebuilding of Jericho.[41] When the suggestion for a return to kingship was made in Parliament by a Presbyterian member in January, 1657, the denunciation of the idea by Samuel Highland well expressed the Baptist attitude.[42] Soon after the revival

[40] Epistle dedicatory, Confession of faith of the Somerset churches, *Confessions of Faith* (Hanserd Knollys Soc.), 67 ff.

[41] Stainer, *Speeches*, 304. There has indeed been an attempt made to represent as a Baptist movement the overtures made to Charles Stuart by William Howard in the summer of 1656. Howard was a Baptist, a member of Knollys's church, and had adopted the views of the Levellers. Gardiner points out that the terms of Howard's propositions, which demanded liberty of conscience and the abolition of tithes, were such as would be likely to be advanced by a coalition of Baptists and Levellers. One would almost be tempted to suspect a Fifth Monarchy element also, from the verbiage of the denunciation of "that grand imposter, that loathsom hypocrite, that detestable traitor, that prodigy of nature, that opprobrium of mankind, that landskipp of iniquity, that sink of sin, and that compendium of baseness, who now calls himself our Protector". It is not at all strange that Howard was able to convert some of his fellow church-members to his cause, but he himself attributes the movement to the Levellers, and it is doubtful if he found among the Baptists many who, setting aside their views on monarchical government, were hopeful of civil or religious betterment from Charles. Gardiner, *op. cit.*, IV, 258; *Hexham Records* (Hanserd Knollys Soc.), 311, 321; Clarendon, *History* (ed. Macray), bk. xv, 103. Of the ten signatures, two certainly, and a third probably, belong to Howard's fellow church-members.

[42] "Are you now going to set up kingly government which for these thousand years has persecuted the people of God? Do you expect a better consequence? Do you expect a thanksgiving day upon this? This will set all the honest people of this nation to weeping and mourning. I desire the motion may die as abominable." Burton, *Diary*, I, 362, cited by Firth, *Last Years of the Protectorate*, I, 121.

of the idea by the presentation of the motion by Christopher Packe rumors arose that "the Anabaptist Churches would publish a Manifesto expressinge theire dislike of present proceedings", and that Baptists and Independents were assembling for a similar purpose at Hull and other places.[43] That these rumors were not unfounded appeared in due course. On April 3 a petition was presented to Cromwell, signed by nineteen Baptist ministers of London, begging him not to yield to the proposed apostasy of restoring the old form of government. Such a step, to their minds, would make the glory of God a byword, would endanger the interests of God's people in general, irrespective of sect; would harden the hearts and strengthen the hands of the enemy, besides grieving the hearts of the most faithful servants of the commonwealth.[44] Among the signatures were those of Jessey, Knollys, and Spilsbury; that of Kiffin, however, did not appear. He was too closely attached to the court party to take a step which would be likely to embarrass Cromwell. Moreover, he had opposed the execution of Charles I, and was presumably not an enemy to monarchy.[45]

Petitions of the same tenor came in from all over the country, from people of different religious affiliations, but the really important opposition came from the army. Here also the Baptists were at the fore. Despite the long-continued complaints of the cashiering of Baptists, there was a goodly number of them left, and, as one observer remarked, they made up in relig-

[43] Bridges to Henry Cromwell, March 10, 1656/7, Lansdowne MSS., 821, fol. 326; Bordeaux despatch, March 12/22, Harleian MSS., 4549, fol. 51.

[44] Nickolls, 142.

[45] Allen to Baxter, May 30, 1659, Baxter Correspondence, IV, fol. 187.

ious zeal what they lacked in numbers.[46] And it would not be far from the truth to say that in every Baptist soldier there was an opponent of monarchy. Thomas Cooper, the eminent Baptist, who was well-known as a supporter of Cromwell, voiced his disapproval of the project while it was in debate. However, after the offer of the crown, he decided that it was his duty to bow to the inevitable, and consequently he joined the group which on March 30 went to express its agreement.[47] Cromwell, understanding the scruples of men who, like Cooper, were subordinating their own views to what seemed the good of the state, as well as of those who, in the army and without, were addressing him against the kingship, based his objections to assuming the crown on their position. He begged "that there may be no hard thing put upon them, things I mean hard to them, that they cannot swallow ".[48] During the next fortnight, however, under pressure of the arguments of the lawyers who believed there could be no satisfactory settlement unless he accepted the change of title, his objections were over-ridden, and he was apparently on the eve of returning a favorable answer when news of the continued opposition in the army made him return to his earlier position. The petition in which the army opposition found its final expression was the product of combined Independent and Baptist activity. It was drawn up by John Owen, at the suggestion of Pride and Desborough, and was presented to Parliament by John Mason, Pride's lieutenant-colonel, a Baptist who secured its twenty-six or twenty-

[46] Bordeaux despatch, May 18/28, 1657, Harleian MSS., 4549, fol. 104 b.
[47] Firth, *op. cit.*, I, 150.
[48] Stainer, *Speeches*, 301.

seven signatures, chiefly among his co-religionists.[49] Fleetwood, Desborough, and Lambert had already informed Cromwell that if he accepted the crown they would withdraw from public employment.

Unwilling to face the defection of his soldiers and generals, Cromwell refused the crown: thus failed the attempt to replace the Protectorate by a monarchy through peaceful means. It would of course be easy to exaggerate the part played by the Baptists in bringing about Cromwell's refusal. It must be realized that it was the separatists generally who objected to the title of king, and not only to that, but also to the proposed state church, with a creed and fixed limitations on toleration, which was provided for by the Petition and Advice. But the opposition of no other single element was so conspicuous, and the protest of the London ministers is especially noteworthy in that, despite the talk of "Anabaptist" disaffection, it was the first Baptist protest addressed to Cromwell which bore anything like an official stamp.

It was not long after the failure of the attempt to settle the crown on Cromwell that the Fifth Monarchy men were again heard from. It has been shown above that the time when they expected the Protectorate to come to an end was the middle of June. A meeting of Fifth Monarchy men held a short time before that date was broken up by soldiers, and some of those present imprisoned. A protest against this treatment stated that these brethren had been engaged in preparation for the Bridegroom's coming, "And not . . . plotting or contriving in a way of Treachery or Designe

[49] Firth, *op. cit.*, I, 191, 192; Bordeaux despatch, May 18/28, 1657, Harleian MSS., 4549, fol. 104 b.

against any City, Town or Castle; the Lives, the Blood, the Persons of any". Such actions they characterized as "base and abundantly below our Principles". To the charge that they had arms, they replied that "although our Brethren, our selves, neither it may be you, see a call to be shedding the blood of any, or even the most vile and wicked, at present", the saints were justified in defending themselves against the attacks of those who would hinder their work, and experience had shown the possibility of such attack. Moreover they held that the Lord's messengers should go armed in order to show their strength.[50]

On the same day that this disclaimer appeared, word came to Thurloe that Harrison, Feake, Canne, and Rogers were holding meetings in which they professed themselves ready for an insurrection, saying that the three and a half years of the witnesses' lying dead was past.[51] Even if the intentions of these men were as far from warlike as the paper just quoted tried to make them appear, such reports are easily understood, if at the meetings such language was used as Rogers employed in a pamphlet issued the month following. It abounded in sentiments such as these: "Is it not high time for the two Witnesses to be uniting, stirring and rising . . . the man among the myrtle trees (Zech. i, 8) on his red horse is already mounted . . . and the slain of the Lord shall be many (Isa. lxvi, 16). Yea, and after the harvest (wherein I hope to be a reaper, a cutter down or a gatherer in) the blood of the vintage

[50] *A Witnes to the Saints in England and Wales*, June 15, 1657 (Thomason). Specific reference is given to the interruption of the funeral services of Pendarvis at Abingdon. See above, note 26.

[51] Information, June 15, 1657, Thurloe, VI, 349.

will be up to the horses' bridles (Rev. xiv, 20). . . . Let us up together all at once and fall on all at once (Numb. xiii, 30) with one mind, as one man (Zeph. iii, 9). Appoint the day, appropriate the duty, and to it." He warned the faithful, however, that "At present I am to bid them BEWARE and PREPARE; beware of running before orders come from Jehovah of Armies, and prepare for them when they come, yea, to make all their arrows ready against Babylon" [52]

While the Fifth Monarchy men were waiting for the sign, the Baptists, pleased with the failure of the kingship project, were silent, although disapproving of the ceremonial by which the second Protectorate was inaugurated. In army circles, also, quiet reigned. Even those most suspected of dissatisfaction showed rather "satisfaction than otherwise", concealing displeasure if they felt any.[53] In December Thurloe scouted as negligible reports of discontent which had come to the ears of Lockhart in Paris: if there were anything in them, he maintained, it would disappear before the renewed activities of the Royalists, "for whatever they differ upon, they will agree against Ch. Stuart and his party, that is certain".[54]

The appearance of calm was, however, deceptive. It was impossible that the sectaries would long endure without protest government according to the Humble Petition and Advice, with its provisions for a state church, supported by tithes, and its limited toleration. And the situation was altered with the assembling of

[52] *Jegar Sahadutha*, July 28, 1657, cited in *Fifth Monarchy Man*, 295-299.

[53] Thurloe to Henry Cromwell, July 17, 28, 1657, Thurloe, VI, 412, 425.

[54] Thurloe to Lockhart, Dec. 14, 1657, Thurloe, VI, 676.

Parliament in January, 1658. The admission of the members excluded by the Council at the beginning of its first session, together with the transfer of some of Cromwell's warmest supporters to the new second chamber, had made the House of Commons, to borrow Masson's effective phrase, strongly anti-Oliverian. A body with markedly republican principles, it showed especial hostility to the newly-established House of Lords, and to any dominance of military influence. Encouraged by the tone of speeches made there, the opponents of the Protectorate began to bestir themselves.

A petition was prepared for presentation to the Commons, the "Other House" being ignored. It stated that the late king had been executed for four things: usurping the powers of Parliament and the control of the militia, abrogating the laws, and raising money without the consent of Parliament. The petitioners begged that these four abuses should not be allowed to return, and suggested measures of prevention. The substance of these measures was: the establishment of a government in which a Parliament of one chamber should be supreme, and which would allow no oppression to tender consciences, and no cashiering of officers except by a council of war. Thus the petition combined the demands of the Commonwealth party, the sectaries, and the army. Its later history shows that it was promoted in part at least by Baptists.[55] The Fifth Monarchy men, too, assisted in the movement, and their churches recommenced their attacks on Cromwell. Rogers, among other things, held him up for execration for having as his only ally the

[55] *A True Copy of a Petition . . . intended to have been delivered to the late Parliament*, March 11, 1657/8 (Thomason). See below, pp. 173 ff.

"Jesuit" Mazarin, and for marrying one of his daughters into a Catholic family.[56] The petition was printed and circulated, and thousands of signatures obtained. The plan was that it should be presented by a committee of some twenty of the signatories, and the anti-Oliverians in the House expected to utilize it as the ground for a debate on the establishment of a republic and the recall of the Long Parliament.[57]

The movement for the petition was a matter of common knowledge. While it was going on came news of Royalist activity, and information that some of the members of the House were in actual correspondence with Charles, while others were tampering with the loyalty of the army.[58] Throughout all this the Commons, instead of taking steps to raise supplies for the pressing necessities of the government, were spending their days trying to decide whether or no they should recognize the "Other House". The day fixed for the presentation of the petition was February 4, and Cromwell saw that he must act. On February 3 he gave orders for the arrest of Hugh Courtney, John Rogers, and John Portman, and their imprisonment in the Tower until further orders, "for attempting to disaffect and exasperate the hearts and spirits of the people, so that thereby they might bring the nation again into blood".[59] On the following day he summarily dissolved Parliament. A few days later he assembled two hundred

[56] Bordeaux to Mazarin, Feb. 4/14, 1657/8, Thurloe, VII, 778; same to same, Feb. 8/18, P. R. O. Transcripts; Smith to Cromwell, Feb. 11, 1657/8, Rawlinson MSS., A 57, fol. 312.

[57] Firth, *op. cit.*, II, 33-34; Catterall, in *Am. Hist. Rev.*, IX, 52-53.

[58] Stainer, *Speeches*, 396-397.

[59] Warrant, Feb. 3, 1657/8, Thurloe, VI, 775; —— to Hobart, Feb. 12, *Eng. Hist. Rev.*, VII, 107 ff.

officers, and made them a speech two hours long. Finding in his own regiment of horse six Baptist officers who refused to be convinced that his government was a righteous one, he told them that it was not for their own good or for the safety of the nation that they should remain in the army under such circumstances, and deprived them of their commissions. The Council of Officers, headed by Fleetwood, presented him with a loyal address; similar addresses came from Scotland, and the danger from army discontent was again dispelled.[60]

In dealing with members of the army, Cromwell could in general count upon that sentiment of loyalty and admiration which they felt for the great commander who had organized the parliamentary forces and had led them to victory. This was not the case when he faced the opposition of the Fifth Monarchy men, and they were making strenuous efforts to lessen his influence upon the people. When Courtney was arrested on the day preceding the dissolution of Parliament, there were found in his room certain pamphlets, enclosed in letters and directed to people in different parts of the country.[61] They were all attacks upon the government, and one was a publication of very recent date. It was addressed to the "Lord's faithfull Remnant", and called upon them to unite, in these days of apostasy. The authors expressed approval of the principles and work of the authors of *A Standard Set Up*, that is, of Venner's party, except that they did not consider it necessary to lay down in advance the

[60] *Clarke Papers*, III, 139 ff.; Thurloe, VI, 786, 789, 793, 806.

[61] *Mercurius Politicus*, Feb. 4-11, 1657/8; *Publick Intelligencer*, Feb. 8-15.

details of the coming government, but were willing to leave that to the "Instruments which the Lord shall set up over his people". They believed that before the personal appearance of Christ all other kingdoms would be destroyed and the Jews brought in. Then came an attack on Cromwell's "usurpation", his triers, his arbitrary actions, his negative voice, his control of the forces, his dissolution of parliaments, illegal imprisonments, foreign expeditions, trade monopolies, control of the press, continuation of tithes. Cromwell's government was likened to that of Charles I, and the assertion was made that the Lord had manifested his displeasure through the failure of the expeditions to the West Indies and the Straits. Cromwell had been deaf to all witness made against him, and it had become the duty of Christians to declare against him and the instruments of his tyranny. Though there were differences of opinion among the Lord's people as to the time of the coming of the kingdom, they were agreed "to Arme against, resist, and openly oppose them, and do our utmost endeavour to force the power out of their hands, and bring them to condigne punishment upon the score of the blood of the Saints, Martyrs, and Prophets of Jesus, as it was by them in the like Case done to the late King: this being the only visible means appointed by the Lord to destroy the Beast with his supporters".[62] The same spirit that pervaded this effusion presided over the pulpits of the party. The

[62] *Some Considerations by way of Proposall and Conclusion, Humbly Tendered for the satisfying and uniting of all the Faithfull in this Day, whose hearts are groaning and sighing for the deliverance of Zion, and appearance of her King, and desiring to separate from this wicked and Adulterous Generation.* This pamphlet did not come into Thomason's hands until March 9, more than a month after copies were found in Courtney's possession.

support promised to Cromwell by the City on March 15 formed the subject of a discourse by Cornet Day. He maintained that this action would be the cause of much bloodshed, and that Cromwell was no magistrate or governor, but a juggler, who deserved to be sawn in pieces.[63] On the first of April the Coleman Street meeting was broken up by the Lord Mayor's guard, and some of the congregation carried off to prison. Among them were Day, Canne, and Feake. Feake was fresh from imprisonment in the Tower, and had shortly before been airing to an audience in the church of Martin's Vintry his grievances on that subject, and attacking, as usual, Cromwell and his government.[64]

One disquieting feature of the Fifth Monarchy agitation at this time was the apparent drawing together of Fifth Monarchy men and Baptists. In the week preceding the imprisonment of Courtney the story appeared in the newspapers, with jesting references to the temerity of the act in view of the inclemency of the weather, that he, with Harrison and his wife and John Carew, had just undergone the rite of baptism. The possible effect of the entrance into Baptist ranks of three such unyielding opponents of the Cromwellian régime was not to be overlooked.[65] This was especially the case now that the Baptists were actually, as organizations, showing an interest in the political situation.

[63] Information, March 18, 22, 1657/8, Thurloe, VII, 5, 18.

[64] Newsletter, April 3, 1658, *Clarke Papers,* III, 146; Canne, *Narrative wherein is set forth the sufferings of John Canne and Wentworth Day.* Before the magistrates Day insisted that if allowed he could prove Cromwell juggler by his own confession, in the old matter of taking away tithes.

[65] *Publick Intelligencer,* Feb. 1-8, 1657/8; Henry Cromwell to Falconbridge, Feb. 17, Thurloe, VI, 810; same to Broghill, n. d., *ibid.,* 790; Bordeaux to Brienne, Feb. 15/25, Harleian MSS., 4549, fol. 339.

It is not surprising that precautions were taken to discover what was done at a general assembly of Baptists which was held at Dorchester in May. Among those present were William Kiffin, Richard Deane of the navy, John Carew, and two Baptist officers from Ireland—Captain Vernon and Adjutant-general Allen. At the first day's meeting about three hundred persons were present. Letters were read from the different churches, giving accounts of their condition and asking about the condition of others. This was for the purpose of considering this " time of apostacy and persecution ". At the second meeting, in the afternoon, there was prayer and preaching. The prayers contained complaints of the " bonds and sufferings of the saints, . . . the time of Syon's affliction, wherein those that have beene glorious lights on the right and left hand, are shutt up in bonds ". The petition was made that " in order to there deliverance, God would put a hooke into the nostrills of, and destroy him, who is the enemy of God and his people ". Another meeting was devoted to the discussion of purely religious matters. Then at a private meeting of the leading men there was carried on a discussion concerning the advisability of joining the Fifth Monarchy party, but owing to the efforts of Kiffin, the proposition was not carried at that sitting. Whether the discussion was renewed at a later meeting the government agents were not able to discover.[66]

When matters had reached the point where a general assembly of Baptist churches was seriously considering affiliation with the Fifth Monarchy party, Cromwell felt justified, apparently, in taking action

[66] Croke to Coplestone, May 15, 1658, Thurloe, VII, 138 ff.

against them as a political body. At any rate he adopted, for an outlying part of his dominions, where the Baptists were not strong enough to make their resentment at his course dangerous, a policy that had the additional advantage of winning the approval of the Presbyterians. The Protector's instructions to the Council in Scotland, issued on June 10, included the direction "to see that no Baptist holds any office of trust, nor practices at law, nor keeps a school".[67] It is not to be wondered at that the Baptists in Scotland did not express concern at his illness during the succeeding months, but appeared to nourish "dark hopes".[68]

Whether, if he had lived, Cromwell would eventually have used toward the Baptists in England any policy savoring so much of persecution on the ground of religion, we can only surmise. However, his growing conservatism in the matter of a state church would certainly have meant the continued widening of the breach between him and that body. On the great point of liberty of conscience his belief remained unchanged, and we have the curious anomaly of the most tolerant man of his age going down to his grave at odds with the two bodies of Englishmen which advocated the widest religious liberty.[69] Yet not entirely at odds. From the outset certain individuals among the Baptists had been among the most uncompromising of his critics. Certain features in his policy had made it possible for these few to influence more and more widely

[67] *Cal. St. P., Dom., 1658-1659,* 61. The relations of the Baptists with the Remonstrant party evidently played a part in this affair. See Beake to Baxter, Oct. 16, 1657, Baxter Correspondence, I, fol. 12.

[68] Langley to Thurloe, Sept. 4, 1658, Thurloe, VII, 371; Pittiloh, *Hammer of Persecution,* 1659 (Thomason).

[69] Baptists and Quakers.

their fellow church-members, until the suspicions thus engendered had made it possible that the question of opposition should be seriously considered in a general council of the church. But the hold that Cromwell had upon the hearts of religious men was a strong one, and there were many Baptists in England, besides those who were his personal friends, who, when he had breathed his last, considered with Steele's emotion "those ejaculatory breathings of his soule for the blessing of love and union amongst the servants of God, amidst their various administrations, particularly praying for them, that were angry with him". And surely all could share Steele's feeling of gratitude that, leaving the world, he left "these nations in peace, which had been so much imbroyled in trouble and misery".[70]

[70] Steele to Thurloe, Sept. 16, 1658, Thurloe, VII, 388. See also Thomas Cooper to Henry Cromwell, *ibid.*, 425.

CHAPTER VI.

IRELAND AND THE PROTECTORATE.

In Ireland, the opposition to the Protectorate came chiefly from Baptist ranks. Although some of the leading Baptists in Ireland were also Fifth Monarchy men, that party does not seem to have had any distinct organization there. In one way this makes the situation for the purposes of our study a simpler one. However, certain features of the position of the Baptists in Ireland, both in relation to the government and to other sects, make the story of their activities there somewhat complicated.[1]

It was natural that under Cromwell and Ireton the Independents and Baptists should have been put into places of trust, and under Fleetwood this tendency continued, in an intensified form, until, with the exception of a few extreme Independents like Fleetwood, Ludlow, Jones, and Hewson, practically the whole administration came to be in the hands of Baptists. A well-informed Independent complained in the fall of 1655 that he knew of at least twelve governors of towns and

[1] As Mr. Firth says in his chapter on this subject, the term Anabaptist was used loosely for all the extreme sectaries, here as in England. *Last Years of the Protectorate,* II, 126. For his purpose it was not worth while to distinguish between this loose use and its exact use to apply to Baptists only. However, it is quite possible in most cases to make the distinction. For example, Hewson, who was closely associated with the Baptists, and whose opposition to the Protectorate was based on much the same grounds, was never called an Anabaptist by those who used the term exactly.

cities, ten colonels, three or four lieutenant-colonels, ten majors, nineteen or twenty captains, two salaried preachers, and twenty-three officers on the civil list, who were Baptists.[2] There were ten Baptist churches, and two of the ministers, Thomas Patient and Christopher Blackwood, ranked among the ablest preachers of the day.[3] Patient had a lectureship in the cathedral at Dublin, and some idea of his abilities may be gained from the fact that he had been able, by opposition direct and indirect, to cause the redoubtable John Rogers to give up his position there and return to England in disgust.[4]

The Baptists were not merely numerous; they were also extremely unpopular. It would be pleasant to be able to prove that when in positions of power they were an exception to Cromwell's accusation that of those who pled for liberty of conscience none were willing to give it. Unfortunately, the testimony against them on this point is unanimous. "I had great opposition in this citty" wrote Edward Burrough the Quaker, from Waterford, "twice opposed by the Rulers, which are Baptists . . . generally the Rulers in this nation are Baptists, but are seated in Darknes, and takes their ease in the flesh, upon their lofty mountaine, and have turned their victory into their owne exaltinge."[5] This was in a private letter, while he publicly proclaimed to the Baptists: "You are as bitter and envious, in blind

[2] Dr. Harrison to Thurloe, Oct. 17, 1655, Thurloe, IV, 90-91. It was even said that soldiers were re-baptized as the way to preferment. *Reliquae Baxterianae*, I, 74.

[3] Vernon to London churches, June, 1653, Ivimey, *History of the English Baptists*, I, 240 ff.

[4] Rogers, *Fifth Monarchy Man*, 29 ff.

[5] E. Burrough to Margaret Fell, 5 of 11 mo. 1655, Swarthmore letters, 789.

zeale as the prophane world; against any that differs from you in Judgement . . . witness at Dublin, Kilkenny, Corke, and else where, where the Servants of the Lord were haled out of your Assemblies and evill entreated, with mockings and cruell words, to your shame forever may this be rehearsed."[6]

Due weight must be given in this connection to the fact that the Quakers were the most troublesome people of their generation, and that they were prosecuted, not merely for their religious opinions, but as disturbers of the peace. Moreover, a particular animosity between the Baptists and the Quakers resulted from the fact that the ranks of the latter were very largely recruited from among the former.[7] But the Quakers were not the only witnesses against Baptist intolerance. One pastor wrote of "the overflowing interest of those, that endeavoured (what in them lay) to null all churches, ordinances, and ministers . . . which were not baptized into the same spirit and way with themselves".[8] Another maintained that "if any Governor, or any in the least command become Anabaptists, they become most cruel tyrants".[9] A critic in 1659 felt that "the

[6] *To you that are called Anabaptists in the nation of Ireland, Teachers and People, who profess yourselves to be the Church of Christ,* 1657 (Devonshire House tracts).

[7] Goadby, *Baptists and Quakers in Northamptonshire,* 13. A Quaker estimate of Baptist tolerance is interesting: "And if we search out your toleration to the bottom, it will be reduced to this Compasse, That none shall be tolerated but those that say as you say, and professe what you professe; and you among your selves are as a kingdom divided that cannot stand, and you are not they which are fit to Rule in the Nation to prescribe Liberty nor give Toleration." Hubberthorne, *Answer to a Declaration,* 1659 (Devonshire House tracts).

[8] T. Taylor to Cromwell, Carrickfergus, Dec. 16, 1655, Thurloe, IV, 286.

[9] R. Easthorpe to Henry Cromwell, June 11, 1657, Lansdowne MSS., 822, fol. 86.

hard treatment the Papists in Ireland have found, and the Presbyterian Scots in the North part of the same Kingdome have lately received from that party, make all other infinitely dissatisfied in their acquiring any power over them"

When all allowance is made for exaggeration and personal bias, citations like these make it evident that the Baptists, deservedly or undeservedly, had so carried themselves as to become extremely unpopular with the men whose religious ideas differed from their own. It would have been against human nature for these men not to make as much as possible of Baptist disaffection, and to side with the force which meant the lessening of their authority.

Another complicating feature of the Irish situation was the question of the transplantation. Fleetwood believed thoroughly in the system by which the Irish were being ruthlessly driven from their lands, and the officers, who were profiting by it, naturally did not care to have it interfered with. It was the Baptist governor of Waterford, Richard Lawrence, who publicly defended the system against the attacks of Gookin and Petty, and the latter cited a number of Baptists as active in opposing his work. This element of self-interest cannot be ignored in a consideration of the struggle to retain Fleetwood as the director of Irish affairs.[11]

In Ireland, as in England, the dissolution of the Little Parliament had been regarded with dismay by the sectaries. The establishment of the Protectorate called

[10] *Interest of England Stated*, 1659 (Thomason).

[11] Petty, *Reflections*, 88 ff.; Fleetwood to Thurloe, June 2, 1654, May 23, 1655, Thurloe, II, 343, III, 468.

forth open criticism, and there was talk of a public protest. Grave rumors of dissatisfaction among the officers come to Cromwell's ears, and he finally sent his son Henry to investigate the situation.[12] By the time Henry arrived, the Baptists of Dublin had received a letter from three of the Baptist ministers in London, beseeching them to be subject to the government, thus doing their duty as Christians, and showing the world that it was wrong in considering Baptists enemies of magistracy.[13] This letter, and the timely summoning to England of two of the grumblers, together with the presence of Henry, had considerable effect, and in March Henry was able to report that all were satisfied, "unless it be some few inconsiderable persons of the anabaptiste judgment, who are allsoe quiett, though not verry well contented". He thought that the difficulty lay in the encouragement they had been given by the deportment of some of those in power, notably Ludlow and John Jones. The former had been especially courted by the Baptists, since his refusal to own the Protectorate, and had been admitted to their private meetings. Henry thought that Fleetwood, also, had been too much inclined to favor the Baptists, though rather "from tenderness than love to their principles".[14]

The Baptists whom Henry referred to as quiet, though not contented, were evidently Quartermaster-general John Vernon, Adjutant-general William Allen, Colonel Philip Carteret, and Colonel Richard Lawrence, the brother of the president of the Council of

[12] See Gardiner, *Commonwealth and Protectorate*, III, 10.

[13] See above, pp. 57-58.

[14] Henry Cromwell to Thurloe, March 8, 1653/4, Thurloe, II, 149; Lloyd to Thurloe, March 13, *ibid.*, 163.

State. The attitude taken by these men was well set forth in a long and rambling letter, abounding in citations from Scripture, which Vernon wrote at this time to his old comrade-at-arms, now at the head of the state. He reminded Cromwell how he had been blessed in the days when he had avoided honors, and contrasted with that early policy his present actions, such as the knighting of the mayor of London. In connection with his present assumption of the title of Highness, he reminded Cromwell that he had once told the writer that the use of the title High and Mighty States by the Dutch was a provoking of the Lord, and would not lead them to prosper. However, he professed certainty that Cromwell had not sought his present high position, and declared that he would rather serve under him than under any other man. He begged that Cromwell would not listen to accusations against Christians, as he knew of but two members of his society besides himself who had expressed scruples on the grounds he mentioned, and these had not spoken of it openly, in the churches.[15]

[15] "When you spoke tremblingly as Ephraim, and with Moses chose affliction with ye people of God, the wisdom you sought with teares, amongst his simple despised ones, directed you and led you safely when (I bare you witnes) you were farre more afraid of haveing the honour from men due unto his name, then of any adversary: and endeavoured with teares, to keep men from thinkeing of you above wt was meet. In wch path god truly honoured you, accordeing to his promise. . . . Ah yor posture and some practices Now seeme to call ye prowd happy (as Mallacki speakes) that of Knighting ye Mayor (on that day, wherein ye lord was soe little honoured and sanctifyed before all ye people) speaks to ye world yor approbation of the former evil Costome of conferring honour upon grounds of vanety. Indeed yor title of Highnes alsoe makes some few soules mourne in secret, in whose hearts yet I am sure ther is noe man nor thinge in this world higher then you and yor welfare are. In scripture it seemes to be ascribed a lone to god, both to be dreaded, and rejoyced in by Saincts (Isay 13. 3, Job. 31. 2).

"And when I call to mynde the perswasion yor Lp. had (and was pleased to express to mee) that ye Dutch provoked ye lord by assumminge

That they had discussed their scruples extensively in private is clear from the great similarity in tone between this letter and one written to Cromwell three days later by Allen, who was Vernon's brother-in-law. He denied even more vigorously than Vernon had done that there was any general dissatisfaction among the Baptists: "Wee can noe sooner Speak (thoug in never so peacable and Christian a way) of these things but we are in England Judged Enemies to the government, ready to rise, nay, up in Arms against it, and what not. Oh my Lord, have you knowne us soe long and yet suspect us soe soone; have we been adictted to such things as these? . . . If God bring you a day of distresse when freinds may best be knowne, you will finde most of those that have been tearmed the most dissatisfied ones here stand by you and your authority . . . and in the mean time, though you may not find them with the

---

the Titles of High and Mighty states, and should not prosper in ym, I am ye more affraid of yor accepting that wch seemes more independent: Some other cares I have concerning you upon my soule, as touching yor makeing and confirmeing promisary oathes, (except onely that engadgement wch to most Christians was least scrupled) and thos many solemne engadgemts and declaracons upon serious prayer soe soon forgotten (wch I noe further imput unto yor Lp. then to beseech you may be sencible of ym before the lord) for they deserve our hearty sorrow, but it never yet hath entered into my heart to think you aspired at, or wilingly accepted yor present power. . . . Nor would I if I coulde be from under yor Governmt, or desire a chainge of it for any man or men I know, or ever heard of now alive . . . yet I beseech yor Lp. to put a difference, and be carefull that you intrench not upon ye Governmt entrusted onely unto Christ, nor easily credit accusations agst Christians, for ye accuser is busy at this day agst yor brethren. I know not a man besides my self and two more in all our socyety in this Contry that have exprest a scruple concerning yor condition, neither have wee either to any dissatisfyed, or ever in the churches. . . . I trust I should abhor my self to be pryvy to an expression against you, unreproved by mee. . . ." Vernon to Cromwell, March 10, 1653/4, Add. MSS., 4156, fol. 47 ff.

Lawrence, being in Waterford, had probably not as yet communicated his grievance.

multitude shouting you up in your titles in the streets, yet will I trust be found Supplicating at the throne of grace for that wisdom for you from above which is first pure and then peacible." [16] To his friends Allen took a less optimistic tone. He considered the dissensions that existed among Christians sent as a judgment from God, and anticipated "but little rest nor much lasting good till he come whose right it is to reigne, . . . and in the meane time it will concern his poor people not to be dreaming of reigning like kings hear on earth, but rather to prepare for that wich was their masters portion". He considered the dissatisfaction in Ireland not as bad as that in England, "and if we may but after all be permitted to live quietly under our rulers, serving God according to our light, I hope we shall owne it as a mercy with them that are over us; if otherwise—which God forbid—we shall not, I trust, be solicitous as to ourselves". [17] He professed that he loved and honored Cromwell, "though this last change with his atendencyes hath more stumbled me than ever any did; and I have still many thoughts of heart concerning it" [18]

Carteret felt that the outlook was gloomy, and seems to have had doubts as to whether he was justified in retaining his commission, but finally decided, probably upon the advice of Allen, that it was permissible to own the government and continue to serve it, but that it was best to have as little as possible to do with public

[16] Allen to Cromwell, March 13, 1653/4, Harleian MSS., 4106, fol. 226 ff.

[17] Allen to Theophilus Hart, April 5, 1654, Rawlinson MSS., A 13, fol. 26; Allen to Caithnes, April 6, Thurloe, II, 215. See also Allen to Standish, April 5, Rawlinson MSS., A 13, fol. 24.

[18] Allen to Hugh Courtney, April 6, 1654, Thurloe, II, 214.

affairs.[19] His brother-in-law, Lawrence, felt that the greatest fear of dissatisfaction in his part of the country was lest " our governors should be led to doe thinges, that may provoke the Lord, and cause him to withdraw his presence from them ".[20]

Since these men kept their opinions from spreading among their fellows, less dissatisfaction came to be expressed, and Patient's congregations were observed to be smaller.[21] In the course of the summer, Allen so far revised his decision to remain inactive as to stand for Parliament; but in Ireland as in England there was a wave of reaction against the sectaries, and he was defeated, along with other Baptists.[22] When it became evident that the new Parliament was not inclined to answer the expectations of the saints, there were expressions of discontent, and rumors of a plot arose, which must have had some foundation, but which were very evidently exaggerated.[23] Allen was among those who were summoned to England on account of these rumors, and he went into retirement in the country there, but soon got himself into trouble by his activities at Baptist meetings, as we have already seen.[24]

The great popularity of Fleetwood was a very important element in keeping discontent in check. His

[19] Carteret to William Allen the merchant, n. d., Rawlinson MSS., A 10, fol. 25; same to Standish, April 10, 1654, *id.*, 23, fol. 105; Allen to Caithnes, April 6, Thurloe, II, 215.

[20] Lawrence to Staynes, April 5, 1654, *ibid.*, 213.

[21] Jennings to Howard, April 5, 1654, *ibid.*

[22] *Severall Proceedings*, Aug. 31-Sept. 6, Sept. 7-14; *Perfect Diurnall*, Sept. 4-11; Egmont MSS., Hist. MSS. Comm., *Reports*, I, 553.

[23] Fleetwood to Thurloe, Sept. 6, 1654, Thurloe, II, 590; Dobbins to Percivale, Sept. 19, Egmont MSS., Hist. MSS. Comm., *Reports*, I, 559; Bordeaux to Brienne, Sept. 21/Oct. 1, Sept. 28/Oct. 8, P. R. O. Transcripts.

[24] See above, p. 78.

reports as to conditions in Ireland were uniformly encouraging, and he considered with satisfaction his own achievements as defender of the government. Yet his preferment of a party whose disaffection might at any moment lead it to cast off the bonds laid upon it by personal loyalty to him could not but cause grave concern to the home government.[25] More important still was the question of the transplantation. It was felt that a change of method was imperative there, and to bring it about, it was necessary to make a change in the administration. Henry Cromwell had been appointed commander-in-chief of the Irish forces in place of Ludlow in August, 1654, and a member of the Irish council in the following December, but he was not sent to Ireland until the summer of 1655. In the preceding April some of the Irish officers began to urge his speedy coming over, and Fleetwood's letters of the same period expressed willingness, even anxiety, for the arrival of his brother-in-law, although they betrayed an undercurrent of dissatisfaction.[26] Cromwell anxiously assured him that there was no intention of superseding him, but intimated that the opportunity was a favorable one for carrying out his plan of visiting England with his wife. This was followed up in July by a positive command to come to England, but it was not until September that Fleetwood finally left Ireland, long after it had become a matter of general report that Henry was to take his place.[27]

[25] Fleetwood to Thurloe, July 27, Sept. 22, 1654; Feb. 2, Mar. 6, 1654/5; June 18, 1655, Thurloe, II, 493, 620, III, 136, 196, 558.

[26] *Ibid.*, and same to same, April 11, 1655, *ibid.*, 363.

[27] For a discussion of Cromwell's policy in this matter, see Gardiner, *op. cit.*, IV, 115 ff.

Henry on his arrival was welcomed with joy by a large element of the population, which felt very strongly about the rule of the " godly party ". They regarded him as sent by a special providence as " a healer of the breaches in this divided nation ".[28] One of the Independent ministers who came over with him believed " that my lord came over upon the wings of faith and prayer, to put honour upon the publique worship of God, and life into his people, and a checke upon some irregular spirits, whome I rather desire to serve in love and pitty, then to censure ".[29] The young commander came over with every desire to conciliate, but with a fixed resolve to rule and not be ruled. In September he wrote home: " Thinges heer are very quiett and peaceable. . . . I have a verry fair correspondency betwixt my selfe and olde freinds. They are pritty plyable. Their shall be noe occation of offence offerred one my parte; yet I must doe my duty." [30] He realized that his youth was a drawback, but meant to discharge his trust faithfully, " and that without giveing any just occasion of offence to any of the people of God; which I may say through his grace [I] have endeavoured to avoide, and I hope it is uppon my harte soe to continue ".[31]

But there was much in his bearing which did cause offense. He attended the regular services at the cathedral, instead of the Baptist meeting which Fleetwood, though not himself a Baptist, had frequented, and the Independent ministers who had come from England

[28] T. Taylor to H. Cromwell, Dec. 6, 1655, Thurloe, IV, 286.
[29] Harrison to Thurloe, Aug. 15, 1655, *id.*, III, 715.
[30] Henry Cromwell to Thurloe, Sept. 18, 1655, *id.*, IV, 40.
[31] Henry Cromwell to the Protector, Oct. 9, 1655, *ibid.*, 74.

with him did not hesitate to attack Baptist doctrine.[32] They did, indeed, approach some of the Baptist leaders to see if they could not be persuaded to join them in worship, but gave up the idea on hearing the conditions under which the Baptists thought it might be arranged. The Baptists stipulated that on days of prayer they should be allowed to speak last, that they might correct anything contrary to the truth which might be said; that there be no singing of psalms; that on the one hand terms of reproach, and on the other, "magnifying titles", should not be indulged in; finally, "That we should not hinder godly men from places of authority and power, because of theire judgements".[33] In this last stipulation lay a further "root of bitterness". It had already become evident that the day was over when the fact that an officer was a Baptist meant that his tenure of his commission was assured.[34]

An agent of Baptist dissatisfaction was Adjutant-general Allen, who, freed from the imprisonment which had followed his activities in Devonshire, was in London. What seemed to him the injustice of that detention had increased his hostility to the Protectorate, and he kept his friends in Ireland informed of the course of events in a spirit which, as can well be imagined, did not err on the side of over-leniency toward the Cromwellian régime. Henry, apprised of this, suggested that he be sent into the country. Thurloe agreed with Henry in his estimate of Allen, and did his best to prevent the success of the applications he was making to be allowed

[32] Newsletter, Sept. 15, 1655, *Clarke Papers*, III, 52.

[33] Dr. Harrison to Thurloe, Oct. 17, 1655, Thurloe, IV, 90.

[34] A Royalist writer stated that Henry "follows ye father's instructions punctually in Ireland, discountenancing that party and cashiering many of ym". Whitby to Nicholas, Oct. 3/13, 1655, *Nicholas Papers*, III, 79;

to return to Ireland. Although Allen had Fleetwood for advocate, it is not likely that he would have obtained the permission he desired had it not been that his wife, whom he had left in Ireland, fell seriously ill. Thereupon, on giving assurances of fidelity and affection, he was allowed to go over.[85] His return, which occurred at about the time of Ludlow's arrest for slipping away to England against Cromwell's orders, was the signal for a new outbreak of discontent.[86] It was felt by the supporters of the government that these murmurings might lead to serious results, unless Cromwell should give "a fitt countenance and authority to the Lord Henry, whereby persons and places may be secured, as there is or shall be occasion".[87]

In pursuance of this idea, Henry's supporters in Dublin drew up a petition in the name of the mayor, aldermen, and others, asking that in case Fleetwood was not speedily to return, Henry should be made lord deputy.[88] Such a slight upon their beloved Fleetwood at once aroused the Baptists and the more extreme among their Independent brethren. Cromwell was scarcely less annoyed than they, since, foreseeing the inevitable dissatisfaction of that element, he wished it

[85] Henry Cromwell to Thurloe, Aug. 29, 1655, Thurloe, III, 744; Thurloe to Henry, Sept, 25, Oct. 23, *id.*, IV, 55, 108; Fleetwood to Henry, Oct. 3, Lansdowne MSS., 821, fol. 26.

[86] "There hath beene many former suspicions of discontents among the officers heere, especially of the baptised churches, and since the securing of the lieutenant generall and the coming of the adjutant generall divers unfit speeches and practices have been discovered. . . . The lord deputy's generall sweetness kept bonds upon some, who have since manifested discontents." Reynolds to Thurloe, Nov. 14, 1655, Thurloe, IV, 197. *Cf.* Thurloe to Henry, Nov. 13, *ibid.*, 191.

[87] *Ibid.*, and Winckworth to Henry Cromwell, Oct. 17, 1655, Lansdowne MSS., 821, fol. 52.

[88] Newsletter, Oct. 27, 1655, *Clarke Papers,* III, 60; Nieuport to the States General, Nov. 1/10, *id.*, IV, 260.

to appear that the return of Fleetwood was merely a matter of time. Moreover, it gave color to the accusation that he was concentrating power in the hands of his immediate family. He closely questioned Hierome Sankey, who was in touch with his brethren in Ireland, and who informed him that, so far as he knew, Henry had done nothing to give offense to the Baptists; that on the contrary he had had letters acknowledging Henry's "faire and frindly cariage to them".[39] Cromwell conveyed to Sankey the impression that he had no intention of laying aside Fleetwood, and both Fleetwood and Sankey intimated to Henry that he would have done well to suppress the petition.[40] As a matter of fact, Henry knew nothing of the movement for the petition until it had been sent; and, when he was informed that a paper of similar import was being circulated among the officers, he promptly took steps to suppress it.[41]

The situation was both a difficult and a delicate one for the young commander-in-chief. He was entirely out of sympathy with these men who were opposing him, and consequently quite unable to fathom their motives. He was convinced that even when they were openly expressing approval of his actions they were

[39] Sankey to Henry Cromwell, Nov. 27, 1655, Lansdowne MSS., 821, fol. 40.

[40] "Though you did not at all countenance, yett if there had been mad[e] a discountenance of the Mayer and Aldermns petition, I thinke it would have done well; we must be true to our principalls, wh. is equally to countenance and en[c]orage all truly godly. And indeed I never knew that the Anab. attempted any such thing or any thing like it." Sankey to Henry Cromwell, Dec. 4, 1655, Lansdowne MSS., 821, fol. 52; Fleetwood to same, same date, *ibid.*, 48.

[41] Ayscue to Henry Cromwell, Dec. 4, *ibid.*, fol. 46; Hewson to Cromwell, Jan. 16, 1656/7, Thurloe, IV, 422; same to same, n. d., Rawlinson MSS., A 5, fol. 249 ff.; Sankey to Henry Cromwell, Dec. 4, 1655, Lansdowne MSS., 821, fol. 52.

slandering him behind his back, and that they wrote calumniating reports of him to England. In this, if we are to believe Sankey and Fleetwood, he did them an injustice; moreover, it is difficult to credit men of the stamp of these religiously-minded soldiers with double dealing. As for their motives, Henry could see in them nothing more than an unbridled desire to rule.[42] In this opinion he was confirmed by the members of other religious bodies in the community.[43]

It would of course be absurd to represent these men as uninfluenced by self-interest or as watching with equanimity the power passing from them, especially when they believed that it was passing into the hands of men less godly, and therefore less able to make good use of it. It was just here that the personal motive became inextricably blended with the religious, and loyalty to Fleetwood the governor, who assured them places and lands, became indistinguishable from loyalty to Fleetwood the saint, whose rule was righteous, no member of whose household discountenanced the godly, and who would not have held a public baptism, with popish ceremonial, for his new-born child.[44] There was another thing to be said for the attitude of such men as Hewson, Vernon, and Allen. Men of Cromwell's generation, his old comrades-at-arms, they did not find it easy to have a stripling set over them, especially when

[42] Henry Cromwell to Thurloe, Nov. 28, 1655, Thurloe, IV, 255; Fleetwood to Henry, Jan. 8, Jan. —, 1655/6, Lansdowne MSS., 821, fols. 70, 80.

[43] See above, pp. 138-139; also Thurloe, IV, 270.

[44] On December 7 Henry's sister Mary wrote him that she had heard that "won is with you . . . ruls much in your family; and truly it is feared she is a descountenanser of the godly people". Thurloe, IV, 293. The public baptism of Henry's child evoked much criticism. W. Staines to Henry Cromwell, May 29, 1656, Lansdowne MSS., 821, fol. 144.

that stripling carried it with a high hand, and apparently set at naught all that they most prized.

Something of this feeling showed itself in a letter addressed to Cromwell by Hewson, his son-in-law Richard Lawrence, and Henry Prittie. They reminded him of their services under him in Ireland, of how fitly Ireton succeeded him there, and how Fleetwood had then taken up the reins of government to the contentment of all the godly. They referred to the way in which Fleetwood had reconciled some of those who had had scruples as to the righteousness of the Protectorate, and declared that, having heard that the promoters of the petitions which Henry, to his credit, had endeavored to suppress, still intended to bring their cause to Cromwell's attention, they wished to enter their own plea. They requested that Fleetwood be continued as lord deputy, and sent back to Ireland as speedily as possible; they declared that in the meanwhile they would be obedient and useful to Henry "in the station he now is in or in any other second place under our present precious lord deputy, your highness shall think fit to confer upon him".[45]

Cromwell was much better able than his son to understand what was passing in the minds of these men. Before their letter reached him he had one on its way to Hewson. It was couched in the friendliest terms, lamented that there should be dissensions in Ireland, and especially that, as was rumored to be the case, any one should fear persecution either from him or from his son. He asked Hewson to write to him frequently, and suggested that he endeavor to make himself serviceable to Henry, and try to bring about union among

[45] Dec. 2, 1655, Thurloe, IV, 276.

the people of God.[46] Hewson in replying assured him that "differances heere is not great, at least very little in appearance. . . . That jelousy bee of persecution from your highnes I never understood, nor feares from my Lord Henry, if he acted his owne principle, were not prevailed by the craft of others that might darken his Lo^pp^s understanding. As for the Annabaptists, though I am not of theire judgment, yet I must doe them the right to informe your Highnes that (if you have true hearted friends in Ireland, which you have many) they are to be numbred in that rank as wel as any. I doe know they are soe farr from feareing persecution from your Highnes that severall of them hath spoke it in my heareing that they owne theire freedome, theire liberty, yea theire safety from persecution to your Highnes. . . . and if ever there should come a time of triall your Highnes would find them thereon for the present government when others it may be would faint in the work". He had already felt bound to "deale faithfully" with Henry, who had accepted his words well. "His Lordship is young and to be pittied: Artificiall compliances and flattering insinuations he cannot be freed from: Stability and Constancy I hope wil increase with him with his experiances: the good Lord keepe him from being puffed upp." [47]

This letter, together with Cromwell's, was made public, and freely circulated in Ireland. When it came into Henry's hands, it can easily be imagined how he chafed at the patronizing references to himself. Nor

[46] Apparently no copy of this letter has survived, but its contents can be gathered from the references to it in Hewson's response, which, with a letter of Henry's, show its date to have been Dec. 4, 1655.

[47] Hewson to Cromwell, n. d., Rawlinson MSS., A 5, fol. 249 ff.

was he inclined to find Hewson's portrait of the Baptists lifelike. He had tried to be moderate, he wrote bitterly to Thurloe, and this letter was his reward. Indeed, nothing better was to be expected from Hewson, who consorted only with " the cheif of our peevish freinds heer, viz, Vernon, Laurence, Carteret, etc. . . . If Coll. Hewson must be beleived (with his three anabaptist sons) I must be made a liar, if not worse ".[48] The sober and godly people feared the Baptists, and groaned under their oppressions: " not longer then this eveninge, at the funeral sermon of adjutant general Allen's wife, where I was invited and expected . . . preached by Mr. Patience, the subject of his discourse was of presumption, and pressing the necessity and excellency of their ordinance of rebaptization ". In spite of what Hewson asserted, they had made a great clamor of persecution.[49] " Can his highness believe ", he wrote a week later, " that the Anabaptists, and especially those heer, to be his best and most faithfull freinds, and that when others will desert him, they will stande by him, as coll. Hewson sayes? . . . But lett the sober good people throughout Ireland be asked their knowledge, they will be able to tell you that when they appeared for the owninge of his highnes, these men did openly deny him, and not only soe, but reproached and reviled those that did owne him, and I am confident have marked him out for revenge, if ever the scale should turne. . . . It is good to use tenderness towarde

[48] Henry is using Anabaptist in the loose sense. Two of Hewson's sons-in-law, Carteret and Lawrence, were Baptists, but the third, John Jones, was an extreme Independent. For his attitude to the Baptists see his *Letters,* 218. He belonged to the faction opposed to Henry, the " Anabaptist " faction.

[49] Henry Cromwell to Thurloe, Dec. 19, 1655, Thurloe, IV, 327.

them. I have done it, and shall still doe it, but shall withall be carefull to keep them from power, whoe, if they hade it in their power, would express little tenderness to those, that would not submitt to their way." He threw light on what Hewson meant in hinting of some who "darken his lordship's understanding", by the statement: "when I have come home at 9 a-clock at night from the councill, I have sometimes founde the good ministers of the citty here, whoe have been very wellcome to me, and for which they are pleased to say my house is preist-ridden".[50] This was the circumstance which did most to prevent a good understanding between Henry and the Baptists: the Baptists were annoyed that the places they had been wont to occupy in the counsels of Fleetwood were now, in those of his successor, filled by Presbyterians and moderate Independents; those worthy men shaking their heads over Baptist intractability, and feeling it their duty to communicate to their host letters containing passages such as the following:

> I heare of some strange passages of your Anabaptists of Dublin to the greife and offence of lord Henry Cromwell. . . . Surely the pride and uncharitableness of that people shall ere long bring them low.[51]
>
> There is a certaine generation amongst us are of a muddie and disturbed temper; and if they cannot get into government and greatnesse, as the Hebrews did into Canaan through Jordan, they will (maugre the promise, which leads against them) attempt it by the way of Munster. Captain Vernon (the church's emissary) has ben abroade: whether proselyteing those of his religion to his present designes, as before he did their judgments to his religion, I knowe not certainely; but

[50] Same to same, Dec. 26, 1655, *ibid.*, 348.

[51] E. Wale to Dr. Harrison, Waterford, 14th of the 10th month, 1655, Thurloe, IV, 314.

confident I am, that somewhat is in agitation and secretly mannaged, which speakes it the more dangerous and to be reguarded. Clonmell, Waterford, Kilkenny, and some other places he has very busily visited. What their consultations have ben is yet darke: however it concernes you to have a speciall care of my lord, and that none of them be aloane with him. Remember Leyden. Though the same principle doe not allwaies produce the very same effect in circumstance, yet give it time, and but a conniveing encouragement, and in substance it will.[52]

The hint of danger to his own person is not likely to have been taken seriously by Henry, but his exasperation was pardonable when he learned that Vernon in one of his sermons had said that it was a judgment for the people of God to be under young or wicked governors, who were apt to be lifted up, and to believe lying reports against the saints. The preacher also remarked that Absalom grasped at unlawful power, and that such men might pretend to be for the saints, but that it was as Pharaoh was for Joseph, and Herod for John the Baptist.[53] Some of the Baptists expressed displeasure at Vernon's tone, but Henry considered it a fair specimen of the treatment he had undergone, although the only provocation that he had given was that he had "not bin subject to their will to doe what they would have imposed uppon me and others".[54]

The personal element certainly entered into the opposition to which Vernon was giving voice. Vernon was suspected to be in some degree acting as the mouthpiece of his brother-in-law Allen, who was at the time behaving with great circumspection. While he was never able to see in the Protectorate anything but an

[52] Letter of H. Warren, Dec. 14, 1655, *ibid.*, 315.
[53] Information, Dec. 19, 1655, *ibid.*, 328.
[54] Henry Cromwell to Thurloe, Jan. 2, 1655/6, *ibid.*, 376.

unrighteous government, the fact that he believed himself to have been severely treated by Cromwell undoubtedly heightened his opposition.[55] There is no evidence that Vernon had any personal grievance at the time, but in the course of the following summer he was complaining of unfair treatment in the cutting-down of his pay.[56] Hewson was piqued at the failure of his application that new commands be given to three officers, Barrow, Richards, and Leigh, whose regiments had been among those that were disbanded. Of these men, Leigh was a Baptist who had expressed approbation of Henry, and Barrow a Baptist who had been opposed to the petition in behalf of Fleetwood and had joined with Hewson in bringing it to Henry's notice. The report that they were present at the framing of Hewson's letter to Cromwell indicates that they were now all three among the malcontents.[57]

Chief among those who might have been expected to be actuated by a sense of personal grievance was Fleetwood, but the difficulty in his case seems to have been rather an excess of amiability, and a too great readiness to believe every one in the right. He was one of those people who through their very goodness and simplicity are the despair of their friends and the joy of those who are wont to use their fellows as tools. To his way of thinking, a member of a gathered church could do no wrong, and his eyes never for a moment penetrated beyond the surface of things. Though he ostentatiously took upon himself the office of healer of

[55] See above, pp. 78, 147.

[56] Fleetwood to Henry Cromwell, Aug. 1, 1656, Lansdowne MSS., 821, fol. 216.

[57] Henry Cromwell to Thurloe, Dec. 26, 1655, Thurloe, IV, 349; Taylor to Harrison, Dec. 17, 1655, *id.*, III, 29.

breaches, his quarters at Wallingford House were notoriously the resort of the disaffected.[58] He was of course consulted in all matters relating to Ireland, and the tenor of his advice to his father-in-law may be judged from the tone of his letters to Henry, to whom he maintained that, although perhaps "some good men are over-hastie", Henry was unduly prejudiced against the very ones w[illegible] were "earnest with the Lord", in his behalf. The real difficulty, he constantly implied, lay in the efforts made by Henry's supporters to cause estrangement between Henry and himself.[59]

Cromwell, however, though his attitude toward the Baptists was far more sympathetic than Henry's, did not allow his views to be influenced by those of Fleetwood. To some extent his first attempt to relieve the strain of affairs in Ireland defeated its own end, for the publication of his letter to Hewson, with the latter's reply, was regarded as a proof that he was siding with Hewson and discountenancing Henry's policy.[60] However, he continued the correspondence, laying especial weight upon the necessity of healing the breaches between the different sects. Upon this task Hewson expressed himself ready and anxious to embark.[61]

Cromwell's next step was to send to Ireland a moderate Baptist, Thomas Cooper, who was strongly at-

[58] Henry sent one of his letters to Thurloe in care of the Independent minister Brewster, who, he thought, "if he does not meet with ill company by the way", will give a fair account of affairs, though he is considered a friend of the Baptists, "having been courted and congratulated". But he begs that Cromwell see him "before he getts to Wallingford House". Thurloe, IV, 327. See also *ibid.*, 348, 373.

[59] Fleetwood to Henry, January, 1655/6, Lansdowne MSS., 821, fols. 70, 74, 80.

[60] Henry Cromwell to Thurloe, Dec. 26, 1655, Thurloe, IV, 348; Dr. Harrison to same, same date, *ibid.*, 349.

[61] Hewson to Cromwell, Jan. 16, 1655/6, *ibid.*, 422.

tached to him, and who was put in command of the forces in Ulster. He hoped for some good effects also from the efforts of Col. Sankey, who had been for some time absent from his regiment, and who returned in company with Cooper.[62] Henry was not unduly enthusiastic about this step, especially since he cherished some doubts relative to Sankey, but hoped that it might do some good. He was convinced that, as Sankey himself put it, nothing but the saddle would satisfy some of his Baptist brethren. " I will keep them from that ", Henry declared, " lest they should make me their asse." [63]

Henry had to be dealt with carefully in these days. Although he was making heroic efforts to exhibit moderation and fairness, he was thoroughly exasperated, and he was convinced that his conduct was being successfully misrepresented in England. Cromwell was not likely to give credence to reflections upon his son. He recognized the weak points of both parties to the quarrel, and give him tactful counsel. On the other hand, he was glad of the opportunity to have a report on the condition of affairs from Cooper, whom he could depend upon to be just and impartial.[64]

Soon after the arrival of Cooper and Sankey, Henry called together some of the dissatisfied officers in their

[62] Thurloe to Henry Cromwell, Dec. 25, 1655, *ibid.*, 343.

[63] Henry Cromwell to Thurloe, Jan. 2, 10, 1655/6, *ibid.*, 376, 408.

[64] " Take heed of professing religion without the power: that will teach you to love all who are after the similitude of Christ. Take care of making it a business to be too hard for the men who contend with you. . . . I have to do with these poor men, and am not without my exercise. I know they are weak, because they are peremptory to judge others. I quarrel not with them but in their seeking to supplant others, which is done by some, first by branding them with antichristianism, and then taking away their maintenance." Oliver to Henry, April 21, 1656, *Letters*, II, 485.

presence. He told them " that they might all of them of that judgement expect equally liberty both in their spirituall and civill concernments with any others ", but that he would not approve of their ruling him, or ruling with him. He then gave them an opportunity to express any grievances they might have against him, "either as a publique person or as a private Christian ". The complaints that were made appeared to Cooper to be unimportant, and based on slight grounds. He thought that the discussion had cleared the air, and that although there were a few persons " soe much out of order in their owne spirits, that noething will please ", there was no fear of a spread of dissatisfaction in the army.[65]

The good results of the presence of Cooper and Sankey appeared in a letter to Cromwell, written soon after this interview, and signed by Henry's supporters among the officers as well as by Fleetwood's. The first half of the letter was devoted to fervent praises of Fleetwood as a " ruler sent from God ", whose " mouth hath spoken wisdome, and his tongue talked of judgment ". The latter half consisted of rejoicings over the sending of Henry, and the whole concluded with the request that " they both be by you set here, as the two pillars att the temple, the one to establish, the other to strengthen . . . as pledges of your affection, and whoe (we trust) will be polished shafts in the Lord's quiver, to strike to the heart wickedness and prophaneness ". The bearer of this rhetorical triumph was instructed to inform Cromwell, when he made the very natural inquiry what it was the writers wanted, that the idea was

[65] Henry Cromwell to Thurloe, Jan. 10, 18, 1655/6, Thurloe, IV, 408, 433; Cooper to Thurloe, Jan. 16, *ibid.*, 422.

that Fleetwood should be sent back, but with the title of lord lieutenant, while Henry should in his absence have the title and powers of lord deputy.[66]

The unanimity shown in this letter was considered a good omen, and indeed so it proved. A calm settled upon the spirits of those who had been so troubled. Allen and Vernon showed some annoyance at the "compliance" of Sankey, but appeared little in public. Henry had, indeed, some trouble with the Baptist officers Axtell and Eyres, but it made only a temporary ripple, and he had the approval of the home government in his handling of them.[67] He followed his father's advice in using efforts to conciliate the Baptists still hostile to the government, assiduously circulating the loyal address of the Welsh Baptists to Cromwell. He endeavored, too, to secure for Ireland the ministry of Spilsbury, the Baptist minister who had so successfully interceded with his brethren the previous year. That worthy divine had, however, just accepted a call from a "very great people" in England, and was not obtainable.[68] One factor in the continuation of peace was the withdrawal of some of the principal malcontents. Vernon and Carteret crossed to England, whence the latter was sent to take up a command in Jersey. Hewson went to London and proceeded to make trouble for Henry there, by disseminating the report that the

[66] The officers in Ireland to Cromwell, Jan. 16, 1655/6, *ibid.*, 421; Instructions, *ibid.* For the subsequent history of the letter see Thurloe to Henry Cromwell, Feb. 5, 1655/6, *ibid.*, 505; Reynolds to same, Jan. 19, Feb. 1, Lansdowne MSS., 821, fols. 26, 85.

[67] Henry Cromwell to Thurloe, Jan. 30, 1655/6, Thurloe, IV, 483; Thurloe to Henry Cromwell, April 28, 1656, *ibid.*, 743; Reynolds to same, Feb. 12, 19, Lansdowne MSS., 821, fols. 89, 93.

[68] Thurloe to Henry Cromwell, Feb. 19, 1655/6, Thurloe, IV, 545; Thomas Goodwin to same, April 6, 1656, Lansdowne MSS., 821, fol. 113.

Independents as well as the Baptists in Ireland were dissatisfied with him.[69] This report the Independents hastened to deny, and Henry's friends in England also labored to make it appear "that other Christians besides Ana. may live in Ireland, and that ministers may be encouraged, and that others may have countenance and justice".[70] If we may judge from their letter to some Welsh churches, the attitude of the Dublin Baptists at this time was one of patient resignation, while their conviction was that it was safest to be prepared for the worst.[71]

Although discontent in the churches was in abeyance, the arrears of pay and other grievances caused discontent among the soldiery, and on that account strenuous efforts were made throughout the summer of 1656 to secure a settlement of the government upon a different basis. Sir John Reynolds, Henry's brother-in-law, and Dr. Harrison were the chief movers in the matter, but they found many obstacles in their way. Fleetwood's feelings had to be considered, and opposition from various members of the Council overcome.[72] Moreover, Cromwell, while he desired to make such a settlement as should "either prevent and make peevish people

[69] Thurloe to Henry Cromwell, May 20, June 16, 1656, Thurloe, V, 45, 122; Henry Cromwell to Thurloe, May 28, *ibid.*, 65; Reynolds to Henry Cromwell, May 27, Lansdowne MSS., 821, fol. 142.

[70] Same to same, June 16, 1656, *ibid.*, fol. 162; *By the Church of God in Dublin, whereof Doctor Samuel Winter is pastour*, June 3, 1656 (Nickolls, 137). The Dublin church spoke in the name of all the Irish Independents.

[71] "Ye are now in prosperous wis; it will be your wisdom to prepare for a storm, for, brethren, whenever did you know the people of God long without persecution? Yea, and that from the powers of the world." Dublin, 12th 4th month, 1656, Ivimey, I, 253.

[72] Dr. Harrison's letters reporting these negotiations are in vol. 821 of the Lansdowne MSS. They employ a somewhat unusual cipher, not difficult except in the case of names, to most of which I find no clue.

quiet, or at least hinder their disquieting and hurting of others ", did not wish to do anything that would make the disaffected party " desperate on a sodaine ", and therefore desired that his intentions should be concealed for a time.[73] Reynolds and Harrison were detained in England, and Anthony Morgan was sent for to give an account of affairs. Henry considered these acts direct slights, and began to say that it would be better for him to retire from Ireland, since he did not have the confidence of his superiors.[74] Thurloe and Fleetwood did their best to pacify him, the latter chiefly by protestations of unchangeable affection, accompanied by rather incoherent recommendations of his Baptist friends.[75] An additional grievance was the unexpected appearance of Vernon in Ireland, although it finally developed that he had come without permission from Cromwell, and to his annoyance. His arrival was the signal for renewed activity among the Baptist malcontents, whose frequent meetings began to cause comment. Vernon boasted of his plain dealing with Cromwell, but expressed the opinion that Henry had been slandered in England, and that both Hewson and Sankey had behaved most unworthily.[76]

In the latter part of August came the report of an intended invasion by the Cavaliers, and the young commander had to give all his attention to preparations

[73] Dr. Harrison to Henry Cromwell, June 10, 17, July 29, 1656, Lansdowne MSS., 821, fols. 155, 164, 214.

[74] Henry Cromwell to Thurloe, July 2, 1656, Thurloe, V, 177; *cf.* Thurloe to Henry Cromwell, June 24, July 1, *ibid.*, 150, 176.

[75] Thurloe to Henry Cromwell, July 8, 15, *ibid.*, 196, 213; Fleetwood to same, Aug. 1, 8, 1656, Lansdowne MSS., 821, fol. 216; 823, fol. 351.

[76] Henry Cromwell to Thurloe, Aug. 6, 20, 1656; Thurloe, V, 278, 327; Thurloe to Henry Cromwell, Aug. 12, *ibid.*, 304.

against such a contingency. While traveling about the island he came to the conclusion that things were in a good and peaceable condition, and on his return to Dublin he found to his surprise that he was beginning to be courted by some of the Baptists. Patient and others came to see him and expressed satisfaction with his management of affairs. He was at a loss to explain this change of attitude, but it was probably due to the influence of the Baptist Steele, an elderly man and a staunch supporter of the Protectorate, who had just arrived in Ireland as chancellor.[77] From England, too, came Baptist commendation. Henry Lawrence, the president of the Council, wrote to assure Henry that he was convinced of his advocacy of the principle of toleration, and gave no credit to rumors of persecution.[78] This was gratifying, coming from the brother of one of the former malcontents: coming from the president of the Council it was perhaps even more gratifying, as presaging support of Henry in the settlement of Ireland.

In October Henry had a valuable champion at Whitehall in the person of Vincent Gookin, the opponent of the transplantation policy. Gookin carried over an ad-

[77] Henry Cromwell to Thurloe, Sept. 29, 1656, Thurloe, I, 731. *Cf. id.*, V, 453.

[78] "I know yr Lordship to bee to much a person of honour and resolve and reason to carry it hardely to different judgements that are of peaceible and quiet Spiritts as to civill affayres, besides that liberty upon the account of conscience is the greate product of this warre, and is certaynely the greate designe that God hath on foote in the worlde that men may have liberty to searve him accordinge to theire understandings, wh. where men ar not in utter darknes I take to bee the onely cement of peace. But my Lorde I need not say much of this subject to a person of yr sense and education and experience, and yr Lordshp may be assured I shall have no ap[ti]tude to receave reports to the prejudice of one I so much esteeme and love." Henry Lawrence to Henry Cromwell, Oct. 9, 1656, Lansdowne MSS., 821, fol. 242.

dress five or six yards long from the " ancient Protestant inhabitants ", and elaborately defended Henry's administration, asking, to Cromwell's amusement, " wheather any person of or from Ireland did ever say any thing to his highness to your prejudice who was not either accidentally by his custome to rule unlimitedly or naturally a man of a proud and Haughty Spirit ".[79] He also presented a long memorial which he had drawn up himself, wherein he set forth the condition of affairs in Ireland. To his mind, nothing lay in the way of a glorious settlement " but what lyes in the minds of a few busy cholericke people, who unjustly thinke themselves as fit to build and setle, as they were to breake and pull down: and in this erraticke confidence doe not only fill many places of publique trust and administration, which would better become wiser and more sober men, but doe impetuously baule and clamour against the preferment of all such, as will not be as mad and tumultuarie as they ". These people had been encouraged by the very means used to quiet them, and had been made to think that they could have any one whom they pleased called away from Henry's side, and detained as long as they pleased, and to believe that the fact that their complaints were given a hearing indicated disapproval of Henry's policy. This had so emboldened them that they had put almost unbearable affronts and slights upon Henry in his own house and before his own servants. These people were few, though they made a great noise, and opposed to them was the great body of the nation, especially the " ancient Protestant inhabitants ", who cherished Henry as the apple of their eyes.[80]

[79] Gookin to same, Oct. 21, 1656, *ibid.*, 246.
[80] Gookin to Cromwell, Nov. 22, 1656, Thurloe, V, 646 ff.

The difficulties referred to by Gookin came to a head a few weeks later, when Allen, Vernon, Barrow, and Axtell waited upon Henry and announced that they had resolved to resign their commissions. Henry took twenty-four hours in which to consider what was his best course, and finally decided to accept their resignations. The result was gratifying. The best friends of the four officers expressed disapproval of their course, the officers themselves did not appear proud of it, and some of the leading Baptists took occasion to express their commendation of his management, and of the liberty which he extended to all churches. He concluded that at last his opponents were not in a position to do any considerable harm.[81]

When the question of the kingship arose, disaffection was expected. Henry wrote to the well-affected officers to look out for any signs of disturbance, and to check any attempts at petitions. Fearing especially the influence of Richard Lawrence and John Jones, encouraged by Hewson, who had returned to Ireland on private business, he made such changes in the disposition of the forces at Dublin as should so far as possible nullify that influence. Allen and Vernon, too, were holding meetings, and Axtell's behavior caused him some uneasiness.[82]

[81] "The Anabaptists and others, whose way and principles were inconsistent with settlement and our interest, do find themselves disabled from doing much harm. My inclination now is, having brought them to good terms, not to crush them quite, lest through despair they attempt things dangerous; and withal, lest others take occasion to become insolent and violent, and so put us to new trouble. Besides, it is against my conscience to bear hard upon any, merely upon the account of a different judgment, or to do anything, that might make them think so." Henry Cromwell to Thurloe, Dec. 3, 17, 24, *ibid.*, 670, 710, 729; Thurloe to Henry Cromwell, Dec. 16, *ibid.*, 708.

[82] Henry Cromwell to Thurloe, March 4, 1656/7, *ibid.*, VI, 94; same to Cromwell, April 22, *ibid.*, 222.

His suspicions of Hewson and Lawrence were only too well founded. It came to light in June that they had been promoting a letter from the officers to Fleetwood, rejoicing in Cromwell's refusal of the crown. They had secured its fifteen signatures, according to Henry, by dubious methods. On the grounds of this action he forbade Hewson and Lawrence to leave for England, and in spite of Thurloe's attempt to make light of the affair, and Fleetwood's defence of Hewson, declared publicly against the project. His objections to what might seem a harmless expression of opinion were based upon the fact that indirect methods had been used, and that the matter did not come up immediately after the refusal of the crown, but much later, when the settlement of the government was well under way.[83] The leading Baptists had addressed to Cromwell a letter of similar import, expressing their approval of his resistance of temptations, and assuring him that "whatsoever report you have heard of either the Church baptized in Dublin, or any other Church in the same faith in Ireland, it is farr from our hearts to disowne the Lord's authority in your Highness, or his worke in your hand; but that you have with cordiall and endeared affections been in our hearts, and the waight of your burden and worke hath (by the praiers

[83] Henry Cromwell to Oliver, June 5, 1657, Add. MSS., 4157, fol. 182; Thurloe to Henry Cromwell, June 16, Sept. 9, Thurloe, VI, 352, 505; Fleetwood to same, June 17, Lansdowne MSS., 822, fol. 98. Lawrence did go to England before the end of the year. Lawrence to same, 1657, *id.*, 823, fol. 7. That this was not the only project appears from a rough draft of a soldiers' address expressing satisfaction with the way the government had been settled. "This we judged our more especiall Duty to make knowne forasmuch as wee have beene more misrepresented for disaffection than others, and forasmuch as that Misaprehension hath emboldened many in their contumacy and opposition against your Highness' government." *Ibid.*, fol. 325.

and teeres (we can truly say) of the most unsatisfied's brother amongst us) been borne before the Lord and the throne of his grace ".[84]

For some reason, perhaps because he had suffered much at Hewson's hands, the latter's project of a letter which, after all, expressed the same sentiments as the address just quoted, was regarded with especial bitterness by Henry. When, three months later, a lieutenant-colonel named Brayfield revived the affair, intimating that the letter had pleased Cromwell, but that Henry was trying, Absalom-like, to steal the affections of his father's people away from him, Henry cashiered him, and in spite of the fact that Thurloe, Broghill, and Cromwell himself wrote, desiring that Brayfield be reinstated, he firmly refused to rescind his action.[85]

All this time the settlement of the government in Ireland was being put off from week to week. Henry offered to step aside, if the delay was due to opposition to him, and when Steele informed him that a petition in his favor had been despatched secretly by his friends, he wrote to Thurloe that it must not be presented, giving reasons which do credit to his character and good sense.[86] Finally, in spite of delays and obstructions, Thurloe was able to announce to Henry in November, 1657, that he had been appointed lord deputy. From

[84] *The humble address of divers of the baptized Christians in Dublin and elsewhere in the behalfe of themselves and their brethren in Ireland* (Nickolls, 148).

[85] Henry Cromwell to Thurloe, Sept. 9, 1657, Thurloe, VI, 505; Thurloe to Henry Cromwell, *ibid.*, 552; Cromwell to same, *Eng. Hist. Rev.*, 1901, 345 ff.; Broghill to same, Oct. 17, Thurloe, VI, 503. In the same connection, with what Fleetwood called Christianlike behavior, he refused to accept the resignation of Carteret. Fleetwood to same, Sept. 15, Lansdowne MSS., 822, fol. 182.

[86] Henry Cromwell to Thurloe, n. d., Aug. 25, Sept. 9, 1657, Thurloe, VI, 446, 481, 505; Thurloe to Henry Cromwell, Aug. 6, *ibid.*, 455.

that time on there was no question of his control of the situation. In February, at the time of his father's cashiering the five Baptist officers in England, a Baptist pastor wrote to him, disowning any part in the transactions of his brethren there, and he felt able to report to the home government "that those people are become very quiett, and I countenance them accordingly, never having other intention then to bring them uppon a levell with others of equall desert".[87] One reason of the change of attitude was very probably the withdrawal of Vernon, who had removed his family to England the preceding summer.[88]

The temper of the Baptist officers who remained in Ireland was shown by the outcome of the discussion on the army address in March, 1658. Though the Baptists were in the majority, and one of them gave voice to fears of a settlement which might permit of a return to kingship, Sankey and Carteret expressed their approval of kingship, if that were the form which best agreed with the constitution, and to Henry's surprise an address favorable to the government as settled by the Humble Petition and Advice was framed. Not more than twelve expressed unwillingness to sign it, and these based their objections upon different grounds. The chief of them, a Baptist, Major Lowe, took such an attitude that his friends and co-religionists censured him for it, and as he was also guilty of neglect of his duties, Henry felt justified in dismissing him from his command.[89]

[87] Henry Cromwell to Thurloe, Feb. 24, 1657/8, *ibid.*, 819.

[88] Vernon to Henry Cromwell, June 22, 1657, Lansdowne MSS., 822, fol. 107.

[89] Henry Cromwell to Thurloe, March 24, April 14, 1658, Thurloe, VII, 21, 71; same to Broghill, March 24, *ibid.*, 22; same to Cooper, May 19, *ibid.*, 142.

The following month there was some rumor of discontent at a meeting of ministers which Henry had summoned to discuss the question of tithes. The trouble was among the Independents as well as the Baptists, and Henry thought the root of the difficulty lay in the actions of no less a personage than his chancellor, Steele.[90] Steele had unquestionably been serviceable in soothing the minds of his Baptist brethren, but he had failed lamentably in tact toward Henry. He had come over to Ireland full of confidence in his ability as a healer of breaches, and with the most benevolent intentions toward the son of his old friend the Protector. But to that high-spirited young man his attitude seemed that of " tutor or guardian to a minor; for at his first coming he . . . read lectures to me of affairs and maxims of state, taught me how to carry myself at the councill, gave me rules how things should be managed at the board, how abroad; and lest I should forget my lesson, gave me three or four sheets in writing, of those rules he thought of most importance ". He represented Steele's offers of assistance as coming when the Baptists were already in so calm a state, that he had declined the proffered aid; whereupon he believed Steele had set about fomenting discontent among the Independents, in order to build up a party, with the expectation of later allaying the disturbance he had created and thus strengthening his influence. The misunderstanding between the two culminated in Steele's decision to resign. He gave as his chief reason the desire to " take better care for his soul's concernment ", but admitted also dissatisfaction with the administration,

[90] Same to Thurloe, May 26, June 9, June 23, July 7, 1658, *ibid.*, 145, 161, 198, 243; Thurloe to Henry Cromwell, June 1, *ibid.*, 153.

as well as embarrassment because in his official position he was not free to look out for the interests of the party of which he was considered the head.[91] Doubtless Henry exaggerated Steele's misdeeds and underestimated his services. Surely, if his fatherly lectures to Henry were as involved and obscure as his letters, we cannot blame Henry for his impatience. Yet that Steele was sincere, like so many bores, there is no reason to doubt; and there is always the presumption that he carried out some at least of his good intentions, and helped allay, and not create, dissatisfaction.

Steele was the last Baptist with whom Henry had to struggle. He had good reason to be proud of what he had accomplished in the island which he had been sent to govern. He had vindicated his father's policy of toleration to all good men, a thing which Oliver, who had a more complicated situation to deal with, was unable to do, and he had made out of an army rent with faction a body which was considered the most valuable asset of the Protectorate in the days of his brother's rule.

[91] Henry Cromwell to Thurloe, June 23, 1658, *ibid.*, 198; Fleetwood to Thurloe, May 2, 1655, *id.*, III, 421. *Cf. id.*, VII, 243, 269.

CHAPTER VII.

Overturning, Overturning, Overturning.

The accession of Richard Cromwell was so peaceful that his supporters were astonished. But the peace was not destined to endure. There was no reason why the critics of Oliver's government should be reconciled to that of Richard. The new head of the state had not, to be sure, any record which could be thought to justify the accusation of apostasy. On the other hand, no close affiliation with matters religious, no earlier rôle as the instrument of God's just judgments, recommended him to the hearts of the saints. And the government was still government by a single person, and by a single person of so much less ability that hopes of success in an attempt to alter it might well be strong.

A Royalist reported that some six hours before Cromwell's death the Fifth Monarchy men sent out emissaries to all parts of England with the news that his condition was hopeless. He believed that they had some project afoot, and that they had chosen Lambert as their commander-in-chief, with Harrison second in command.[1] In London, Feake railed against the government from the pulpit, and "Chillenden, Spencer, and other Anabaptists" indulged freely in criticism.[2] Later in the month the report came from Exeter that

[1] Barwick to Charles II, n. d., Thurloe, VII, 415.

[2] Newsletters, Sept. 4, 6, 1658, *Clarke Papers,* III, 162, 163; Thurloe to Henry Cromwell, Sept. 7, Thurloe, VII, 374; Bordeaux to Mazarin, Sept. 30/Oct. 10, P. R. O. Transcripts.

Carew, Vernon, and Allen were planning a great meeting of their party.[8]

Had these men still held their commands in the army, their reported activities would have been more disquieting, and the hopes they raised in the minds of the Royalists would have been more sanguine. For it was upon the attitude of the army that the fate of Richard's Protectorate hung, and it was the army's discontent which brought about his downfall. Exactly how much of the dissatisfaction among the soldiers was due to Fifth Monarchy and Baptist agitation it is impossible to estimate, but contemporary opinion laid a good deal of stress upon it, and gave those elements considerable credit, or discredit, for the events which brought about the change of government. It is certainly necessary to recognize, from this time onward, a lowering in the plane of motives, a greater emphasis on place and power, on soldiers' pay and soldiers' privilege, than in the days of Oliver. Personal ambition on the part of the officers, the soldier's jealousy of the civilian: these were perhaps the most potent forces, but religious considerations were still the controlling motives of many, and for those whom self-interest directed they furnished frequently a convenient cloak.

It was discontent with the succession of the civilian Richard to his father's position as commander-in-chief, which prompted the first army petition, but it was in the form of prayer meetings that the gatherings of the inferior officers continued, after Richard had reproved them for their action. The dissatisfaction expressed

[8] Coplestone to Thurloe, Sept. 11, 1658, Thurloe, VII, 385; Intelligence, Sept. 18/28, *ibid.*, 398.

in these meetings took the form of references to the late apostasy, and to the existing opportunity of returning to the good old cause. At Wallingford House, too, where the superior officers met under the leadership of Fleetwood and Desborough, it was not considerations of the unfitness of civilians to meddle with military affairs which went upon record, but resolutions to "looke backe to what they had sworne and promised".[4]

Henry Cromwell perceived clearly the danger in the unauthorized meetings of officers, and likewise looked with suspicion at the Savoy conference, just opening. "What a hurly-burly is there made", he wrote to Fleetwood. "A hundred Independent ministers called together! A Council, as you call it, of 200 or 300 officers of a judgment! . . . Will not the loins of an imposing Anabaptist be as heavy as the loins of an imposing Prelate or Presbyter? And is it a dangerous error that dominion is founded on grace when it is held by the Church of Rome, and a sound principle when it is held by the Fifth Monarchy?"[5]

The struggle as to the government began on February first, when Thurloe brought into the House his bill for the recognition of the Protectorate. It was while the debates upon this bill were going on that an incident occurred, unimportant in itself, but significant, since it showed the position of the parliamentary majority, and the alignment of the elements opposed to Richard's government. On February 8 William Kiffin, and other gentlemen "of good affection to the Commonwealth", men with "honest, old faces", were observed in the

[4] *Clarke Papers*, III, iv.
[5] Henry Cromwell to Fleetwood, Oct. 20, 1658, Thurloe, VII, 454.

lobby of the House with a petition. They were requested to wait until the debates were concluded. A week later, when the Protectoral party had carried its bill, and Richard had been duly recognized as Protector, and as general of all the armies of the Commonwealth, the petition was received. It was presented by Samuel Moyer, " Commonwealths men, Levellers, 5th monarchs attending ". The petition turned out to be the same one which had played such an important part in the last days of the preceding Parliament, and was generally regarded as an application for the establishment of a republic. Although the petitioners were scornfully referred to as " only those of Prayse God Barebones gang ", the presence among them of Kiffin, lately the staunch supporter of Cromwell, and such respected citizens as Moyer and Berners, shows that they represented an element of standing and solidity in the community. The House politely assured them that some of the grievances enumerated in their petition were already in debate, and that whatever else in it was suitable for consideration by the House should secure attention in due time.[6] They were also told that the House expected the petitioners, in accordance with the expressions in their petition, to acquiesce in its resolutions. Despite the efforts of Hazelrigge, Vane, Lambert, and others, a motion to thank the petitioners for their pains was lost by one hundred votes, and they retired " not a little troubled ".[7]

[6] Clarges to Henry Cromwell, Feb. 8, 15, 1658/9, Thurloe, VII, 609, 617; Barwick to Hyde, Feb. 16, *ibid.*, 615; *Commons Journals*, VII, Feb. 9, 15; Aungier to Henry Cromwell, Feb. 15, Lansdowne MSS., 823, fol. 218; Burton, *Diary*, III, 152, 288. Clarges said that there were 40,000 signatures!

[7] T. Gorges to Dr. Gorges, Feb. 16, 1658/9, Lansdowne MSS., 823, fol. 227; Mabbott, Intelligence, Feb. 15, *ibid.*, fol. 222; Annesley to Henry Cromwell, Feb. 15, *ibid.*, fol. 213; Burton, *Diary*, III, 288-296.

The disappointment felt by these worthy men in the attitude of Parliament must have been sensibly increased as the weeks went on, and there were no signs of intention to follow up the policy foreshadowed by Richard, whose "Proclamation in behalf of Ministers of tender consciences" had elicited a grateful address from a number of Baptist congregations, which regarded it as a sign of intention to follow in his father's footsteps.[8] Those who favored a state church were in a decided majority in the House, and it early became evident that its religious policy would be a conservative one. In fact, practically the only side of its activities which were of a kind to find favor with the sectaries was its release on the grounds of illegal imprisonment of some of the men sent into confinement by Oliver.

Among these were Portman, who had been in the Tower since the discovery of the Fifth Monarchy plot of 1657, and Overton, who had been in prison since the winter of 1655-1656. When the latter was brought up to London he was accorded an ovation which reminded one observer of the days of Prynne, Bastwick, and Burton.[9] It is probable that the effect of such events was greater in awakening ideas of the possibilities of tyranny in one-man government, than in enhancing with

[8] The humble and hearty address of sundry Churches of persons baptised into the Name of the Lord Jesus. *Mercurius Politicus*, Feb. 10-17, 1658/9.

[9] *Commons Journals*, Feb. 3, 26, March 16. Newsletter, March 12 [?], *Clarke Papers*, III, 184. Concerning Portman's case Gorges wrote to Henry Cromwell: "This Imprisonment is voted illegal and unjust, thus your Excelly sees that the Indulgence of your Renowned father hath another interpretation uppon it, had his Highness proceeded with that sort of men as he did with another Generacion he had better secured the nation from those vipers that gnaw his blessed memory with the most poysoned Teeth of design and mallice." n. d., Lansdowne MSS., 823, fol. 235.

the sectaries the popularity of Parliament. At any rate, a tendency already noted continued, and the sectaries, together with the republicans outvoted in the House, began to pin their hopes upon the army. Significant of this was a circumstance related by Arthur Annesley to Henry Cromwell at this juncture. It was that " Dr. Owens hath gathered a church in the Independent way, and the lord Fleetwood, Lord Desborough, Lord Sidenham, Berry, Goffe, and divers other were admitted members since my last, which hath divers constructions put upon it, and is not that I can heare very well liked at Wh. H." [10]

Those at Whitehall might well look askance at the new church. From that time forward Dr. John Owen played a prominent part in army councils and deliberations. It was he who conducted the devotional exercises at the great meeting of officers in April, which brought about the breach between army and Parliament. He was one of the ministers who accompanied the officers when, instead of dissolving their assembly at Richard's command, they adjourned to Wallingford House, and there his counsels must have had weight in the consultations.[11]

Whatever may have been the motives which ruled the officers' actions, their power to shape events depended upon the attitude of their troops. And when the soldiers of the regiments in town, including Richard's own

[10] March 15, 1658/9, *ibid.*, fol. 251. That Desborough had been working to gain the support of the sectaries had been observed as early as the preceding November. Intercepted letter, Nov. 5, 1658, Thurloe, VII, 496.

[11] In spite of Orme's refusal to believe that Owen had any part in these proceedings, the references in correspondence and newsletters leave no doubt that Dr. Owen of Christ Church was the man in question. See Orme, *Life of Owen*, and *Dict. Nat. Biog.*

regiment, obeyed Fleetwood's orders to meet at St. James's, instead of the Protector's orders to rendezvous at Whitehall, they were undoubtedly influenced in their action by the belief that they were following not merely the champion of army independence of civilian control, but the champion of religious liberty against a regime which refused to recognize it. It was this action of the soldiers which forced Richard to put himself into the hands of the army and dissolve his Parliament, thus virtually bringing his Protectorate to an end.[12]

Whatever their influence in the events which had substituted the rule of a group of officers for the rule of Protector and Parliament, the sectaries felt confident that now at last attention would be paid to the counsels of the saints, and they lost no time in proffering them.[13] Four days after the dissolution of Parliament an aid to the deliberations of the Council of Officers was tendered by "a People who through Grace have been hitherto kept from the Great Apostacie of this day . . . a willing People, and their number not a few, who will stand by them with their lives and Estates, for that Good old Cause"; the good old cause being a free Parliament, godly magistrates, liberty of conscience, and abolition of tithes.[14] Feake made public a timely account of the rise of the Fifth Monarchy party, giving

[12] Ludlow, II, 63 ff.; *Clarke Papers,* III, 189 ff.; *Cambridge Modern History,* IV, 450 ff.

[13] The Baptists were represented on the Council of officers by Cooper, Sankey, Lilburne, Packer, and Okey.

[14] *A true Copie of a Paper delivered to Lt. G. Fleetwood . . . the 26 day of the second Moneth, called April, 1659* (Thomason). The authors consider the dissolution of the late Parliament providential, speak admiringly of the Little Parliament, and advise the army to regain the point reached in 1650, when King Jesus was owned.

his interpretation of the " Best Cause under Heaven ", and representing the Fifth Monarchy men as a peculiar people, " waiting for the word of command from their Leader, to execute the vengeance written against Babylon, for being drunk with the bloud of the Saints, and with the bloud of the martyrs of Jesus ".[15] One set of petitioners asked for the re-assembling of the godly party in the Little Parliament, and there was a good deal of talk, in the churches and at the prayer meetings of the inferior officers at St. James's, of a Sanhedrim of seventy godly men.[16] However, as a perusal of the pamphlets of the day makes perfectly clear, by far the most popular embodiment of the " good old cause " was the remnant of the Long Parliament which Cromwell had dissolved in 1653.[17] It was advice for the restoration of this body that the Council of Officers, not at all inclined to any further experiments at government by the saints, thought worthy of acceptation.

It is easy to understand why the Commonwealth party favored the restoration of the remnant of the Long Parliament, but by what mental processes had that body, whose expulsion had been greeted with rejoicing in 1653, become the darling of the sectaries' hearts in 1659? Considerable light on this question is

[15] *Beam of Light,* May 2, 1659 (Thomason).

[16] *A Faithfull Searching Home Word;* Thurloe, VII, 666; *Clarke Papers,* III, 214; IV, 21.

[17] *To his excellencie the Lord Charles Fleetwood . . . from several Thousand of faithful Friends to the Good old Cause,* April 26; *The Humble Representation of divers well-affected Persons of the City of Westminster . . . ,* April 27; *Petition of the well-affected to the Good Old Cause about Southwark,* April 30; *Twelve Plain Proposals,* April 28; *Some Reasons Humbly Proposed . . . ,* April 28; *A Declaration of the Well-affected to the Good Old Cause,* May 2; *Five Proposals,* May 3. These are all in the Thomason collection.

shed by a pamphlet published by William Allen just at this time. In it he gave an account of the meeting of officers at Windsor in the spring of 1648, when, according to Allen, Cromwell had told them that if they wished to understand why they were not prospering in their designs they must consider when it was that, as an army, they had departed from the right path, and must then return to it. They had decided that it was when they had begun negotiations with the king. After this decision, and the giving up of that policy, the Lord had blessed them in all things. Allen next proceeded to point out that the army had again forsaken the right path, and had become a hissing and a byword, but that, if it would turn back again, it would again be blessed. It must go back to the time when the Lord had prospered it, and listen to the advice of those who had never apostatized.[18] It is interesting to note that the declaration by which the officers recalled the Long Parliament remnant followed this reasoning with some exactitude. It stated that the existing state of affairs was due to backsliding and receding from righteous paths; that all efforts to better affairs had by the hand of God been rendered unavailing; and that the people had finally looked back and perceived that the Long Parliament had the right spirit, and had been blessed in its work.[19]

Thus the change of government took place under auspices which made it natural that the sectaries should be considered instrumental in the work. For the part taken by Baptists, we have the testimony of a London

[18] *A Faithful Memorial of that Remarkable Meeting of Many Officers of the Army in England, at Windsor Castle, in the Year 1648*, in Somers, *Tracts*, VII.

[19] *Declaration, id.*, VI, 504.

Baptist minister. William Allen, the General Baptist, who must not be confused with the author of the *Faithful Memorial,* writing to Richard Baxter about some negotiations for accommodation which had been going on between Baptists and Presbyterians, said: "As for the late change, I beleeve the Annabaptists have been so little concerned in the active part of it, as, if rightly understood, will amount to no just ground of scruple to others to afford them in general their comunion." [20] The whole letter in which these words occur is occupied with clearing the Baptists of charges made against them. The passage therefore is a proof of the existence of an impression that the Baptists had been instrumental in the change of government; and the purpose for which it was written makes it certain that no more conservative estimate of their position would be possible.

Whatever their active part in establishing the new order, Baptists on all hands manifested approval. The General Baptists of sixteen counties, meeting at Aylesbury, expressed unqualified approbation, and volunteered a suggestion that the government, when finally settled, take the form of a commonwealth.[21] A group

[20] Allen to Baxter, May 30, 1659, Baxter Correspondence, IV, 187. He continues, "Nor doe I think it will take those Anabap. off their prosecution of christian agreemt among differing brethren, whose hearts were inclined to it before". However, Baxter's statement of the case is that, when Independents and Baptists had come to terms with the Presbyterians on a set of propositions, "the turne set them up, and they were too high for accommodation". Baxter to W. Mewe, Aug. 6, *ibid.,* 281.

[21] *The humble Petition of the Baptized Congregations assembled at Ailsbury in the county of Bucks, from several parts of the Nation on behalf of themselves and the several congregations they are related to in Kent, Sussex, Surrey, Hampshire, Dorsetshire, Somerset, Berks, Wilts, Bucks, Hertford, Bedford, Nottingham, Devon, Lincolnshire, and Herefordshire. Commons Journals,* VII, May 26, 1659; *Post,* May 24-31, 1659.

of Particular Baptists in Kent also sent congratulations, with a hint concerning the abolition of tithes.[22] John Canne, the Fifth Monarchy Baptist, had in print three days before the assembling of Parliament *A Seasonable Word to the Parliament Men, to take with them when they go into the House,* in which he told them explicitly: " It is desired and expected by the Godly, that you will be mindful of the great reproach which hath layn these five or six yeers upon the Name of God, and the holy profession of the Gospel. It will be little comfort to many of your friends, to see the Civil Rights and Liberties of the people restored, and nothing done to the vindication of God's glory, which hath suffered so much through the Late Apostacie." He asserted that it was more important to give Jesus Christ his rights than the people their civil rights; that if they made it their work to prepare the way for him he would protect them, and that the essential principle of the " good old cause " was " No king but Jesus ". He warned them that " there are people which fear God more than men, and will not be partakers of other mens sins; these were they, who in the strength of the Lord, held forth a publike Testimony against the Apostacie, and kept alive the Good Old Cause; yea, let me tell you, you had not sate where you now do, if the Spirit of God in these men had not shaken the very foundation of the last Government ". Reminding them that one of the complaints against them before had been that they preferred unworthy men to places of trust, he enjoined

[22] *The hearty Congratulations and humble Petition of thousands of well-affected Gentlemen, Freeholders, and Inhabitants of the County of Kent, and City of Colchester* (Thomason). *Animadversion . . . with a seasonable Caution against the Petition of the Kentish Anabaptists,* June 20, 1659 (Thomason); *Commons Journals,* VII, June 4.

them henceforth to prefer only worthy ones, hinting that such men do not seek places but wait to be sought out.[23]

Two days later Samuel Moyer appeared in the House with an address which expressed the hope that the opportunity of pursuing the Lord's work would not be neglected, and that the government might be so settled "that it may not be too long trusted in any Man's hands: that it may not be perpetuated to Men: For we have found it by woful Experience, that the best of Men, be they what they will, if they have Power long in their Hands, they may too much exalt themselves ".[24]

The restored Parliament, in these early days, showed its appreciation of the importance of conciliating the sectaries, however little it might fancy their suggestions. This time Moyer and his fellows did not have to go away without any thanks for their pains. The following day the policy of employing good men was inaugurated by the appointment of Canne as official newswriter, in place of Marchamont Needham.[25] The co-operation of the saints was its reward. In his first issue Canne printed, above his own name and those of two other Baptist pastors, Jessey and Edward Harrison, an *Invitation to the Lord's people, throughout the three Nations, to provoke them to a Holy Rejoycing in the Lord and exalting his Name, for his late Salva-*

[23] *A Seasonable Word to the Parliament-Men, To take with them when they go into the House: Wherein is showed, The first part of their present Work, and what is expected from them, to satisfie their true and real Friends. Likewise a Watchword, how they prefer not again such Persons to Places of Trust who have lately Betrayed the Priviledges of Parliaments, and the Just Rights of the People, into the hand of a Single Person,* May 20, 1659 (Thomason).

[24] *Commons Journals,* VII, May 12, 1659.

[25] *Ibid.,* May 13.

tion begun, and the good hopes given of Reviving his work again in the midst of us. The recent changes were referred to as the work of an overturning Providence, which had subverted the throne of iniquity and defeated the combinations of Achitophels, thereby encouraging the saints to hope that the day of redemption was drawing nigh. A day of commemoration was suggested, and Christians advised to pray, among other things, that a spirit of wisdom and judgment be granted to those that were to rule.[26]

At first it must have seemed to the sectaries that such a spirit had been granted. On May 10, a committee was appointed to consider the cases of those who had been "imprisoned for conscience sake".[27] On June 14, a petition for the abolition of tithes was answered by the statement that Parliament would continue the system "till they can find out some other more equal and comfortable Maintenance for the Ministry and Satisfaction of the People: Which they intend with all convenient speed". But once more the question of tithes was to be the signal for the parting of the ways. That same day, the resolution to refer the matter of tithes to a grand committee resulted in a tie, and was carried only by a vote of the Speaker.[28] On the day set for the discussion, it was postponed for another week. The same day a petition from Hull, from "many, who

[26] *Publick Intelligencer,* May 9-16, 1659; *Weekly Intelligencer,* May 10-17. On July 11 Canne published, regretfully, his decision that in consideration of "the people's weakness", he will not as yet substitute the terms 1st day, 2d day, etc., for the nomenclature in use "till the Scripture Language be better understood, which in time will be the most usual Language in the world". *Publick Intelligencer,* July 4-11, 1659.

[27] *Commons Journals,* May 10.

[28] *Ibid.,* June 14.

through Grace, have been kept sensible of, and mourned for and under the late Apostacy from the Good old Cause", was read, and there being found "Things in it of several Natures", there was a division on the question of thanking the petitioners. Colonel Rich and Sir Henry Vane were tellers for the yeas, and the motion was carried by only five votes. A week later, a Quaker petition against tithes was presented, whereupon the House passed a resolution, which was ordered printed and published throughout the nation, "That this Parliament doth declare, That, for the Encouragement of a Godly, Preaching, Learned Ministry, the payment of Tythes shall continue as they are now, unless this Parliament shall find out some other more equal and comfortable Maintenance". The word *unless* had been substituted for the word *until,* by vote of the House, without a division.[29]

This was a significant *volte face,* and gave every reason for the growth of doubts in the minds of the sectaries as to the fitness of a body become so conservative on such a fundamental point, to settle the form of government. However, there was an impression that the resolution had been voted unexpectedly, when many who would have opposed it were absent.[30] It was always possible, moreover, to fall back upon the hope of the influence which could be exerted by the army, and there was a daily increasing probability that its influence would be exerted in the right direction.[31]

[29] *Ibid.,* June 21, 27.

[30] *Faithfull Searching Home Word,* 1659 (Thomason).

[31] Those who were skeptical as to both Parliament and army had the opportunity to subscribe to a scheme evolved by the ingenious Dr. Peter Chamberlen, Doctor of Physic and incidentally Baptist and Fifth Monarchy man. He proposed to set up Christ's kingdom through the instru-

For the army was assuming a character increasingly sectarian. With Richard's overthrow had come the demand that the places left vacant by the weeding out of his supporters should be filled by men who had suffered under the Protectorate. Overton, Rich, Alured, and others had made haste to present themselves at Wallingford House and profess their willingness to serve the new government, if only as private soldiers. New commissions were given them, and in the reorganization of the forces during the following summer commissions were likewise issued, or re-issued, to Okey, Packer, Saunders, Gladman, Streater, Richard Lawrence, John Mason, Spencer, Brayfield, Axtell, Allen, Vernon, Lawson, Cooper, Barrow, Wigan, Goodgroom, and Sankey—to mention only those whose names have appeared elsewhere in these pages. In the reorganized militia, too, the sectaries enrolled themselves in numbers so considerable as to attract attention. Commissions in the London militia were accepted by such well-known Baptists as William Kiffin, John Fenton, Jeremy Ives, Edward Leader, George Gospight, and John Canne.[32]

---

mentality of a parliament elected by congregations, and announced that he had £500,000 pledged for this work. *The Declaration and Proclamation of the Army of God*, June 9, 1659; *A Scourge for a Denn of Thieves*, June 26, both in Thomason.

[32] *Scout*, May 20-27, 1659; *Cal. St. P., Dom., 1658-1659*, 375, 394; *1659-1660*, 12-13; *Commons Journals*, June 8 ff. "Of late they receive in all the sublimated Saints into the army, which Pride and some others cashiered; and there is talk of an underhand list of 7,000 men upon the fifth monarchy account. It is so reported by some of that party; whether in reality or vaunt, I know not. If the former, then all those persons which flock so fast to London, under pretence of petitioning against tythes, may possibly have another errand." Barwick to Hyde, June 21, Thurloe, VII, 687. See also, Intercepted letter, July 22, *ibid.*, 704.

This warlike zeal of the sectaries in joining the militia was due to rumors of Royalist activity, and the signs of Presbyterian sympathy with that party. It naturally caused all manner of reports of Anabaptist and Fifth Monarchy plots. Many if not all of these were set on foot by those who wished to utilize popular prejudice for political purposes. One evening early in June, the mayor of London sent to Fleetwood, "to be further communicated or kept in silence as in your good wisedome shall seeme meete", a broadside brought to him by some terrified citizens, announcing that the Fifth Monarchy men were "Arm'd, Officer'd, and every way in a Readiness, upon the word given them, to surprise and suppress the Army, to Fire the City, and to Massacre all considerable People of all sorts . . . Beware, Tuesday next". Vane, it was stated, was at the head of the plot, and had told a friend that the army must be suppressed, or Parliament could not sit long; that this was to be the work of the new militia.[33] From Devonshire came a story of a whole town roused from sleep by the report of a plot of Fifth Monarchy men, Baptists, and Quakers to cut the throats of all the godly in the nation.[34] Canne countered this with the tale of a plot to murder all the Independents and Anabaptists in Gloucester. It may have been the publication of this tale, which was promptly denied by the

[33] *An Alarum to the City and Souldiery*, June 6, 1659 (Thomason); Ireton to Fleetwood, June 6, Tanner MSS., 51, fol. 74.

[34] *Scout*, June 22-July 19, 1659. It was perhaps in connection with similar rumors that Cornet Day was accused of having used seditious words during a service attended by his regiment in Westminster Abbey. The Council of State examined him, but set him at liberty. *Commons Journals*, July 28; *Cal. St. P., Dom., 1659-1660*, 47; *Particular Advice*, July 22-29.

mayor, that furnished Parliament an excuse for removing Canne from the post of intelligencer.[85]

The listing of the sectaries was seen to have been of value when the Royalist plot came to a head; and when Lambert had marched to deal with the only serious outbreak, that of Sir George Booth in Cheshire, they were very active in filling up the ranks of the three volunteer regiments which Parliament put under the command of Vane, Skippon, and White.[86]

When the danger from the Royalists was over, Parliament could turn its attention to the consideration of the form the government should take. To the flood of pamphlets which supplied it with advice on this great subject the Fifth Monarchy party, as would be expected, furnished its quota. The first to appear proposed the proclamation of Christ as head, and the erection of such a government as was contemplated by the godly party in the Little Parliament.[87] John Rogers came forward in a guise unwontedly moderate, deploring the extreme to which Feake and other rigid Fifth Monarchists went, in not recognizing the right of the people to choose their representatives. He distinguished between the two sorts of Fifth Monarchy men, and asserted that the rational ones desired a

[85] *Mercurius Politicus,* Aug. 4-11; *Commons Journals,* Aug. 13; *Publick Intelligencer,* Aug. 22. Sometime between August 13 and November 8, Canne became one of the editors of the two papers, *Occurrences from Forraign Parts,* and *Particular Advice from the Office of Intelligence.* See *Occurrences,* Nov. 8-15, 1659, for Canne's announcement.

[86] *Scout,* Aug. 5-12, 1659; *Cal. St. P Dom., 1659-1660,* 94, 156; Bordeaux to Mazarin, Aug. 11/21, 15/25, P. R. O. Transcripts; Phillips, *Continuation of Baker's Chronicle,* 424 John Wigan, the Fifth Monarchy Baptist, thought he observed a tendency to discriminate against Fifth Monarchy men. Letter, July 27, *Cal. St. P., Dom., 1659-1660,* 46.

[87] *The Fifth Monarchy, or Kingdom of Christ, in opposition to the Beast's, Asserted,* Aug. 23, 1659 (Thomason).

Christian commonwealth, with Christ at its head, where the rule of saints as saints did not exclude the rule of men as men. "Nor are we of opinion that this government under the seventh Trumpet [38] is initiated or matriculated by the personal appearance of Jesus Christ; but all we hold is, that the most holy, able, wise, pious, and (every way) qualified persons, men fearing God, hating covetousness, of the highest capacity, reason and latitude to all . . . and of the liveliest courage for the Cause and Interest of our dearest Jesus and of the whole Body, be set up over us. Not that they should be all such, or none but such (for that we cannot expect) but to do our best to find some such." [39]

Unquestionably Rogers had in his eye at least one such man, who was already doing his best to secure a righteous settlement. Since Sir Henry Vane had been his fellow-prisoner in Carisbrooke Castle, Rogers had given him his enthusiastic support.[40] Their friendship may have had something to do with the persistent connection of Vane's name with most of the rumors of Fifth Monarchy agitation during this period. Apparently Vane had been able to moderate some of Rogers's views, while his mystic idealism brought him into sympathy with some of the notions of Rogers concerning the kingdom of Christ. Passages in Vane's writings show his firm belief in a visible kingdom of Christ on earth, and his conviction that the setting up of

[38] Revelation, xi, 15, 16.

[39] *A Christian Concercitation with Mr. Prin, Mr. Baxter, Mr. Harrington, For the True Cause of the Commonwealth,* Sept. 20, 1659 (Thomason).

[40] Since his experiences in the Isle of Wight, Rogers had undergone imprisonment in the Tower from Feb. 3 to April 16, 1658. The restored Long Parliament had given him the chaplaincy of Fairfax's regiment, which he held at the time of Booth's rising.

that kingdom would be the best solution of England's difficulties.[41] The practical side of his nature, however, prevented his allowing any plans for establishing such a kingdom from interefering with practical politics as he conceived them. What he was working for was a truly republican form of government, and for furthering his ends he was astute enough to encourage the allegiance of the Fifth Monarchy men as well as of other extreme sectaries, with many of whose views he sympathized. Frequently they gave him their support for quite different motives, as was the case when they backed up his opposition to the proposed engagement against a single person: the Fifth Monarchy men because they believed it would engage them against Christ's kingship; some, at least, of the Baptists because of scruples against all oaths.[42]

Vane's name was mentioned, though apparently without reason, in connection with a Fifth Monarchy petition presented to Parliament September 17, and later published in the form of a broadside. It declared strongly against government by a single person, and expressed the belief that the recent troubles marked the preparation for the rule of Christ. The petitioners asked that Parliament employ none who had been honored by the Protector, and that tithes be abolished and liberty of conscience allowed.[43] With a policy that

[41] *The Retired Man's Meditations*; citations in Hosmer's *Life of Vane*.

[42] Rogers, *Fifth Monarchy Man*, 310; Ormond, Advices, Sept. 12, 1659, Carte MSS., 213, fol. 301; Bordeaux to Mazarin, Sept. 19/29, P. R. O. Transcripts; same to same, n. d., *ibid.*, fol. 67 b. After the Restoration, Henry Denne and Jeremiah Ives took part in the discussions on the lawfulness of oath-taking by Christians. See *Catalogue of Thomason Tracts*.

[43] *An Essay toward Settlement upon a sure foundation*, Sept. 19, 1659 (Thomason).

savored, as a critic suggested, rather "of the Serpentine subtilty and guile then of the simplicity and innocency of the Dove", the petitioners put at the head of the list of signatories the name of John Owen; it was not, however, Dr. John Owen, the well-known Independent, but an obscure individual of the same name.[44] The other names were, with a few exceptions, those of well-known Fifth Monarchy men, Baptists, and Levellers.

It was not alone the sectaries who plied Parliament with suggestions. Besides the schemes of Milton, Prynne, Baxter, and other amateur constitution-makers of various persuasions, there were the productions of Harrington and his Rota, and, more formidable because of the power behind them, there were the various army schemes.[45] The unwillingness of Parliament to proceed with the settlement, in accordance with any of these ideas, or even along lines of its own, caused general dissatisfaction, but again it was army discontent which overthrew the government.[46] The series of events which began with the Derbyshire petition and ended with the blockading of the Parliament House by Lambert, and the establishment of a committee of safety, was the work of the army faction alone. The men who had brought back the Rump, as it began to be derisively called, had driven it out again, and the destiny of the nation was again in the hands of its soldiery.

[44] Johnson, *Examination of the Essay*, 1659 (Bodleian). The names signed were as follows: John Owen, Henry Jessey, Vavasor Powell, John Vernon, Hugh Courtney, William Allen, Philip Pyncheon, John Portman, Clement Ireton, Robert Rumsey, P. Goodicke, R. Price, James Hitt, John Wigan, H. Danvers, Richard Goodgroom, Henry Parsons, Robert Overton, Richard Saltonstall, Wentworth Day.

[45] See Masson, *Milton*, V, 480 ff., 605 ff.

[46] A sop was thrown to the sectaries on October 8 by the appointment of Praise-God Barbone to be comptroller for sequestrations. *Commons Journals*, VII, 794.

How far was the change due to, or favored by, the sectaries? Men spoke of the officers who had done the work as "anabaptists and millenaries, or saints", and represented Lambert as supported by Vane and the "desperate sectaries".[47] The sectaries, however, were not at one in the matter. Those who held republican or Levelling views were true to the principles of parliamentary government, and refused to support their comrades against the Rump. Overton would not countenance the officers' petition, and Okey, Alured, Saunders, and Streater were among the officers who addressed to Fleetwood a letter of remonstrance, begging him as a professor of religion to restore the Long Parliament.[48] Praise-God Barbone, too, headed a faction in the City which never wavered in its support of Parliament.[49]

On the other hand, the revolution had been carried through under the authority, nominally at least, of Fleetwood, though he was probably then, as always, merely the tool of abler men. On the new committee of safety, which declared for the abolition of tithes and asked for the prayers of the godly, the leading spirit was Vane. These two men of approved godliness must have kept a respectable following of sectaries, while the confidence of moderate Baptists was unquestionably given to three Baptist members of the committee, Henry

[47] Mordaunt to Charles II, Oct. 11, *Carte Papers*, II, 223 ff.; Bordeaux to Mazarin, Oct. 20/30, P. R. O. Transcripts.

[48] Thurloe, VII, 771 ff.

[49] See below, p. 196. Kiffin, however, with Packer and Spencer, believed Parliament was for Sir George Booth's party, and against liberty of conscience. E. D., *A True relation of the Case Between the ever Honourable Parliament and the Officers of the Army*, Oct. 16, and *The Declaration of the Officers . . . Examined and Condemned*, Nov. 25 (Thomason).

Lawrence, Robert Bennet, and William Steele.[50] We should expect to find the sectaries in the army supporting the military revolution, in general, and an indication that this was the case is supplied by incidents in connection with Monck's position. It had been Monck's assurance that he would support Parliament which emboldened that body to take a firm stand with the officers, and to cashier Lambert and the other eight officers, thus bringing about Lambert's *coup d'état* and its own downfall. When, after hearing of these events, Monck reiterated his decision to stand by Parliament, the men whom he put into prison for murmuring at his announcement were spoken of as "most of the Anabaptist officers". It was a well-known Baptist, Richard Deane, sent by Fleetwood with letters to Monck, whom the latter sent back to England on suspicion of having carried on intrigues among his soldiers; and the twenty-four privates and six corporals whom he later discharged for their disaffection were all or most of them members of the same Baptist church.[51] The imprisoned officers were in correspondence with members of the London militia, and at a meeting of the commissioners of that body Kiffin, Moyer, Fenton, Jessey, and others secured the passage, by a close vote, of a resolution to send a letter to Monck

[50] There was a report that the subaltern officers were dissatisfied with the committee, and wished to reject six of the nominees, substituting for them Harrison and five other extreme sectaries. There was especial objection to Lambert, on the ground that he was not religious. Bordeaux to Mazarin, Oct. 27/Nov. 6, 1659, P. R. O. Transcripts.

[51] *Post,* Nov. 1-8, 1659; *Weekly Intelligencer,* same date; *Faithful Intelligencer,* Nov. 29-Dec. 3; Monck to Fleetwood, Nov. 7, *Clarke Papers,* IV, 105, and note 1. Robson to Monck, Nov. 29, *ibid.*, 160. Timothy Wilkes, one of Monck's commissioners, was a member of Feake's church. He was suspected of having betrayed Monck's interests to the army party. Berners to Hobart, Nov. 29, *ibid.*, 299.

expressing a dislike of his proceedings, telling him that he could not depend on the support of the militia, and asking him to release the officers he had imprisoned. At a subsequent meeting, this vote was reversed, and an attempt was made to keep the matter a secret, but the letter got into print, and naturally enough, in view of the names of the promoters, the whole project was considered a Baptist one.[52]

On the whole, the conservative estimate of the Baptist position may again be supposed to be the one given by William Allen the minister, who wrote: "However the so-called sectarian party, having their eye so much upon the Army, as their only visible security, are thereby under a great temptation to make the best of a bad matter and to cast in their lot at a venture with the Army, yet some there are of them that are so farr dissattisfied . . . with the late proceedings of the Army, as that they dare not doe any thing that lookes like an espousing of their quarrill against those whose authority over them, they had so lately acknowledged as supreame."[53] The man in the street, however, made no

[52] —— to Clarke, Nov. 3, 1659, *Clarke Papers,* IV, 91; Newsletter, Nov. 5, *ibid.,* 101; *Scout,* Nov. 4-11.

[53] Allen to Baxter, Nov. 8, 1659, Baxter letters, IV, fol. 274. See also same to same, Dec. 30, *id.,* I, 189, where he speaks of having remonstrated with Fleetwood himself. A publication by another Baptist pastor expressed the sentiment that the Parliament had only been recalled to meet a temporary exigency; that "most of the eminent good things they did were by force squeezed from them", and that some other body, chosen for the present situation, would be as lawful an authority as it, and more likely to answer the desires of all good people. *Eighteen Questions Propounded, to Put the great Question between the Army and their dissenting Brethren, out of Question, (Viz.) Whether the best way to secure the Government of these Nations, in the way of a Free-State, without a Single Person, King, or House of Lords; Together with our Liberties, as Men and Christians, Be either to Chuse a New and Free Parliament, or else to Restore the last Long Parliament. Published by Jer. Ives,* Nov. 21, 1659.

such distinctions, but classed the sectaries, and especially the Baptists, as supporting the army in a body. "Whether ever any Commonwealth will trust the Baptized Churches again", ran a query, "seeing they have dealt thus perfideously with the Honourable Parliament, who (as the Fathers of the Nation) were pleased to put part of the Militia into their hands, for the security of the Priviledges of Parliament, and Freedoms of all men, against Domestic and Forraign Enemies: yet they have malitiously and shamefully betrayed their Trust, in opposing the Parliament, from whom they had their Commissions; and have sided with those Traytors which interrupted the Parliament in October 13, 59, which will be as a Brand upon the Churchmen for ever, except they come in, and now appear with General Monck, and the rest of the true English men, for the re-establishing the Parliament."[54]

Besides such reflections upon the Baptists there were reports, spread by Royalists and people obsessed by thoughts of Münster and John of Leyden, that the Anabaptists were planning an appeal to arms.[55] Reflections thus cast upon them as a denomination some Baptists felt needed a specific denial. A declaration signed by the leading Particular Baptists of London, and by some General Baptists, was issued December 12. It stated that, while they could not pretend to justify all the actions of every individual member of their denomination, any more than Independents or Presbyterians could, the practice of Baptists was "to be obedient to Magistracy in all things Civil, and willing to live peace-

[54] *The Northern Queries from the Lord General Monck, his Quarters,* Nov. 7, 1659 (Thomason).

[55] Bordeaux to Mazarin, Dec. 12/22, 15/25, P. R. O. Transcripts.

ably, under whatever Government is, and shall be established in this Nation". They denied the reports that they entertained designs against those who held different religious views, or that they desired to tolerate civil or ecclesiastical miscarriages under pretence of liberty of conscience, or that they had intentions against the peace of the city, and expressed the hope that any pretending to be Baptists who caused breaches of the peace would be duly punished.[56]

Those Baptists who were Commonwealth men, if they concurred in this declaration, must have made the mental reservation that the committee in charge of affairs was not an established government, and indeed the events of the following fortnight justified them in such an opinion. Lawson, Overton, Rich, Okey, Alured, Eyre, Streater, and Saunders distinguished themselves as champions of the interrupted Rump, and received marks of that body's gratitude when the military government was proved a failure, and the officers were forced to reseat the twice-expelled remnant at Westminster. Thanks to them, the sectaries might have laid claim to the distinction of having had a part in the setting-up of every form of government tried in England throughout the whole period.

But there the end came. With the second restoration of the Long Parliament coincided the disappearance of the sectaries as a political force. The behavior of the restored Rump was, naturally, triumphant. The sec-

[56] *A Declaration of several of the People called Anabaptists, in and about the City of London.* December 12, 1659 (Guildhall library). Two protests were made against this declaration by Baptist bodies, but one was entirely on the grounds of its limiting toleration to Protestant Christians, the other opposed taking any part in affairs of government, beyond verbal testimony. See above, p. 8.

taries who had not been active on its behalf were weeded out in that prompt reorganization of the army wherein, it was said, scarce one officer in ten retained his command.[57] This, with the skilful manipulation of the forces by Monck somewhat later, took away from the sectaries any possibility of power to do overturning work in the future.

One group, however, raised its voice to the last. On the day following the tumults in the city, by which Londoners signified their desire that Parliament fill up the vacancies in its ranks, Praise-God Barbone appeared in the House to clear himself and his followers from the blame of any participation in the outbreak, and to present a petition. He said in making the presentation that the petitioners were such as had always adhered to the Parliament, and were ready to defend it against all attacks. The petition was a request that all clergymen and officials should be obliged to take an oath against Charles Stuart. The petitioners were thanked for " this their love and care of the Commonwealth ", but that evening the apprentices showed their opinion of such love and care by breaking all the windows in Barbone's house in the Strand.[58]

This petition played directly into the hands of the Royalists. Straightway appeared a host of burlesque

[57] Firth, in *Cambridge Modern History,* IV, 548. A pamphlet rejoicing over the return of the Rump said, " The Anabaptist was thicker in office than any other persuasion, but immediately before this turn, yet could hee not keep it, nor stem the tyde, when the turn came ". *A Coffin for the Good Old Cause,* Feb. 2, 1659/60 (Thomason).

[58] Rugge, *Diurnall*; *Commons Journals,* Feb. 9, 1660; Text of the petition in *The Picture of the Good Old Cause drawn to the Life,* July 14, 1660. *Cf. That Wicked and Blasphemous Petition of Praise God Barebone*; *The Illegal and Immodest Petition of Praise-God Barebone.* All in Thomason tracts.

petitions and mock manifestoes, which held the Baptists up to ridicule, generally representing them as mad fellows, sometimes suggesting that their madness might be dangerous.[59]

As usual there was no difficulty in stirring up a panic. William Kiffin and three other Baptists were one day arrested and their houses searched for arms. They were released after three days, but report had it that the Anabaptists had been preparing to rise and cut the throats of all who were not of their judgment, and that enough arms for a thousand men had been found. All this was in spite of the fact that the newspapers stated that the arrest had been a mistake, and gave a list of the arms found, which consisted of two drums, one partizan, five old pikes, and six swords. A fortnight later the General Baptists felt it necessary to deny the persistent rumors that a supply of arms had been found; that the Baptists had gathered " knives, hooked knives, and the like ", for the purpose of murdering all who held other views on religious matters than their own.[60] The panic was by no means confined to London, and did not die out until the reorganization of the militia had taken arms away from the sectaries.[61]

[59] *The Humble Petition and Recantation of many dissatisfied Persons commonly known by the name of Anabaptists* (Brit. Mus.); *Life and Approaching Death of William Kiffin,* March 13; *Phanaticke Intelligencer,* March 24; *Phanatique League and Covenant,* March 24; *An Humble Petition on the behalf of many Thousands of Quakers, Fifth Monarchy men, Anabaptists, etc.,* Feb. 14 (Thomason). One bore such an appearance of genuineness that the Baptists thought it necessary to have it denounced as a libel: *A Serious Manifesto and Declaration of the Anabaptist and other Congregational Churches,* Feb. 28, 1659/60 (Thomason); *Mercurius Politicus,* Feb. 23-Mar. 1.

[60] *Ibid.*; Rugge, *Diurnall*; *Letter sent to . . . the Lord Mayor* (Thomason); *Confessions of Faith* (Hanserd Knollys Soc.), 119.

[61] *Letter from Shrewsbury,* March 1, 1659/60 (Thomason); Phillips, *Continuation,* 435, 438.

Although it was the Baptists who were regarded as the most dangerous sectaries during these last days of the Commonwealth, the Fifth Monarchy men were not entirely inactive. As early as the preceding November one of them had pointed out that the logical outcome of the assembling of a Parliament would be the restoration of the Stuarts.[62] Another a few days later had presented to the army committee *A Claim for Christ and his Laws, which is apprehended to be the Good Old Cause, by several well-wishers thereunto.* This suggested that Christ be proclaimed king and lawgiver, that no laws not in accordance with the Scriptures be enacted, and that only men of a right spirit be chosen to take part in the government.[63] William Allen had once more attempted to arouse the old spirit in the army, but by that time Monck had taken care that such appeals could arouse no effectual response.[64]

After the secluded members had been admitted, and the House had become a Presbyterian body, it could of course no longer claim the support of any body of sectaries, and doubtless many of them joined in the risings of groups of citizens and soldiers in different parts of the country, which were so easily put down by Monck's remodelled army.[65] While the elections for the Convention Parliament were going on, attempts were made to make it appear that there was a concerted movement under way. Among the state papers are some inter-

[62] *A Reply to Mr. William Prinne,* Nov. 26, 1659 (Thomason).

[63] Printed by Canne in *Occurrences from Forraign Parts,* Nov. 27-Dec. 7, 1659. See also *A Faithfull Searching Home Word,* Dec. 13 (Thomason).

[64] *Word to the Army,* 1660 (Brit. Mus.).

[65] Williamson to Cheverel, March 2, Ormonde MSS. (Hist. MSS. Comm., *Report,* 1902, 334); Barwick to Hyde, March 6, 14, Thurloe, VII, 854, 861.

cepted letters, very evidently forgeries, which purported to reveal a plot of incredible dimensions, headed by Desborough, and carried on by the best-known of the Levellers, Baptists, Commonwealth men, and Fifth Monarchists.[66] Warrants were issued for the arrest of Courtney, Allen, and Vernon, either in this connection or in the belief that they were planning to assist Lambert; and Praise-God Barbone, summoned before the Council of State, pledged that he would take no action against the government.[67] There were reports of fanatic activity in Yarmouth, Cardiff, and Lyme Regis, and when on April 9 Lambert escaped from the Tower and led an abortive rising in Northamptonshire, a number of sectaries flocked to his standard. The greater number stayed quietly at home, however, and apparently did not even busy themselves with the committal of their grievances to paper; although the scarcity of pamphlet literature of that description can be ascribed partly to the activity of the government in prosecuting publishers. The redoubtable Livewell Chapman was at the time a fugitive from justice on that account.[68]

This quietness of the sectaries, their "stupid consternation", was very noteworthy. The explanation given by a Royalist was that "God had disarmed their spirits of that violence that had so long possessed them, even to their personating a concurrent Contentment in this strange mutation of affairs".[69]

Whether their silence was merely that of despair, or whether they, like the great majority of Englishmen,

[66] *Cal. St. P., Dom., 1660,* 407, 409 ff.; *Parliamentary Intelligencer,* April 2-9, 1660.

[67] Phillips, *Continuation,* 440; Rugge, *Diurnall.*

[68] *Parliamentary Intelligencer,* March 26-April 2, April 2-9, 16-23, 1660; *Mercurius Politicus,* April 19-26.

[69] Phillips, *Continuation,* 441.

tired of the confusion of the past months, and of rapidly succeeding changes of government, saw in the return of monarchy the possibility of a return to peace and stability, to uninterrupted trade and reasonable prosperity, the Baptists no longer interfered in public affairs, hoping perhaps that, if they lived peaceably, a grateful monarch would not deny them liberty of conscience. The Fifth Monarchy men had not, indeed, given up the struggle, as Venner's plot the following year was to show. But for the time being they were quiescent, comforting themselves, it may be, with the thought that He who in the last few months had overturned so many governments which had failed to heed the warnings of the saints, would never allow the crown of England to remain long upon the head of Charles Stuart.

Such were the activities of Baptists and Fifth Monarchy men from Little Parliament to Convention Parliament. How far were they important in their effect upon the history of England?

The Little Parliament failed when it did because the moderate men who made up the majority of its members were unable to carry with them the small body of religious enthusiasts who were striving to remould the government on Scriptural lines. These men knew not compromise, and their preachers throughout the Parliament's life kept before them the ideals for which they were striving, and held up to execration any signs of departure from those ideals. To ultimate failure the Little Parliament was foredoomed; but if the two factions had been able to pull together for a few months longer, Cromwell would not have been driven to the adoption of a hastily-formed constitution, based on military power and abounding in imperfections; and the Protectorate, with a more workable Instrument of Government, would have had better chances of success. Cromwell himself declared that it was the Fifth Monarchy men who had directed the policy of the radicals, and by their extravagance rendered the success of the experiment impossible.[70] And, although investigation shows that the Fifth Monarchy men were unable to bring the other radicals to the adoption of the more extreme features of their policy, we have seen that it was the refusal of the whole radical wing to compromise on the subject of tithes, a matter on which Baptists and Fifth Monarchy men agreed, which brought to an end the Little Assembly.

When the Protectorate was established, the violent opposition of the Fifth Monarchy preachers was one of the reasons which led Cromwell to issue the ordinance on treason, and the existence of that ordinance, in its turn, forced him, unless he was willing to see men put to death for proclaiming their honest convictions, to keep men in prison without trial. This refusal of a legal trial was one of the strongest arguments that came to be used against the Cromwellian régime. If Cromwell had been willing to use harsh measures with hostile preachers and pamphleteers, he might have been able to stem the swelling tide of opposition, but his very leniency became a weapon against him, and their continual agitations, both in and out of prison, kept constantly before the people the real as well as the fancied defects of the Protectorate, and prevented it from gaining a hold upon their affections. The Levellers and the

[70] April 21, 1657. Stainer, *Speeches,* 329.

Commonwealth men were working to the same end, and not without effect, but in that age it was the appeal made upon religious grounds which could count upon the most enthusiastic response.

The unrestrained language of the Fifth Monarchy writers and preachers, their bitter attacks upon him from the pulpit and from the press, were not merely a continual source of sorrow and embarrassment to Cromwell; their extravagances of idea and of language destroyed his belief in the priesthood of believers, and strengthened his growing conviction that an organized church and a regulated ministry were necessary for the peace of the state. This it was that brought upon him the opposition of the Baptists.

That opposition, however, was slow in growing. We have seen that the Baptist churches, as organizations, took little public action against the Protectorate. In 1654 the General Baptists of all England formally recognized the Protectorate; in the same year the leading Particular Baptists of London expressed their approval of the government, and the churches of Baptist soldiers in Scotland sent Cromwell a loyal address. Expressions of satisfaction with his government came from various churches after the dissolution of the first Protectorate Parliament, and in 1656 the General Baptists again counselled submission to the government, and some of the Welsh churches expressed approval of its righteousness. Throughout this time individual Baptists like Canne, Simpson, Powell, Hobson, Vernon, and Allen could be cited as disturbers of the peace, but on the other hand, Kiffin, Richardson, Steele, Henry Lawrence, John Spilsbury, and Thomas Cooper made equally strenuous, if less conspicuous efforts to serve the government and to maintain the peace. As far as the Baptists, as Baptists, had a political program it was based upon advocacy of the principles of liberty of conscience and voluntaryism in religion, and they showed a willingness to accede to any form of government which gave promise of maintaining those principles. But when the defects of the Instrument of Government, and the prevailing discontent, gave rise to the attempt to remedy the situation by re-establishing the monarchy, the Baptists, who saw in that form of government the absolute denial of their most cherished principles, went into opposition. That opposition, voiced as it was by fighting Baptists as well as by praying ones, played a not unimportant part in the refusal of the crown. When it developed that the failure of the kingship did not mean the triumph of religious liberty, the Baptists as well as the Fifth Monarchy men were bound to be true to their principles, and it was at this point that the efforts of the latter to have their program officially adopted by the former showed signs of a possible success.

From the beginning the Baptist churches had been a great recruiting ground for the Fifth Monarchy men, unsuccessful as these were in gaining their official support. The majority of the churches represented in the Fifth Monarchy manifesto in the fall of 1654 were Baptist, the work of Powell in Wales was chiefly among Baptist churches, the whole Welsh movement being generally considered a Baptist one, and the Norfolk agitation of 1656 was for the most part Baptist. The proportion of Baptists among the Fifth Monarchy men cannot be estimated exactly, but the indications show that the number was steadily increasing throughout the days of the Protectorate. It is easy to see how to Cromwell and his supporters the fact that behind the fanatics in the pulpits, and likely to be swayed by their arguments, lay this great silent body in the army and in civil life, would seem not the least of the perils that menaced the government. The opposition of a class of men whose sincerity he respected added its weight to the burden of Cromwell during the closing days of his life, and well-nigh drove him to abandon that advocacy of religious tolerance which distinguished him above all the men of that age.

After Cromwell's death, Baptists and Fifth Monarchy men took part in all the changes of government which were bringing England nearer and nearer to the return of that absolutism which was more than all else abhorrent to them, and they thus contributed no little toward bringing about what was to them the final catastrophe. Unable to realize that the Protectorate was their only bulwark against the return of the Stuarts, they worked for its overthrow, and then persuaded themselves that the restoration of the mutilated Long Parliament was the next step toward the establishment of a satisfactory Commonwealth. The conservatism of the religious policy adopted by that body, once reseated, convinced many of them, probably the majority, that its recall had been a mistake, and the activities of their divided forces furnished substantial assistance to the Royalists, by giving them an opportunity to utilize the popular prejudice against Anabaptists, and thus divert attention from their own projects.

Yet the division of the sectarian forces indicated merely a difference of opinion as to the best means to be employed, none at all as to the ultimate end to be gained. It is a noteworthy fact that throughout the whole period the Fifth Monarchy men and the radical Baptists had pointed out, in their pamphlets and in their sermons, that once, and once only, had England placed its destinies in the hands of men who might have established a righteous government—the " faithful remnant " of the Little Assembly. The only explanation they could find for the failure of that experiment was that England was not ready for it—that its people were not yet sufficiently enlightened. The counsels of the Fifth Monarchy men were counsels of perfection, and they proffered them to an imperfect world. Mr. Gardiner has pointed out that the nominated Parliament touched the high-water mark of Puritanism; that with the establishment of the Protectorate the ebb had set in. Therein lies the importance of the men we have been studying. As the Anabaptists of Germany carried the principles of the Reformation to their logical conclusion, so these Englishmen of the seventeenth century carried to their logical conclusion the principles of Puritanism. Refusing to barter with evil, refusing to compromise or to give ground, they stood for the ideal of a perfect state, and in the struggle to realize that ideal they succeeded only in contributing to the failure of the compromise represented by the Protectorate, and in aiding the re-establishment of the absolutism of the Stuarts.

BIBLIOGRAPHICAL NOTES.

THE most valuable body of material for this study has been the *Thurloe Papers,* of which the originals are in the Bodleian Library. Comprising, as they do, letters and papers from all sources, representing, and—since they were not intended for the public eye—frankly expressing all shades of opinion, they shed a flood of light upon what the members of the two parties thought, and upon what others thought of them. Because of the suspicion with which Baptists and Fifth Monarchy men were regarded, an especially close watch was kept upon their correspondence, and a large number of their letters are to be found here, as well as numerous reports, from outsiders, of their assemblies and activities. Some of the most illuminating of these are among the papers not published by Birch when he edited the *Thurloe Papers.* A few have been published since, notably two in the preface to volume II of Professor Firth's edition of the *Clarke Papers.* Supplementing these are the papers of a similar nature, collected by Birch and probably originally in the same collection, which are now among the Additional MSS. in the British Museum.

The four volumes of the *Clarke Papers,* edited by Professor Firth for the Camden Society, and the volume from the same collection issued under the title of *Scotland and the Protectorate,* shed much light on the activities of Baptists and Fifth Monarchy men in the army, and furnish such news regarding their parties as it was judged wise to put into newsletters for military perusal. Some useful letters are to be found among the Carte, Tanner, and Clarendon MSS., and among the *Nicholas Papers*. Yet, since the Royalists seldom took the trouble to distinguish between the various kinds of Independency, these letters are of much less value for the present purpose. Similarly the French ambassador Bordeaux, though extremely well-informed as to events, was apt to make a most comprehensive application of the term Anabaptist. The letters of Thurloe to Pell, of which the most important were published by Vaughan, are much more exact in this respect. The correspondence of Henry Cromwell, which was probably preserved by his private secretary, Petty, and through him passed into the hands of the Shelbourne family, from whom the British Museum purchased it, is absolutely invaluable for the situation in Ireland, although unfortunately the letters for the most part represent only the side hostile to the Baptists. The letters of John Jones give some glimpse of the other side of the picture. The Baxter correspondence in the Dr. Williams Library sheds light on the attitude of the more liberal Presbyterians, and on their efforts at accommodation with the Baptists, Men of all sorts and conditions wrote to Baxter, and on every possible subject. The letters of William Allen, the Baptist minister and merchant, which are in this collection, make frequent references to the political situation. His point of view was that of the Baptist verging toward Presbyterianism. The Swarthmore Letters, among the manuscript collections of the Society of Friends in Devonshire House, show the Baptists as they appeared to the Quakers, and for this point of view the *Journal* of Fox is useful. Cromwell's letters are of course indispensable, though few deal directly with the Baptist problem. The speeches, too, are most important, especially in exhibiting his change of opinion regarding the Fifth Monarchy.

The papers edited by John Nickolls from among Milton's State Papers include some letters, but are chiefly important for the addresses from Baptist churches, showing the positions definitely adopted by congregations at different times. In this connection should be mentioned the collections of addresses, confessions of faith, and similar documents brought conveniently together by the Hanserd Knollys Society, though all of them are available elsewhere. Useful also have been the volumes of documents issued by the Baptist Historical Society under the editorship of Dr. Whitley. Grey, in his *Examination of Neale's Puritans,* and Peck, in his *Desiderata Curiosa,* print some useful documents. From the *Reports* of the Historical Manuscripts Commission have been gleaned scattered references from widely differing collections, and for matters of fact the *Calendars of State Papers* and the *Journals of the House of Commons* are a mine of information.

The records of individual churches are extremely useful for tracing the spirit and interests of the Baptists, but with very few exceptions they contain no references to political affairs. The incompleteness of the records, and the prudence of omitting anything that might later get the church into trouble, weigh against the argument that since the records are silent the churches did not discuss these affairs. For instance, the manuscript records of the Baptist church that met in Lothbury, which are for the most part in the handwriting of Dr. Peter Chamberlen, give only two half-pages of notes bearing on political affairs, and these refer to a single discussion; yet we know that this church took a definite stand in the Fifth Monarchy interest. The records in Somerset House throw light on the affiliations of individuals, and sometimes contain slight bits of information on other matters, but for the most part consist merely of statistics.

The great collection of pamphlets, broadsides, and newspapers in the British Museum, known as the Thomason Tracts, is singularly rich in material for our subject. We find there what the men we are studying chose to tell the world of themselves and their opinions, and what their opponents and apologists chose to publish about them. The principal Fifth Monarchy men who published over their own signatures were, for the early years, William Aspinwall and John Spittlehouse; throughout the period, John Rogers, and the Baptists John Canne and Christopher Feake. Of the moderate Baptists, Samuel Richardson wrote in defense of the government, Jeremiah Ives championed parliamentary government, Thomas Collier and Henry Denne religious toleration, while John Tombes confined himself to doctrinal matters. The Fifth Monarchy Baptist, William Allen, was well enough known as a critic of the government to have his name borrowed for the famous pamphlet, *Killing No Murder*. Thomason's aim was to preserve a copy of every pamphlet and newspaper that came from the press, and he added to the value of his collection by marking on each the date on which it came into his hands, which was, whenever possible, the date of publication. In the majority of cases where

Thomason's dates can be compared with the dates of publication, they have been proved correct; it has accordingly been thought advisable to give them in all cases where the exact date might be of value. The appearance of the excellent catalogue of the collection, edited by Mr. Fortescue, has made it no longer imperative to give the press numbers of these tracts; they are, however, included in the bibliography, though not in the foot-notes. The names of publishers are usually given when they appear, as they frequently supply a clue to the nature of the tract. Henry Hills, a prominent Baptist, usually brought out Baptist productions, and Francis Smith, a General Baptist, during the latter part of the period published General Baptist literature. John Streater's prosperous business was also begun in the latter days of our period, but he published republican rather than Baptist works. As might be expected, the collection is far richer in Fifth Monarchy than in Baptist productions, and these were usually brought out by one or other of the ultra-republican printers, Livewell Chapman and Giles Calvert; less frequently by Thomas Brewster, who was a great purveyor of Quaker literature. Hills and Field were the official printers of the Protectorate, and the works printed with the names of both men are usually of an official character. In the same way the newspapers reflected the prejudices of their editors. The *Scout* and *Post,* edited as they were by a Baptist, looked with a very favorable eye upon the sectaries, and the *Perfect Diurnall* was also of a liberal tone. *Mercurius Politicus* and the *Publick Intelligencer* were government organs, and anti-sectarian to a degree: from October, 1655, till the last days of the Protectorate they were the only newspapers in existence, and consequently the only newspaper references to Fifth Monarchy men and Baptists during that time are such as served the government's purpose. From the middle of May till the middle of August, 1659, however, these papers were edited by a Fifth Monarchy Baptist, who later had a hand in the two papers, *Particular Advice* and *Perfect Occurrences.* Rugge's *Diurnall* supplements the newspapers for the period immediately preceding the Restoration, but adds little of value for us. Much useful information regarding the newspapers is contained in Williams's *History of English Journalism,* but its value is seriously impaired by the ultra-royalist prejudices of its author.

From the contemporary historians and memoir writers little can be gleaned concerning our sectaries. The republican Ludlow, though he had many friends among the Baptists, had little interest in them as a political factor. Though Mrs. Hutchinson and her husband were both Baptists, she is singularly dumb regarding her co-religionists, except for two slighting references. Clarendon has the Royalist aloofness, and when he does mention Anabaptists confounds them with Levellers and Quakers. Phillips, Bate, and Heath trouble very little about them. The theological writers of the period persisted in imputing to their fellow-countrymen the practices attributed by Bullinger and other Continental historians to Anabaptists, and after reading Edwards' *Gangraena,* Blome's *Fanatick History,* the *Relation of several Heresies,* or the *Short History of the Anabaptists of High and Low Germany,* one does not wonder that it took little to make the average Englishman wake at night with the fear of an Anabaptist knife at his throat.

The first place among the secondary authorities belongs, of course, to Samuel Rawson Gardiner, the exhaustiveness of whose researches in all fields makes the work of the gleaner a somewhat thankless one. The continuation of the work left incomplete by his death, down to the last days of Oliver's Protectorate, has been done by the man who, next to Gardiner, was best fitted for the task. It is true that the interest of Professor Firth is rather in political and military than in religious history, but his apparently unlimited knowledge of all the parties and personages of the times renders his work of inestimable value. Masson's *Life of Milton* has charm of style in addition to its many other admirable qualities, and Godwin's work is still useful on account of his intimate acquaintance with the pamphlet literature. The work of Ranke is misleading on our special subject unless it is constantly borne in mind that he uses the term Anabaptist to cover all advanced phases of Independency; and Guizot's knowledge of the sectaries was vague.

Among special studies, Rogers's *Some Account of the Life and Opinions of a Fifth Monarchy Man* is careful and accurate on the whole; Glass's monograph on the Barbone Parliament is fruitful of information, though irritating because of insufficiently specific references. Simpkinson's *Thomas Harrison* is notable for this fault, and is every way inferior to the briefer biography by Professor Firth.

Of the church histories, Dr. Shaw's is practically the only one unmarred by theological bias, and unfortunately he leaves the sectaries severely alone. For one who has the courage to struggle through the bewildering medley of document and comment for which Hanbury is responsible, there is some reward. The work of Neale is painstaking to a degree, as is that of Stoughton.

Among purely Baptist histories, the monumental work of Crosby is still without a rival. It is based on the study of manuscript material, much of which is no longer available, and the author makes an heroic effort after impartiality, but without conspicuous success. Ivimey leans heavily on Crosby, and Evans on both, but neither seems to have emulated his attempt to be fair. Ivimey quotes freely from the *Thurloe Papers,* but shows no hesitation in picking out a favorable sentence from a mass of hostile context, in triumphant vindication of the party therein attacked. As a corrective, we have Lewis's steady refusal to see anything good in Anabaptism or Anabaptists. The copy of his work in the Bodleian, interleaved with additions for a later edition, and the accompanying collections, contain information, but it must be used with caution. Wilson, in his *Dissenting Churches,* seems to have been content to found his statements on Crosby. Little can be said for the later Baptist historians, though there is an occasional exception, such as Culross, who in his *Hanserd Knollys* endeavors to use all the sources. The recent studies of the churches in various localities, too, usually represent painstaking research. Barclay's *Inner Life,* from the Friends' standpoint, represents much research, but abounds in inaccuracies. Weingarten's admirable work is a model, and worthy of all emulation for impartiality, accuracy, and erudition. The pages devoted to our subject by Gooch are extremely well done, and his whole study is most suggestive for our purpose.

BIBLIOGRAPHY.

I. SOURCES.

A. Manuscript.

1. collections.

Baxter, Richard, Correspondence, 6 vols., Dr. Williams Library, Gordon Square, London.

Birch Collection (Additional MSS., 4101-4478), British Museum.

Bordeaux Letters (transcripts), Public Record Office, London (cited as P. R. O. Transcripts); Harleian MSS., 4546-4549, British Museum.

Carte MSS., Bodleian Library.

Clarke MSS., 27, 50, Worcester College Library, Oxford.

Cromwell, Henry, Correspondence (Lansdowne MSS., 821-823), British Museum.

Pell Papers (Lansdowne MSS., 745-755), British Museum.

Swarthmore Letters, Friends' Library, Devonshire Square, London.

Tanner MSS., Bodleian Library.

Thurloe Papers (Rawlinson MSS., A 1-73), Bodleian Library.

2. single works.

Book of the Acts and other Businesses of the Church [in Lothbury], (Rawlinson MSS., D 828), Bodleian Library.

Register Book of the Congregations of Jesus Christ in and about Speldhurst and Ponsonby in Kent (Additional MSS., 36,709), British Museum.

Registers of Dissenting Churches, Somerset House, London.

Rugge, Thomas, Diurnall (Additional MSS., 11,116), British Museum.

B. Printed.

1. collections.

Baillie, Robert, *Letters and Journals,* 2 vols., Edinburgh, 1775.

Calendars of State Papers, Domestic, 1652-1660, 9 vols.

Carte, T., *Collection of Original Letters and Papers . . . 1641-1660*, 2 vols., London, 1739.

Clarendon Papers, *Calendar*, by W. D. Macray, Oxford, 1872.

Clarendon State Papers, 3 vols., Oxford, 1767-1786.

Clarke Papers, edited by C. H. Firth (Camden Soc. and (vols. III, IV) Royal Hist. Soc.), 4 vols., 1891-1901.

Commons, House of, *Journals*.

Congregational Historical Society, *Transactions*, London, 1901-1907.

Cromwell, Oliver, *Letters and Speeches*, Carlyle's collection, edited by Mrs. S. C. Lomas, 3 vols., London, 1904.

Cromwell, Oliver, *Speeches*, edited by C. L. Stainer, London, 1901.

Grey, Zachary, appendix of documents in his *Examination of . . . Daniel Neal's History of the Puritans*, 3 vols., London, 1736-1739.

Hanserd Knollys Society, *Publications*, London, 1846, 1854.

Harleian Miscellany, 10 vols., London, 1808-1813.

Historical MSS. Commission, *Reports*.

Jones, John, *Correspondence* (Lancashire and Cheshire Historical Soc.), 1860-1861.

Massachusetts Historical Society, *Collections*.

Nicholas Papers (Camden Soc.), 3 vols., 1886-1897.

Nickolls, John, *Original Letters and Papers of State addressed to Oliver Cromwell . . . Found among the political collections of Mr. John Milton*, London, 1743 (cited as Nickolls).

Peck, Francis, *Desiderata Curiosa*, London, 1779.

Scotland and the Protectorate, edited by C. H. Firth (Scottish Historical Soc.), Edinburgh, 1899.

Somers, John, *Collection of scarce and valuable tracts*, 13 vols., London, 1809-1815.

Thurloe, John, *A Collection of State Papers*, edited by Thomas Birch, 7 vols., London, 1742 (referred to as Thurloe).

Vaughan, Robert, *The Protectorate of Oliver Cromwell* (selections from the Pell correspondence), 2 vols., London, 1839.

Whitley, W. T., ed., *Minutes of the General Assembly of the General Baptist Churches in England, with kindred records*, vol. I, 1654-1728, London, 1909.

2. SINGLE WORKS.

Pamphlets in the Thomason collection are designated by their number, and their dates, when in brackets, are those placed on them by Thomason when he acquired them. Pamphlets in the general collection of the British Museum are designated by B. M.

An Alarum to the City and Souldiery—God grant they may not neglect it, [June 6] 1659 (669. f. 21. 44).

Allen, William, *The Captive Taken from the Strong,* London, Livewell Chapman, 1658 (B. M.).

A Word to the Army, Touching their Sin and Dutie, London, Chapman, 1660 (B. M.).

An Animadversion upon the Late Lord Protector's Declaration for the distressed Churches of Lesna, &c. Together with a seasonable Caution against the Petition of the Kentish Anabaptists, for too large a Toleration in religion, London, [June 20] 1659 (E. 988. 5).

Animadversions upon a Letter and Paper, first sent to His Highness by certain Gentlemen and others in Wales, [Jan. 28] 1656 (E. 865. 5).

The Anabaptists' Catechisme: with all their Practices, Meetings, and Exercises, the names of their pastors, their doctrines, disciples: a catalogue of such dishes as they usually make choice of at their feasts (i. e. love feasts usually held at an inn) how and by whom they are dipped, &c. published according to the order of their conventicles. Printed for R. A., [Sept. 11] 1645 (E. 1185. 8).

The Anabaptists Faith and Belief Opened, London, [Sept. 12] 1659 (669. f. 21. 72).

The Anabaptists late Protestation, or their Resolution to depart the City of London, [April 2] 1647 (E. 383. 11).

An Answer to a Paper entituled: A True Narrative of the Cause and Manner of the Dissolution of the late Parliament, London, G. Calvert, [Dec. 12] 1653 (E. 725. 20).

An Antidote against the Infection of the Times, or, A Faithfull Watch-word from Mount Sion, to prevent the ruine of Soules. Published for the good of all by the appointment of the Elders and Messengers of the severall Churches of Illston, Abergevenny, Tredinog, Carmarthen,

Hereford, Brodwardin, Cledock, and Llangors, meeting at Brecknock upon the 29 and 30 daies of the Fift moneth 1656, London, Brewster, 1656 (E. 892. 10).

Archer, Henry, *The Personall Reign of Christ upon Earth,* B. Allen, [Jan.] 1642 (E. 180. 13).

The Arraignment of the Anabaptists Good Old Cause, with the manner and proceedings of the Court of Justice against him, J. Morgan, [March 22] 1660 (E. 1017. 32).

Ashton, Thomas, *Satan in Samuel's Mantle, or, the cruelty of Germany acted in Jersey, Containing the Arbitrary, Bloudy, and Tyrannical proceedings of John Mason, of a baptised Church,* London, T. R., 1659 (Bodleian).

Aspinwall, William, *A Brief Description of the Fifth Monarchy, or Kingdome, that shortly is to come into the World. And a prognostic of the time when this fifth Kingdome shall begin.* Pr. by M. Simmons, and sold by Livewell Chapman, [Aug. 1] 1653 (E. 708. 8).

——— *An Explication and Application of the Seventh Chapter of Daniel,* London, Chapman, [March 20], 1653/4 (E. 732. 2).

——— *The Legislative Power is Christ's Peculiar Prerogative Proved from Isaiah ix, 6, 7,* London, Chapman, [Aug. 20] 1656 (E. 498. 4).

——— *A Premonition of Sundry Sad Calamities Yet to Come,* London, Chapman, [Nov. 30] 1654 (E. 818. 7).

——— *Thunder from Heaven against the Back-sliders and Apostates of the Times.* Pr. for L. Chapman, [April 14] 1655 (E. 831. 26).

——— *The Work of the Age,* London, Chapman, [April 14] 1655 (E. 832. 1).

Baillie, Robert, *Anabaptism, the true Fountaine of Independency, Antinomy, Brownisme, Familisme, and the most of the other Errours which doe trouble in the Church of England, unsealed,* 1646.

——— *A Dissuasive from the errors of the time, wherein the tenets of the principal sects are drawn.*

The Banner of Truth Displayed: or a Testimony for Christ, and against Antichrist. Being the Substance of severall Consultations, holden, and kept by a Certain Number of

Christians, who are waiting for the Visible appearance of Christ's Kingdome, in and over the World, London, [Sept. 24] 1656 (E. 888. 4).

Bartlet, Richard, *The New Birth: in which is brought forth the New Creature, with a description of the true marks and characters thereof.* Pr. by W. H. for L. Blaiklock, [Sept. 7] 1654 (E. 1503. 2).

Bate, G., *Elenchus Motuum Nuperorum in Anglia,* London, 1663.

Baxter, Richard, *Reliquae Baxterianae,* London, 1696.

Blome, Richard, *The Fanatick History, or an Exact Relation and Account of the Old Anabaptists and New Quakers,* 1660 (E. 1832. 2).

Bridge, William, *Christ's coming Opened in a Sermon before the Honorable House of Commons in Margaret's Westminster: May 17, 1648. Being the day appointed for the great Victory in Wales,* London, Peter Cole, 1648.

Browne, Captain John, *A Brief Survey of the Prophetical and Evangelical Events of the last Times,* London, Gertrude Dawson, [Feb. 3] 1655 (E. 826. 18).

Bunyan, John, *Grace abounding to the chief of sinners,* London, 1666.

Burrough, Edward, *To you that are called Anabaptists in the nation of Ireland,* 1657 (Friends' Reference Library, Devonshire House, London).

Burton, Thomas, *Diary of the Parliaments of 1656-1659,* 4 vols., London, 1828.

Canne, John, *The Acts and Monuments of our late Parliament,* 1659 (E. 1000. 19).

——— *A Narrative, wherein is set forth the sufferings of John Canne, Wentworth Day, John Clarke . . .* London, 1658.

——— *A Seasonable Word to the Parliament-Men, to take with them when they go into the House,* London, Chapman, [May 20] 1659 (E. 983. 1).

——— *Truth with Time: or certain reasons proving that none of the seven last plagues or evils are yet poured out,* London, 1656.

——— *A Voice from the Temple to the Higher Powers, wherein is shewed that it is the duty of Saints to search the Prophecies of Holy Scripture which concern the Later Times.* Pr. by M. Simmons, [June 13] 1653 (E. 699. 16).

——— *A Second Voyce from the Temple.* Pr. by M. Simmons, [Aug. 15] 1653 (E. 710. 19).

The Case of Colonel Matthew Alured; or, a short account of his sufferings. Submitted to the consideration of the Parliament and Army. Pr. for L. Chapman, [May 23] 1659 (E. 983. 25).

The Cause of God, and of these Nations, Sought out, and drawn forth from the Rubbish of the Lusts and Interests of Men, London, 1659 (Boston Public Library).

Certain Quaeries Humbly presented in way of Petition by many Christian people throughout the County of Norfolk and City of Norwich to the Lord General and Council of War. Pr. for Giles Calvert, 1649 (E. 544. 5).

[Chamberlen, Peter], *The Declaration and Proclamation of the Army of God owned by the Lord of Hosts in many victories. Whereunto is annexed 17 necessary proposals for settling of good judges in every city, taking off the excise, and payment of the souldiers.* Second ed. Pr. by J. Clowes for the author, [June 9] 1659 (E. 985. 26).

——— *Legislative Power in Problemes. Published for the Information of all those who have constantly adhered to the Good Cause: and for the Reformation of all those who had embraced the Bad Cause,* London. Pr. by John Clowes, [Dec. 3] 1659 (E. 1079. 1).

——— *A Scourge for a Denn of Thieves,* London. Pr. by J. C. for the Author, [June 16] 1659 (E. 986. 23).

Chillenden, Edmund, *Preaching without Ordination; or, a Treatise proving the lawfulnesse of all Persons to preach and set forth the Gospel,* 1647 (E. 405. 10).

A Coffin for the Good Old Cause; or, A Sober Word by way of Caution to the Parliament and Army, [Feb. 2] 1659 [1660] (E. 1015. 3).

Coker, Matthew, *A Prophetical Revelation given from God himself,* London, Cottrel, 1654 (E. 734. 7).

Collier, Thomas, *Certaine Queries: or Points now in Controvercy examined and answered by Scripture*, 1645 (E. 1183. 5).

——— *A Discourse of the true Gospel Blessedness in the New Covenant.* Pr. by H. Hills, 1659 (E. 1801. 2).

The Copie of a Paper Presented to the Parliament: and read the 27th of the fourth Moneth, 1659, London, Calvert, 1659.

A Copy of a Letter from an Officer of the Army in Ireland, to his Highness the Lord Protector, concerning his changing of the Government, [1656] (E. 881. 3). The letter is signed R. G.

Cornewell, Francis, *The Vindication of the Royall Commission of King Jesus against Pope Innocensius the third, that enacted by a decree that the Baptisme of Infants should succeed Circumcision*, 1644 (E. 10. 15).

Covell, William, *A Proclamation to all, of all sorts, high and low, rich and poore, wherein is proclaimed the Law-Royal (i. e. the Rights of the People), which in keeping thereof is true Liberty. Given forth by force and power for every one to observe upon pain of death*, [1654] (669. f. 19. 30)

Croope, J., *Conscience-Oppression: or, A Complaint of wrong done to the People's Rights, being a Word necessary and seasonable to all Christians in England*, [Feb. 24] 1656 [1675] (E. 903. 8).

A Cry for a right Improvement of all our Mercies. With some Cautions touching the election of the (expected) New Representative, T. Brewster and G. Moule, 1651 (E. 643. 23).

The Cry of a Stone, or a Relation of Something spoken in Whitehall, by Anna Trapnel, being in the Visions of God, 7 to 19 Jan. 1653 [4] (E. 730. 3).

A Declaration of a small Society of Baptized Believers, undergoing the name of Free-Willers, about the City of London. Pr. for Henry Adis, 1660 (669. f. 22. 66).

A Declaration of divers Elders and Brethren of Congregationall Societies in and about the city of London, decrying and disclaiming two bookes: the one called "A Cry": the other called "A Model of a new Representative." Wherein their judgements touching the qualifications of electors, and eligible persons, are tendered to consideration, Chapman, 1661 (E. 644. 7).

A Declaration of Several Baptized Believers, walking in all the Foundation Principles of the Doctrine of Christ, mentioned in Heb. 6, 1, 2, London. Pr. by G. D., Jan. 12, 1659.

A Declaration of several of the Churches of Christ, and Godly People in and about the citie of London, concerning the Kingly Interest of Christ, and the present sufferings of his cause and Saints in England, London, Chapman, [Sept. 2] 1654 (E. 809. 15).

A Declaration of several of the People called Anabaptists, In and about the City of London, London, Henry Hills, 1659 (Guildhall Library).

A Declaration of the Officers of the Army in Scotland to the Churches of Christ in the three Nations, Edinburgh, Oct. 20, 1659 (E. 1005. 7).

A Declaration of the Well-affected to the Good Old Cause, for the return and session of the Long Parliament interrupted by the late Protector. Directed to the surviving Members of that Parliament, May 2, 1659 (669. f. 21. 27).

Decrees and Orders of the Committee of Safety of the Commonwealth of Oceana, London, [Nov. 12] 1659 (E. 1010. 3).

Dell, William, *The Stumbling Stone, wherein the University is reproved by the Word of God,* London, Giles Calvert, [April 20] 1653 (E. 692. 1).

Denne, Henry, *The Quaker no Papist,* London, Francis Smith, [Oct. 16] 1659 (E. 1000. 13). Defends Catholics as well as Quakers.

The Downfall of the Fifth Monarchy. Or, The personal Reign of Christ on Earth, confuted, London, [April 20] 1657 (E. 1637. 3).

Edwards, Thomas, *Gangraena,* London, 1646.

England's Settlement, upon the Two solid foundations of the Peoples Civil and Religious Liberties, London, [Sept. 12] 1659 (E. 995. 17). A plea for toleration.

Erbery, William, *The Bishop of London, the Welsh Curate, and Common Prayers, with Apocrypha In the End,* London,

[Jan. 8] 1652 [3] (E. 684. 26). William Erbery was a Welsh fanatic, at one time a Baptist, a sometime Agitator, an apostle of toleration and of church unity, whose method was that of ridicule of sectarian differences.

——— *A Call to the Churches; or, a Packet of Letters to the Pastors of Wales presented to the Baptized Teachers there,* [Feb. 19] 1653 (E. 688. 7).

——— *The Madman's Plea, or a Sober Defence of Captain Chillingtons Church, shewing the Destruction and Derision ready to fall on all the baptized Churches, not Baptized with Fire,* London, [Oct. 28] 1653 (E. 715. 17).

——— *The Man of Peace: or, The Glorious appearance of the great God in his People, rising as a Man of War, to waste the Assyrian: that is, the Mighty Oppressor,* J. Cottrel, [Feb. 14] 1654 (E. 729. 11).

——— *An Olive-leaf; or, Some Peaceable Considerations To the Christians meeting at Christ's-Church in London,* London, J. Cottrel, Jan. 9, 1654 (E. 726. 5).

——— *The Sword Doubled To cut off both the Righteous and the Wicked,* London, Giles Calvert, 1652/3 (E. 671. 13).

An Essay toward Settlement upon a sure foundation, being a testimony for God in this perillous time by a few who have been bewailing their own abominations, London, Giles Calvert, [Sept. 19] 1659 (669. f. 21. 73). Fifth Monarchy manifesto.

Evans, Arise, *The Bloudy Vision of John Farley, interpreted by Arise Evans. With another vision signifying peace and happiness. Also a refutation of a pamphlet published by one Aspinwall, called, A brief Description of the fifth Monarchy,* [Dec. 10] 1653 (E. 1498. 1).

——— *The Declaration of Arise Evans . . . With his Prophetick Proposals, touching Mr. Feak, and Mr. Simpson, and the rest of the discontented and Independent Party, foretelling, the great Change that will happen in this present Year, 1654, and the wonderful Things that will befal the Anabaptists,* London, G. Calvert, [Feb. 9] 1654 (E. 224. 1). These two pamphlets were written by an ex-Baptist, a Welshman, who imagined himself inspired, at this time, to defend Cromwell. Later he went over to Charles Stuart.

Mr. Evans and Mr. Pennington's Prophesie concerning seven yeers of Plenty and seven yeers of famine and pestilence. Together with the coming of the Fifth Monarchy, [Jan. 12] 1655 (E. 823. 6).

The Faithfull Narrative of the late Testimony and Demand made to Oliver Cromwel, and his Powers, on the Behalf of the Lords Prisoners, in the name of the Lord Jehovah, [March 21] 1655 (E. 830. 20).

A Faithfull Searching Home Word, intended for the view of the remaining Members of the former Old Parliament, in the time of their late Second Sitting at Westminster. Shewing the Reasonableness and Justness of their first Dissolution. Printed in the first year of the Army's endeavouring to deal treacherously with the Faithfull Friends of the Cause a second time, after their first and Second Dissolution of the late long Parliament, [Dec. 13] 1659 (E. 774. 1).

Feake, Christopher, *A Beam of Light, shining in the midst of much Darkness and Confusion: Being (with the Benefit of Retrospection) an essay toward the stating (and fixing upon its true and proper Basis) the Best Cause under Heaven: viz. the Cause of God, of Christ, of his People, of the whole Creation, that groans and waits for the Manifestation of the Son of God,* London, Chapman, [May 2] 1659 (E. 980. 5).

——— *Hymne at Christ Church,* Aug. 11, 1653 (E. 710. 13).

——— *The New Non-Conformist, who having obtained help of God, doth persist unto this very day,* London, Chapman, [May 24] 1654 (E. 737. 1).

——— *The Oppressed Close Prisoner in Windsor-Castle, his Defiance to the Father of Lyes, In the strength of the God of Truth . . . As also, a Seasonable Word, concerning the Higher Powers: concerning the payment of Taxes and Tribute-money by the Saints to those Powers, and how far a Minister of the Gospel may inter-meddle in State-Affairs,* London, Chapman, [Dec. 19] 1655 (E. 820. 10).

Featley, Daniel, *The Dippers Dipt, or, the Anabaptists duck'd and plung'd over Head and Eares at a Disputation at Southwark,* 1645 (E. 268. 11). The seventh edition came out in January.

[Fell, John], *The Interest of England stated: or, A faithful and just Account of the Aims of all Parties now pretending,* [July 22] 1659 (E. 763. 4).

The Fifth Monarchy, or Kingdom of Christ, in opposition to the Beast's, Asserted, London, Chapman, 1659 (E. 993. 31).

Fox, George, *Journal,* London, 1694.

Gilbert, Claudius, *The Libertine School'd, or, A Vindication of the Magistrate's Power in Religious matters. In answer to some Fallacious Quaeries scattered about the City of Limrick by a Nameless Author, about the 15 Dec. 1656* (E. 923. 4).

Goodwin, Thomas, *A Sermon on the Fifth Monarchy,* London, Chapman, [Sept. 22] 1654 (E. 812. 9).

——— *The World to Come, or, The Kingdome of Christ Asserted.* Pr. and to be sold in Pope's Head Alley and in Westminster hall. London, [May 15] 1655 (E. 838. 13). These two pamphlets are reprints by a Fifth Monarchy man of three sermons preached a number of years earlier.

[Griffith], Alexander, *Strena Vavasoriensis. A New-Years-Gift for the Welch Itinerants: or, A Hue and Cry after Mr. Vavasor Powell,* [Jan. 30] 1654 (E. 727. 14).

A Ground Voice, or some Discoveries offered to the view, with certain Queries propounded to the Consideration of the whole Army in England, Scotland, and Ireland, Officers and Common-Souldiers, Horse and Foot. With Certain Queries to the Anabaptists in particular that Bear any Office, either in Court or Army, under the present self-created Politick Power, [Nov. 16] 1655 (E. 860. 1).

Heath, John, *A Brief Chronicle of the late Intestine War,* London, 1663.

——— *Flagellum,* London, 1663.

Hammon, George, *Truth and Innocency Prevailing against Error and Insolency . . . by way of answer to Mr. Hezekiah Holland. Whereunto is added a Second Part: wherein is proved, That all the Laws and Statutes of King Jesus (in his last Will and Testament) are practicable,* London, [May 2] 1660 (E. 1022. 4). Hammon was the pastor of the General Baptist church at Biddenden, in Kent, and held

16

pronounced Fifth Monarchy views. The first part of this pamphlet is doctrinal.

The hearty Congratulation and Humble Petition of thousands of well-affected Gentlemen, Freeholders, and Inhabitants of the County of Kent, and City of Canterbury, London, Chapman. June, 1659 (669. f. 21. 45). Congratulates Parliament, asks for liberty of conscience and abolition of tithes.

Homes, Nathaniel, *The Resurrection Revealed.* Imprimatur, Joseph Caryll and Peter Sterry, Oct. 1653. Reprinted, London, 1833. Use of Fifth Monarchy ideas, by one not in sympathy with Fifth Monarchy party.

Hubberthorne, Richard, *An Answer to a Declaration put forth by the general Consent of the People called Anabaptists. In and about the City of London. Which Declaration doth rather seem a begging of Pardon of the Cavaliers, then a Vindication of that Truth and Cause once contended for,* London, Simmons, 1659. Quaker attack.

The Humble Advice, and tender Declaration or Remonstrance of several thousands of men fearing God, in the County of Durham, Northumberland, and the adjacent parts of Westmoreland and Cumberland, with the North part of Yorkshire; To the Lord General Monk, and those with him, London, Henry Hills [Nov. 2, 1659] (669. f. 21. 87).

The Humble Petition and Recantation of many Dis-satisfied Persons, commonly known by the Name of Anabaptists, London, James Johnson, 1660 (B. M.). A libel, ridiculing Baptists.

The Humble Petition of Many Thousand Citizens and inhabitants in and about the City of London, London, Chapman, Feb. 15, 1658[9] (E. 968. 6).

The Humble Petition of several Colonels of the Army, [Oct. 18] 1654 (669. f. 19. 21).

The Humble Representation and Address to His Highness of several Churches and Christians in South-Wales and Monmouthshire. Presented Thursday, January 31, London, Henry Hills and John Field [1656] (E. 866. 3)

The Humble Representation of some Officers of the Army, To the Right Honourable Lieutenant General Fleetwood, Nov. 1, 1659 (E. 1005. 8).

Hutchinson, Lucy. *Memoirs of the life of Colonel Hutchinson,* edited by C. H. Firth, London, 1906.

Hyde, Edward, Earl of Clarendon, *History of the Rebellion and Civil Wars,* edited by Macray, Oxford, 1888.

The Illegal and Immodest Petition of Praise-God Barebone, Anabaptist and Leather-seller of London, London, H. Mason, [Feb. 25] 1660 (669. f. 23. 62).

Ives, Jeremy, *Eighteen Questions Propounded, to Put the great Question between the Army and their dissenting Brethren, out of Question. (Viz.) Whether the best way to secure the Government of these Nations, in the way of a Free-State, without a Single Person, King, or House of Lords; Together with our Liberties, as Men and Christians: Be either to Chuse a New and Free Parliament, or else to Restore the last Long Parliament,* London, Francis Smith, [Nov. 21] 1659 (E. 1010. 12).

J[essey], H[enry], *The Lords Loud Call to England: being a true relation of some Judgments of God by Earthquake, Lightening, etc.,* Printed for L. Chapman and Francis Smith, [Aug. 14] 1660 (E. 1038. 8).

Johnson, Edward, *An Examination of the Essay: or, an Answer to the Fifth Monarchy,* London, W. Thomas, 1659.

Josselin, Ralph, *Diary,* 1616-1683, Royal Historical Society, *Publications,* Camden, 3d series, XIV.

Kiffin, William, et. al, *A Letter sent to the Right Honourable the Lord Mayor of London by Lieut. Col. Kiffen, Capt. Gosfright, Capt. Hewling and Lieut. Lomes, touching the seizing of their persons. Also shewing the forgery and falsehood of a pamphlet intituled, A Manifesto and Declaration of the Anabaptists.* Pr. by H. Hills, 1660 (669. f. 23. 72).

ΚΛΕῚΣ ΠΡΟΦΗΤΕΊΑΣ, *or The Key of Prophecie, whereby the Mysteries of all the Prophecies from the Birth of Christ until this present are unlocked, and the speedy Resurrection of King Charles the II out of banishment is foreshewn,* [Jan. 28] 1660 (E. 774. 2).

Lane, Edward, *An Image of our Reforming Times: or, Jehu in his proper Colours,* London, Chapman, [Aug. 14] 1654 (E. 808. 11). A Fifth Monarchy production, comparing Cromwell to Jehu.

L'Estrange, Roger, *The Dissenters' Sayings, The Second Part,* London, 1681 (Boston Public Library).

A Letter from Shrewsbury, setting forth the Design which the Anabaptists and Quakers had to secure the Castle, and to have received five hundred more unto them in opposition to the Parliament, London, T. H., [March 1] 1659 [60] (669. f. 23. 71).

A Letter of Addresse to the Protector Occasioned by Mr. Needham's reply to Mr. Goodwins book against the Triers. By a Person of quality [1657] (E. 923. 7). A vindication of Independents and Baptists. The letter is signed D. F.

The Life and Approaching Death of William Kiffin, Extracted out of the Visitation Book by a Church Member, London, [March 13] 1659 [60] (E. 1017. 4). A libel.

Llanvaedonon, William, *A Brief Exposition upon the second Psalme,* London, Chapman, [June 23] 1655 (E. 844. 9).

A Looking Glass for, Or An Awakening Word to, The Superior and Inferior Officers, with all others, belonging to the Armies of England, Scotland, and Ireland: more especially to those, who have the least Spark of grace or Principle of true honesty remaining in them, wherein is set before them some passages in severall of their Declarations, speciously pretending for the Rights and Liberties of the People [Oct. 22, 1656] (E. 891. 1).

Ludlow, Edmund, *Memoirs,* edited by Firth, 2 vols., Oxford, 1892.

A Model of a new Representative. Wherein is shewn what are the men that are conceived meet to be the choosers of, and chosen unto the places of Parliament-men in the next representative. Pr. for G. Calvert, [Oct. 15] 1651 (E. 643. 13).

Moderation: or Arguments and Motives tending thereunto. Humbly tendred to the Honourable Members of Parliament. Together with a brief Touch of the reputed German Anabaptists, and Munster tragedy. By S. T., London, Henry Hills, [Feb. 3] 1660 (E. 1015. 8).

Moor, Thomas, jr., Mercies for Men: prepared in, and by, Christ, even for such as neither know them nor him. A discourse delivered at the Munday meetings at Black Friers. Printed by R. I., 1654 (E. 744. 1).

More, John, *A Trumpet sounded; or, the Great Mystery of the Ten little Horns unfolded. Being as a candle set up in the dark Lanthorn of Daniel. Consisting of two parts. The First of which was sent to the Lord Protector so-called.* July 29, 1654.

Nedham, Marchamont, *Interest will not Lie: or, A view of England's True interest. In refutation of a pamphlet entituled The Interest of England Stated,* [Aug. 17] 1659 (E. 763. 5).

No Return to Monarchy: and Liberty of Conscience secured, without a Senate, or any imposing power over the people's representatives. Humbly tendered to the consideration of the Parliament, upon occasion of the Army's thirteenth proposal. By a True Lover of the Common-Wealth, and a Real Friend to the Honest Interest, [June 6] 1659 (E. 985. 16).

The Northern Queries from the Lord Gen. Monck his Quarters, sounding an Allarum to all Loyall Hearts and Free-born English-men . . . Printed in the Year of England's Confusions, and are to be sold at the Sign of Wallingford House, right against a Free Parliament [Nov. 7, 1659] (E. 1005. 15).

Osborne, John, *An Indictment against Tythes, or tythes no wages for gospel ministers,* London, Chapman, [July 18] 1659 (E. 989. 28).

Pagitt, Ephraim, *Heresiography,* 3d ed., London, 1647.

Peace Protected and Discontent Disarmed, London, [April 11] 1654 (E. 732. 27). John Goodwin's seventeen queries reprinted, with others added. Upbraids Fifth Monarchy men, especially those who signed the Declaration of 1651.

Pendarves, John, *The Fear of God . . . A Sermon preached unto the Church of Christ meeting in Petty France, 10 day, 6 mo. 1656,* London, Chapman, [April 3] 1657 (E. 907. 3).

A Perfect Diurnall, or the Daily Proceedings in the Conventicle of the Phanatiques, March 19, 1660 (E. 1017. 21).

The Petition of Divers Gathered Churches, And other wel affected, in and about the City of London, For declaring the Ordinance of the Lords and Commons, for publishing

Blasphemies and Heresies, Null and Void. Also, a seasonable Premonition to the Churches of God in the Countrey, that acknowledge the Holy Scriptures the only Word of Faith, and believe that God so loved the World . . . More especially to the thirty congregations, whose Faith and practice is extant. Printed for William Larner, 1651. Reprinted, 1655 (E. 856. 3).

Petty, Sir William, *Reflections upon some persons and things in Ireland, by letters to and from Dr. Petty. With Sir Hierome Sankey's Speech in Parliament.* Pr. for J. Martin, Ja. Allestreye and T. Dicas, [April] 1660 (E. 1915. 1).

Phanatick Intelligencer, [March 24] 1659 [60] (E. 1017. 42).

A Phanatique League and Covenant. Solemnly enter'd into by the Assertors of the Good Old Cause. Printed for G. H. the Rumps Pamphleteer-General, [March 14, 1660] (669. f. 24. 11).

Phillips, Edward, *Continuation of Baker's Chronicle,* London, 1670.

The Picture of a New Courtier, drawn in a Conference, between Mr. Timeserver and Mr. Plain heart. In which is discovered the abhominable Practices and horrid hypocrisies of the Usurper, and his time-serving Parasites. . . . In which a Protector having been in part unvailed, may see himself discovered by I. S. a Lover of Englands dear bought Freedomes, [April 18, "cast about the streets"] 1656 (E. 875. 6). By John Streater?

The Picture of the Good Old Cause drawn to the Life in the Effigies of Master Praise-God Barebone, London, [July 14] 1660 (669. f. 25. 57).

Pittiloh, Robert, *The Hammer of Persecution: or The Mystery of Iniquity, in the Persecutions of many Good People in Scotland, Under the Government of Oliver Late Lord Protector, And continued by others of the same Spirit. Disclosed, with the Remedies thereof,* London, Chapman, [July 25] 1659 (E. 993. 4).

Postlethwaite, Gualter, *A Voice from Heaven: or, A Testimony against the remainders of Antichrist Yet in England: And in particular, the Court of Tryers for Approbation of Ministers,* London, Chapman, [April 15] 1655 (E. 1498. 3).

The Prophets Malachy and Isaiah Professing to the Saints and Professors of this Generation of the Great Things the Lord will doe in this their Day and Time . . . By a well-wisher to the Kingdom of our Lord Jesus, London, Chapman, [Sept. 22] 1656 (E. 888. 2). Prefaces by Feake and Pendarves.

The Protector, So called, In Part Unvailed, London, [Oct. 24] 1655 (E. 857. 1).

Records of a Church of Christ meeting in Broadmead, Bristol, 1640-1657, Hanserd Knollys Society, London, 1847. Cited as Broadmead Records.

Records of the Churches of Christ, Gathered at Fenstanton, Warboys and Hexham, 1644-1720, Hanserd Knollys Society, London, 1854. Cited as Hexham Records.

A Relation of severall Heresies, discovering the Originall Ringleaders, and the time when they began to spread. Published according to Order, by a well wisher of Truth and Peace, London. Pr. by J. M., [Jan. 3, 1656] (E. 863. 2). Account of Anabaptists taken chiefly from Bullinger.

A Reply to Mr. William Prinne his unsafe Expedient for the settlement of these Nations by restoring the ancient Nobility. Printed for Francis Smith, [Nov. 26] 1659 (E. 1010. 8).

The Revelation Unrevealed. Concerning the Thousand-years Reigne of the Saints with Christ upon Earth. Laying forth the weak Grounds, and strange Consequences of that plausible, and too much received Opinion, London, John Bisse, Jan. 1650 (E. 1346, 1).

•*A Reviving Word from the Quick and the Dead, to the Scatter'd Dust of Sion: or, A Breathing of the Spirit of Life, in a Few Dry Bones, that begin to Rise and Rattle, In and about this City of London; by a Solemn Declaration, for an Immediate Uniting of All Saints into One Body, upon the Growing Principles of Grace, and Kingdome of our Lord Jesus, in every Administration thereof,* London, Calvert, [Oct. 11] 1657 (E. 926. 2). Signed by Edward Edmonds and others.

Richardson, Samuel, *An Apology for the Present Government, and Governour,* London, Calvert, [Sept. 30] 1654 (E. 812. 18).

——— *Plain Dealing: or The Unvailing of the opposers of the Present Government and Governors. In Answer of several things affirmed by Mr. Vavasor Powell and others,* London. Printed by E. C., [Jan. 23] 1656 (E. 865. 3).

Rogers, John, *Διαπολιτεία. A Christian Concercitation with Mr. Prin, Mr. Baxter, Mr. Harrington, For the True Cause of the Commonwealth,* London, Chapman, [Sept. 20] 1659 (E. 995. 25).

——— *To his Excellency the Lord Generall Cromwell, A few Proposals, relating to Civil Government,* Robert Ibbitson, [April 27] 1653 (669. f. 16. 97).

——— *To His Highnesse Lord General Cromwell, Lord Protector, &c. The humble Cautionary Proposals of John Rogers, Minister of the Gospel according to the Definition of the Spirit (now) at Thomas Apostles,* 1653 (669. f. 17. 71).

——— *Jegar-Sahadutha: An Oyled Pillar. Set up for Posterity,* [July 28, 1657] (E. 919. 9).

——— *Mene, Tekel, Perez . . . a Letter written to, and lamenting over, Oliver Lord Cromwell,* Bern [1654].

——— *Sagrir, Or Doomesday drawing nigh, with Thunder and Lightning to Lawyers,* London, Calvert, [Nov. 7] 1653 (E. 716. 1). Copious extracts from these pamphlets of Rogers are given in Edward Rogers' *Life and Opinions of a Fifth Monarchy Man.*

The Serious Attestation of many Thousands, Religious and well disposed People, living in London, Westminster, Borough of Southwark, and parts adjoining, March 26, 1657 (669. f. 20. 52). Against kingship.

A Serious Manifesto and Declaration of the Anabaptist, and other congregational Churches, London, Hardy, [Feb. 28] 1660 (669. f. 23. 65 *). A libel.

A Short History of the Anabaptists of High and Low Germany, London. Printed by T. Badger for Samuall Brown, 1642 (E. 148. 5).

Sighs for Righteousness: or the Reformation this day calls for stated in some sad and serious Queries proposed to our Rulers, London, [June 2] 1654 (E. 738. 14).

Some Considerations By way of Proposall and Conclusion, Humbly Tendered. For the satisfying and uniting of all the Faithfull in this Day, whose hearts are groaning and sighing for the deliverance of Zion, and appearance of her King. And desiring to separate from this wicked and Adulterous Generation, [March 9] 1657 (E. 746. 3).

Some Mementos For the Officers and Souldiers of the Army, [Oct. 19, 1654] (E. 813. 20).

Some Reasons Humbly Proposed to the Officers of the Army, For the speedy Re-admission of the Long Parliament, Who setled the Government In the way of a Free State, London, Chapman, [April 28] 1659 (E. 979. 8).

Spanhemius, Frederick, *Englands Warning by Germanies Woe: or an historicall Narration of the Originall, Progresse and Sects of the Anabaptists in Germany and the Low Countries.* Pr. by J. Dever and R. Ibbitson for John Bellamie, [Nov. 23] 1646 (E. 362. 28).

The Speeches and Prayers of some of the late King's Judges, 1660.

The Spirit of Persecution Again broken loose, by an Attempt to put in Execution against Mr. John Biddle Master of Arts, an abrogated Ordinance of the Lords and Commons for punishing Blasphemies and Heresies. Together with, A full Narrative of The whole Proceedings upon that Ordinance against the said Mr. John Biddle and Mr. William Kiffin, Pastor of a baptised Congregation in the City of London, London, Richard Moone, [July 21] 1655 (E. 848. 27).

Spittlehouse, John, *An Answer to one part of The Lord Protector's Speech, or A Vindication of the Fifth Monarchy-men,* London, Chapman, 1654 (E. 813. 19).

——— *The Army Vindicated, In their late Dissolution of the Parliament: With several Cautions and Directions in point of a New Representative,* London, Richard Moone, [April 24] 1653 (E. 693. 1).

——— *Certaine Queries Propounded to the most serious Consideration of those Persons Now in Power. or any others whom they doe, or may concerne,* London, Chapman, [Sept. 11] 1654 (E. 809. 14).

——— *An Explanation of the Commission of Jesus Christ in relation to the Gifts, Work, and Maintenance of his Ministers.* Pr. by J. C. and sold by R. Moone, [Sept. 22] 1653 (E. 713. 15).

——— *The first Addresses to the Lord General with the Assembly of Elders elected by him and his Council for the management of this Commonwealth. Containing certain rules how to advance the Kingdom of Jesus Christ over the face of the whole Earth.* Pr. by J. C. for himself and Richard Moone, [July 5] 1653 (E. 703. 19).

——— *A Warning Piece Discharged, or, Certain Intelligence communicated to the Lord General Cromwel, in relation to the election of a New Representative,* Richard Moone, [May 19] 1653 (E. 697. 11).

[Spriggs, William], *A Modest Plea for an Equal Commonwealth, against Monarchy,* Giles Calvert, [Sept. 28] 1659 (E. 1802. 1).

A Standard Set Up, whereunto the true Seed and Saints of the most High may be gathered together . . . , [May 17] 1657 (E. 910. 10).

Strange and Wonderful News from Whitehall, or the mighty visions proceeding from Mistress Anna Trapnel, London, R. Sele, [March 11] 1654 (E. 224. 3).

Streater, John, *A Glympse of That Jewel, Judicial, Just, Preserving Libertie,* London, Calvert, [March 31] 1653 (E. 690. 11).

[———] *Secret Reasons of State in reference to the affairs of these nations at the interruption of this present Parliament anno 1653, discovered. With other matters worthy of observation, in Jo. Streater's case, this being a narrative of his two years troubles at the beginning of the late Monarchie erected by General Cromwel,* [May 23] 1659 (E. 983. 24).

Taylor, Jeremy, *Liberty of Prophecying,* 1646.

That wicked and Blasphemous Petition of Praise-God Barbone, and his Sectarian Crew: Presented to that so called, the Parliament of the Commonwealth of England, Feb. 9, 1659, for which they had the Thanks of that House: Anatomized.

Worthily stiled by his Excellency the Lord Generall Monck, Bold, of dangerous Consequence, and Venemous . . . Printed for Philo-Monarchaeus [April 4, 1660] (E. 1019. 15).

Tillinghast, John, *Generation Work: The Second Part,* London, Chapman, [March 7] 1654 (E. 1491. 1).

——— *Knowledge of the Times: or the resolution of the question how long it shall be unto the End of Wonders.* Pr. by R. I. for L. Chapman, Dec. 9, 1654 (E. 1467. 1).

Trapnel, Hannah, *A Legacy for Saints: being several experiences of the dealings of God with Anna Trapnel. Written with her own hand.* Printed for T. Brewster, [July 24] 1654 (E. 806. 1).

A True Catalogue, Or, An Account of the several Places and most Eminent Persons in the three Nations, and elsewhere, where, and by whom, Richar Cromwell was proclaimed Lord Protector of the Commonwealth of England, Scotland, and Ireland . . . all which is chiefly presented to the view of the true Friends to the Cause and Interest of Christ in the Three Nations and elsewhere, but more especially to those very, very, hardly a few among them now sitting in Parliament. Printed in the First Year of the English Armies small & scarce beginning to return from their almost six years great Apostacy [Sept. 28, 1659] (E. 999. 12).

A true Copie of a Paper delivered to Lt. G. Fleetwood, In the presence of divers Officers of the Army: to be communicated to the General Council of Officers: From a People who through Grace have been hitherto kept from the Great Apostacie of this day. Wherein The Good old Cause Is Stated, According to the Armies own Declarations and former Ingagements. And likewise here is declared, That if the Army (by the Lord's good hand assisting them) shall now begin where they left the work of the Lord, & faithfully carry on that Good Old Cause, There are a willing People, and their number not a few, who will stand by them with their lives and Estates, London, Chapman, Apr. 26, 1659 (E. 979. 4).

A True Copy of a Petition Signed by very many Peaceable and Well-affected People, Inhabiting in and about the City of London, and intended to have been delivered to the late

Parliament. Now presented to the Publick view and consideration of all men: With a brief Apology in the behalf of the Petitioners. By a Friend to the Common-Wealth, and a Cordiall Well wisher to the righteous things prayed for in the Petition, by E. H., London. Pr. for the author, and to be sold by Livewell Chapman, [March 11] 1658 (E. 936. 5).

A True Relation of the State of the Case Between the ever Honourable Parliament and the Officers of the Army. By a Lover of his Countrey and Freedom, E. D. Printed by J. C., [Oct. 16] 1659 (E. 1000. 12).

The True Magistrate, or the Magistrate's Duty and Power in matters of Religion, London, Brewster, Oct. 3, 1659. (E. 1000. 1).

A True Narrative of the Proceedings in Parliament, Council of State etc. from Sept. 22 until this present time, Dec. 2, 1659. Printed by John Redmayne (E. 1010. 34).

A True State of the Case of Liberty of Conscience in the Commonwealth of England. Together with a Narrative of John Biddle's sufferings, London. Printed for Richard Moone, [July 14] 1655 (E. 848. 12).

Twelve Plain Proposals offered to the Honest and Faithful Officers and Souldiers of our English Army. Pr. by J. C. for Livewell Chapman, London, [April 28] 1659 (669. f. 21. 26). Against monarchy.

Twelve Queries, humbly presented to the serious Consideration of the High Court of Parliament about the two soul-oppressing yokes of a Forced Maintenance and Ministry, London, S. Clowes, [Sept. 10] 1653 (669. f. 17. 49).

Vane, Sir Henry, *The Retired Mans Meditations, or the Mysterie and Power of Godlines. Shining forth in the Living Word,* London, Brewster, 1655.

Vindiciae Magistratuum, Or, a Sober Plea for Subjection to Present Government According to the Command and special Direction of God himself, in his Holy Scriptures. By the meanest of the Lord's tenderers of his great Honour, and weal of his Saints, London, Hills, [June] 1658 (E. 2120. 1). The preface is signed C. D.

A Warning for England, especially for London, in the famous history of the frantick Anabaptists, their wild preachings and practises in Germany, [Feb.] 1642 (E. 136. 33).

Whitelocke, Bulstrode, *Memorials,* 4 vols., Oxford, 1853.

A Witnes To the Saints in England and Wales, to whom our God has given Grace and Glory, and the shield of his salvation: Who have their conversations in this crooked and perverse Generation. By some of the Mourners in Zion, [June 15, 1657] (E. 915. 2).

3. NEWSPAPERS.

All in the Thomason Collection.

Certain Passages of Every Daies Intelligence. By Henry Walker, printed by Clowes. January, 1654-September, 1655. A continuation of *Moderate Publisher.*

The Faithful Post. By D. Border, printed for George Horton, March, 1653-June, 1655. Between June and September, 1653, opposition copies published, and after November, 1653, known successively as *Great Britain's Post, Grand Politique Post,* and *Weekly Post.*

The Faithfull Scout. By D. Border, printed by Robert Wood. December, 1650-June, 1653. Known April-June, 1653, as *Armies Scout.* Border was a Baptist, and the *Post* and *Scout* were consequently favorable to the sectaries in general, and the Baptists in particular.

Mercurius Politicus. By Needham, January, 1653-May, 1659, and August, 1659-April, 1660. Between May and August, 1659, by John Canne. Printed by M. Simmons; later by T. Newcombe. Official organ of the government.

The Moderate Intelligencer. Printed by Robert Wood. May, 1653-April, 1654.

Moderate Publisher of Every daies Intelligence. By Henry Walker, printed by John Clowes. January, 1653-January, 1654.

The Observator. By Needham, printed by T. Newcombe, October-November, 1654.

Occurrences from Foreign Parts. By Oliver Williams *et al.* John Canne had a hand in it after August of 1659. Printed by J. Macock. June, 1659,-March, 1660.

The Parliamentary Intelligencer. By H. Muddiman and G. Dury. December, 1659-April, 1660. In Monck's interest.

Particular Advice from the Office of Intelligence. By Oliver Williams et al. (including Canne). Printed by J. Macock. January, 1659-July, 1660. Called *Exact Accompt* after Jan. 6, 1660.

A Perfect Account of the Daily Intelligence. By B. D., printed by Bernard Alsop. January, 1651-September, 1655.

A Perfect Diurnall of some Passages and Proceedings of and in Relation to the Armies. Printed by Griffin Rushworth, Pecke. December, 1649-September, 1655.

Perfect Occurrences. January-June, 1654.

The Publick Intelligencer. The Monday issue of *Mercurius Politicus.*

Severall Proceedings of State Affairs. By H. Scoble and H. Walker, printed by R. Ibbitson. September, 1649-September 1655. At different times, *Severall Proceedings in Parliament, Perfect Proceedings,* and *General Proceedings.*

The Weekly Intelligencer of the Commonwealth. By R. Collings [?], printed by R. Austin for R. C. July, 1650-September, 1655.

II. LATER WORKS.

Bagwell, Richard, *Ireland under the Stuarts and during the Interregnum,* 2 vols., London, 1909.

Banks, C. E., "Thomas Venner," *New England Historical and Genealogical Register,* 1893.

Barclay, Robert, *The Inner Life of the Religious Societies of the Commonwealth,* London, 1876.

Bernstein, E., *Kommunistische und demokratisch-sozialistische Strömungen während der englischen Revolution des 17 Jahrhunderts.* In Bernstein, Hugo, et al., *Die Geschichte des Sozialismus,* Bd. 1, Th. 2, Stuttgart, 1895.

Bogue, David, and Bennett, James, *History of Dissenters,* 4 vols., London, 1808-1812. Vol. I.

Catterall, R. C. H., "The Failure of the Humble Petition and Advice," *American Historical Review,* IX.

Crosby, Thomas, *History of the English Baptists,* 4 vols., London, 1738-1740.

Culross, James, *Hanserd Knollys,* London, 1895.

Davies, David, *Vavasor Powell,* London, 1896.

Davis, J., *History of the Welsh Baptists,* Pittsburgh, 1835.

Dexter, Henry M., *As to Roger Williams,* Boston, 1876.

Dexter, H. M., *The Congregationalism of the last three hundred years,* New York, 1880. Contains a monumental bibliography.

Dictionary of National Biography.

Dodd, J. A., "Troubles in a City Parish under the Protectorate," *English Historical Review,* 1895.

Doel, W., *Twenty Golden Candlesticks,* London, 1890.

Evans, B., *The Early English Baptists,* 2 vols, 1862-1864.

Firth, C. H., "Anarchy and the Restoration" in *Cambridge Modern History,* IV, Cambridge, 1906.

——— "Cromwell and the Crown," *English Historical Review,* 1893.

——— *Cromwell's Army,* London, 1902.

——— *The Last Years of the Protectorate,* 2 vols., London and New York, 1909.

———"The Later History of the Ironsides," Royal Historical Society, *Transactions,* n. s., vol. XV, 1-45, London, 1901.

——— *Life of Thomas Harrison,* American Antiquarian Society, Worcester, 1893.

——— *Oliver Cromwell and the Rule of the Puritans in England,* London, 1900.

Fitzmaurice, Lord Edmond, *Life of Sir William Petty,* London, 1895.

Fortescue, G. K., ed., *Catalogue of the Pamphlets, Books, Newspapers and Manuscripts relating to the Civil War, the Commonwealth, and Restoration, collected by George Thomason, 1640-1661,* 2 vols., London, 1908.

Gardiner, S. R., *History of the Commonwealth and the Protectorate,* new ed., 4 vols., London, 1903.

Glass, H. A., *The Barbone Parliament,* London, 1899.

Goadby, J. J., *Baptists and Quakers in Northamptonshire, 1650-1700,* Northampton, 1882.

Godwin, William, *History of the Commonwealth of England,* 4 vols., London, 1824-1828.

Gooch, G. P., *History of English Democratic Ideas in the 17th Century,* Cambridge, 1898.

Guizot, F., *Histoire du Protectorat de Richard Cromwell,* 2 vols., Paris, 1856.

Hanbury, Benjamin, *Historical Memorials relating to the Independents or Congregationalists,* 3 vols., London, 1839-1844.

Ivimey, Joseph, *History of the English Baptists,* 4 vols., London, 1811.

Lewis, John, *A Brief History of the Rise and Progress of Anabaptism in England,* London, 1738.

Marsden, John B., *History of the Later Puritans,* London, 1872.

Masson, David, *Life of John Milton,* 7 vols., London, 1859-1894.

Neal, Daniel, *History of the Puritans,* 3 vols., London, 1837 (1st ed., 1732-1738).

Noble, M., *Memoirs of the Protectoral House of Cromwell,* 2 vols., 1787.

Orme, William, *Memoirs of the Life, Writings, and Religious Connexions of John Owen,* London, 1820.

——— *Remarkable Passages in the Life of William Kiffin,* 1823.

Palmer, A. M., *History of the Older Nonconformity of Wrexham* (1888).

Parliamentary History, London, 1812.

Pike, G. H., *Ancient Meeting Houses,* London, 1870.

Ranke, L. von, *History of England,* 6 vols., Oxford, 1875.

Rees, Thomas, *History of Protestant Nonconformity in Wales,* London, 1861.

Reid, J. S., *History of the Presbyterian Church in Ireland,* 2 vols., London, 1837.

Rippon, John, *Baptist Annual Register,* 1793-1802.

Rogers, Edward, *Some Account of the Life and Opinions of a Fifth Monarchy Man,* London, 1867.

Shaw, W. A., "The Commonwealth and the Protectorate," in *Cambridge Modern History,* IV, Cambridge, 1906.

Shaw, W. A., *History of the English Church during the Civil Wars and under the Commonwealth,* 2 vols., London, 1900.

Simpkinson, C. H., *Thomas Harrison,* London, 1905.

Stoughton, J., *History of Religion in England,* London, 1881.

Tallack, W., *George Fox, the Friends, and the early Baptists,* London, 1868.

Taylor, Adam, *History of the English General Baptists,* 2 vols., London, 1818.

Weingarten, Hermann, *Die Revolutionskirchen Englands,* Leipzig, 1868.

Williams, J. B., *History of English Journalism to the foundation of the Gazette,* London, 1908.

Wilson, Walter, *History and Antiquities of Dissenting Churches . . . in London . . .,* 4 vols., London, 1808-1810.

Wilson, Walter, "Dissenting Churches," MS. collections in Dr. Williams Library.

INDEX.

www.ingramcontent.com/pod-product-compliance
Lightning Source LLC
LaVergne TN
LVHW050612100826
845148LV00011B/1564

* 9 7 8 1 5 9 7 4 0 3 8 0 1 *